CONTESTED
WATERS

CONTESTED WATERS

The STRUGGLE for RIGHTS and RECONCILIATION in the ATLANTIC FISHERY

edited by FRED WIEN and RICK WILLIAMS

Nimbus Publishing Limited
3660 Strawberry Hill Street, Halifax, NS, B3K 5A9
(902) 455-4286 nimbus.ca

Printed and bound in Canada
NB1662

Editor: Marianne Ward
Design: John Van Der Woude

Library and Archives Canada Cataloguing in Publication

Title: Contested waters : the struggle for rights and reconciliation in the
     Atlantic fishery / edited by Rick Williams and Fred Wien.
Names: Williams, Rick, 1945- editor. | Wien, Fred, editor.
Identifiers: Canadiana (print) 20220262152 | Canadiana (ebook)
     20220285942 | ISBN 9781774711149 (softcover)
     ISBN 9781774711347 (EPUB)
Subjects: LCSH: Fisheries—Nova Scotia. | LCSH: Fishery law and
     legislation—Nova Scotia. | LCSH: Fishery policy—Nova Scotia. |
     LCSH: Lobster fisheries—Law and legislation—Nova Scotia. | CSH:
     First Nations—Fishing—Nova Scotia. | CSH: First Nations—Fishing—
     Law and legislation—Nova Scotia.
Classification: LCC SH331 .C66 2022 | DDC 333.95/609716—dc23

Canada   NOVA SCOTIA    Canada Council Conseil des arts
for the Arts du Canada

Nimbus Publishing acknowledges the financial support for its publishing activities from the Government of Canada, the Canada Council for the Arts, and from the Province of Nova Scotia. We are pleased to work in partnership with the Province of Nova Scotia to develop and promote our creative industries for the benefit of all Nova Scotians.

CONTENTS

IV. MI'KMAW VOICES

V. COMMERCIAL HARVESTER AND COMMUNITY VOICES

VI. CURRENT ISSUES

INTRODUCTION

by FRED WIEN and RICK WILLIAMS

When violent conflicts between Mi'kmaw and non-Indigenous fish harvesters broke out in the fall of 2020 in Southwest Nova Scotia, it brought to mind similar incidents that took place in the Maritimes in the immediate aftermath of the Supreme Court's 1999 decisions in the *Marshall* case. The first of those decisions recognized the Treaty Right of the thirty-five Mi'kmaw, Wolastoqey (Maliseet), and Peskotomuhkati (Passamaquoddy) Nations in the region to conduct self-regulated fisheries to earn moderate livelihoods, and the second affirmed the overarching authority of the federal Department of Fisheries and Oceans (DFO) to regulate First Nations fishing activities in situations where conservation and other significant public interests were at risk. However, Supreme Court decisions also require the federal government to consult the *Marshall* First Nations (i.e., Mi'kmaq, Wolastoqiyik, and Peskotomuhkati) on any proposed infringements on their self-governance rights and to provide solid justification for such interventions, such as risks to the sustainability of the lobster resource.

Many people in the Maritimes and beyond, in both Indigenous and non-Indigenous communities, were appalled by the violence and racism they witnessed on their television screens in the fall of 2020, but they also had difficulty making sense of what was going on because the issues involved are

Mi'kmaq and Maliseet First Nations and the Peskotomuhkati

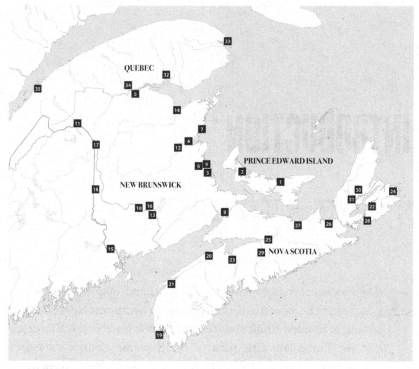

1. Abegweit
2. Lennox Island
3. Bouctouche
4. Eel Ground
5. Ugpi'ganjig (Eel River Bar)
6. Elsipogtog (Big Cove)
7. Esgenoôpetitj (Burnt Church)
8. Fort Folly
9. Indian Island
10. Kingsclear
11. Madawaska Maliseet
12. Metepenagiag (Red Bank)
13. Oromocto
14. Pabineau
15. Peskotomuhkati Nation at Skutik
16. Saint Mary's
17. Tobique
18. Woodstock
19. Acadia
20. Annapolis Valley
21. Bear River
22. Eskasoni
23. Glooscap
24. Membertou
25. Millbrook
26. Paqtnkek
27. Pictou Landing
28. Potlotek (Chapel Island)
29. Sipekne'katik (Indian Brook)
30. Wagmatcook
31. We'koqma'q (Waycobah)
32. Gesgapegiag
33. Gespeg
34. Listuguj
35. Wolastoqiyik Wahsipekuk (Viger)

so complex. It was impossible to explain in a sound bite or short newspaper article the many issues in the dispute, the different kinds of Aboriginal and Treaty Rights involved, the history of how Indigenous Peoples, for whom fishing had long been central to their way of life, lost access to the resource, and the protectiveness felt by non-Indigenous harvesters regarding the commercial fishery. Then there are the complexities of the fishing industry itself, the resource sustainability issues, the different ways of controlling fishing effort, the local rules and customs governing the conduct of fishing, and the relationships between commercial harvesters and fish buyers and processors.

In creating this book, then, our first goal was to provide readers with broader perspectives on the historical roots of the conflict, on the structure, economic value, and management of the fishing industry overall, and on the ongoing development of First Nations fisheries since the *Marshall* decisions. We also felt it important to give voice to the differing perspectives of First Nations leaders, non-Indigenous fish harvester groups, academic researchers, and other expert observers regarding the legal issues and policy questions underlying the conflict. And a third objective was to explore possible pathways to resolving some of these issues.

This book is divided into six segments. The first provides an overview of First Nations fisheries and the wider commercial fishery as context for the many issues that have arisen. This segment is also intended to challenge with facts certain partisan arguments that are not supported by facts, such as charges by non-Indigenous leaders that allowing First Nations moderate livelihood fishing would devastate fisheries resources, or claims by some Indigenous leaders that First Nations have seen no advances in the recognition of their fishing rights in the two decades since the Supreme Court ruled on the *Marshall* case.

To start off, Rick Williams, who has worked extensively with inshore fishing organizations in the Maritimes, provides an overview of the commercial inshore fishery as it is currently organized, managed, and conducted. He discusses matters such as the number of owner-operators fishing in the region, the value of landings from lobster and other species, and the incomes earned from fishing. In another chapter, he describes the development since the *Marshall* decisions of three distinct First Nations fishing sectors: fishing for food, social, and ceremonial purposes within an Aboriginal Right recognized by the Supreme Court in its 1990 *Sparrow* decision and applied across the country; the communal-commercial fishery, wherein First Nations, with financial and other supports from the federal government, now own and operate significant numbers of regular commercial fishing enterprises; and the recent initiatives by *Marshall* First Nations to develop smaller-scale, self-regulated commercial fishing to allow larger numbers of community members to earn moderate livelihoods.

Both this chapter and another, by Joseph Quesnel and John Paul, who, respectively, are associated with the Macdonald-Laurier Institute and the Atlantic Policy Congress of First Nation Chiefs, document the impressive economic benefits that the *Marshall* First Nations have derived from the development of their communal-commercial fisheries as measured by capital investments in boats and gear, by levels of employment, and by new revenues flowing to communities. Providing additional context, Fred Wien, who has written extensively about Mi'kmaw economic history, describes different stages of that history from the earliest days to the present. His chapter pays particular attention to the systemic factors that excluded the Mi'kmaq in Nova Scotia from access to their traditional fishing activities and the marine habitat.

Section II turns specifically to the complexities of the lobster fishery, which is the dominant sector within the Atlantic fishery and offers the best opportunities for First Nations communities to generate jobs, incomes, and new revenues for their communities from engagement in fishing. However, the unique characteristics of the lobster industry—how, where, and when it is conducted—create certain challenges for expanding First Nations participation. In his chapter on this topic, Rick Williams describes why it is difficult for new entrants to gain a foothold on local fishing grounds where unwritten rules are often enforced to manage the intense competition for a limited resource.

One of the unresolved issues is the lack of clarity over who has the authority to regulate fishing for moderate livelihood by First Nations harvesters. In their chapter, Shelley Denny, a Mi'kmaw biologist, and Lucia Fanning with the Marine Affairs Program at Dalhousie University point to the legal complexity that exists: the Department of Fisheries and Oceans has authority over regular communal-commercial fishing, but the Mi'kmaq Treaty Right prevails in the regulation of commercial fishing for moderate livelihoods—unless DFO can claim a clear and demonstrably justified purpose for intervening, after consultation. There is sharp disagreement between DFO and First Nations on the limits of this authority.

Anthony Charles from Saint Mary's University makes the point that when rules were being developed to constrain fishing effort, First Nations were excluded from the process. However, they are now developing their own rules through community-based fishing management plans that incorporate Traditional Knowledge about responsible fishing. Charles has several suggestions about how the Mi'kmaq can increase their presence in the fishery under the umbrella of moderate livelihood without placing unsustainable pressure on the resource.

In another chapter focused on the lobster fishery, Jim Jones, a former senior official in the Department of Fisheries and Oceans, describes some innovative ways in which First Nations communities can expand fishing for a moderate livelihood without threatening the sustainability of the resource and the livelihoods and economic interests of non-Indigenous harvesters.

The third segment of the book contains three chapters that clarify and provide context for the *Marshall* decisions. Jane McMillan, who was with Donald Marshall Jr. when he was charged with fishing eel out of season, writes about "Junior's" background, his love of fishing, and his motivation in exercising his Treaty Rights at the time. Three lawyers from the McInnes Cooper law firm—Jeffery Callaghan, Lucia Westin, and Dan Vanclieaf—provide a succinct primer on the Supreme Court's *Marshall* decisions, what they said and what issues remain unresolved. And to conclude, Naiomi Metallic and Constance MacIntosh, both faculty members at the Schulich School of Law at Dalhousie University, argue that "[w]hile the court in *Marshall*...acknowledged Canada could lawfully 'regulate' the Treaty Right, regulate does not mean Canada may legislate and limit the Treaty Right in whatever way it sees fit."

The fourth segment of the book contains chapters that express Mi'kmaw perspectives on the development of First Nations fisheries and the moderate livelihood right. We begin with two interviews with Mi'kmaw Elders. The first is with Albert Marshall from Eskasoni First Nation who challenges the term "moderate livelihood." "If we are fishing in moderation," he says, "it means we are being held back. Rather, it should be that we are fishing to enable future generations access to a healthy, vibrant ecosystem." Kerry Prosper, an Elder from the Paqtnkek Mi'kmaq Nation, recalls the times when he and other Mi'kmaq from the community would be harassed by fish and game officials for exercising their Treaty Right to hunt and fish, even when that occurred within reserve boundaries. The third chapter in this segment shares public statements issued by the Assembly of Nova Scotia Mi'kmaw Chiefs on the violence experienced by the Mi'kmaw fishing community in the fall of 2020 and on their positions on Treaty Rights and the failure of the federal government to meet its duty to consult as affirmed by Supreme Court decisions.

As noted above, one area of strong disagreement between First Nations leaders and non-Indigenous harvesters and their organizations is the issue of self-determination over Indigenous fisheries. As a pertinent example, Amber Giles, a specialist in fisheries management from Wolastoq territory, and her co-authors describe how Mi'kmaw traditions and community values govern the way harvesters from the Eskasoni First Nation fish for eels. In a speech to the Senate of Canada, reproduced here, Senator Daniel Christmas, who has had senior decision making roles at Membertou First Nation, makes the point that the Mi'kmaq have been exercising self-management and conserving the fisheries resource for millennia, applying the Mi'kmaw traditional law called *Netukulimk*.

Section v gives examples of commercial harvester and community voices. It begins with public statements made by non-Indigenous commercial harvester leaders and their organizations. They express frustration at having no say in government decisions on First Nations fishing rights that have wider impacts on licensing, quota allocations, and the management of different fisheries. While expressing support for the continuing development of First Nations fisheries and rejecting violence and racism, they strongly emphasize the need for a single, unified regulatory system defined and enforced by DFO.

In the fall of 2020, Allister Surette, the president and vice-chancellor of Université Sainte-Anne, was appointed as the Special Federal Representative to serve as a neutral third party and advise on how to rebuild trust between commercial fish harvesters and First Nations in Southwest Nova Scotia. In the chapter that contains an interview with him, he describes the roots of the conflict and delineates possible paths forward.

Two further chapters round out this segment. We describe an initiative carried out in Southwest Nova Scotia in the 2018–19 period aimed at improving dialogue and understanding between Mi'kmaq First Nations and non-Indigenous harvester groups. The combined group met fourteen times over two years, providing a model for dialogue that would benefit both sides. In addition, an interview with fisheries consultant Gilles Thériault, a founder of the Maritime Fishermen's Union and long-time advisor to First Nations, explains how the communal-commercial fisheries have evolved in New Brunswick in the post-*Marshall* period.

In the final segment of the book, we turn to particular issues or flashpoints that continue to divide participants in the inshore fishery, and we explore ideas for their resolution. One inescapable reality is that First Nations are struggling to make gains in the face of the biological limits characterizing commercially exploited species. In her article, Susanna Fuller, who works for Oceans North, highlights the challenges involved in balancing Indigenous Rights in the context of declining and vulnerable fish populations.

A second issue we explore in this segment is the reality of racist expression and behaviour at the grassroots level. Fred Wien and Jeff Denis, a sociologist at McMaster University and an expert on racism, argue in their chapter that acts of racism came to the forefront in the fall of 2020, as they did shortly after the *Marshall* decision in 1999–2000, as a response to sharpened competition for resources and the perception in the non-Indigenous community that their access to the resource and their way of life were threatened. Some in the community used racist animosity toward the Mi'kmaq as a tool in the struggle, both to demean the humanity of perceived "outsiders" and to mobilize support among their community members.

Another "hot button" issue not yet resolved is the giant step taken by Membertou First Nation and some other Mi'kmaw communities in partnership with a multinational seafood company to purchase Clearwater Seafoods, the largest shellfish-processing company in Canada. The fear among non-Indigenous harvesters and their organizations is that Clearwater will use its new partnership with First Nations to get around government rules that until now have largely prevented processing companies from also harvesting fish in inshore fisheries for lobster, crab, and other valuable species. Drawing on his own research, Ryan Stack, a PhD candidate in social accounting at Queen's University, reviews the details of this purchase.

Finally, this segment contains a record of conversations with several Mi'kmaw leaders, including the Mikmaw Grand Chief Norman Sylliboy, Senator Daniel Christmas, Member of Parliament Jaime Battiste, and

Regional Vice-Chief for the Assembly of First Nations, P. J. Prosper. They discuss the merits of proceeding with two initiatives: the establishment of an Atlantic First Nations Fishing Authority and the creation of one or more dialogue tables to bring First Nations and non-Indigenous harvester leaders together.

The concluding chapter summarizes the critical issues and flashpoints that will have to be better managed in the short term, and hopefully resolved over time, if peace with justice is to be achieved in the inshore fishery. Drawing on insights and ideas from the articles collected here, we offer strategic advice to leaders in First Nations, non-Indigenous harvester groups, and government for new initiatives to address these challenges.

OVERVIEW

The **COMMERCIAL FISHERY** and the **DEVELOPMENT** of **FIRST NATIONS FISHERIES**

An **OVERVIEW** of **COMMERCIAL FISHERIES**

by RICK WILLIAMS

T he Supreme Court's 1999 *Marshall* rulings recognized the rights of Indigenous communities in the Maritime provinces and the Gaspé Region of Quebec to harvest and sell fish for commercial purposes. This in turn required the federal government to take immediate steps to expand Indigenous participation in the existing commercial fishery. At the time, almost all commercial fishing licences and quotas were already allocated to non-Indigenous harvesters, so the accelerated development of Indigenous commercial fishing required the transfer of fishing rights and opportunities from non-Indigenous "rights holders" to First Nations communal ownership. Other chapters will examine how these changes are being pursued and the often difficult interactions among Indigenous and non-Indigenous groups and government decision makers in this process. For readers who are not familiar with the fishing industry and how it is structured and managed, this chapter describes the structure of the commercial fishery and its economic value for the region.

THE INSHORE FISHERY IN THE MARITIMES AND QUEBEC

In 2018 the Canadian fish-harvesting industry generated $3.7 billion in total plant gate revenues (or "landed value") flowing to fish-harvesting enterprises and fishing communities. Of that total value, 65 percent, or

$2.4 billion, was landed by fleets in the three Maritime provinces and Quebec, and of that an estimated $2 billion was landed by independent owner-operated inshore and midshore vessels.[1] Industrial fleets with large offshore vessels virtually disappeared from Canadian waters after the catastrophic groundfish collapse in the 1990s. Today the commercial fishery in Canada is overwhelmingly an industry comprising small and medium-sized owner-operated enterprises (SMES).

Within this picture, shellfish fisheries are dominant. In 2019, before the COVID pandemic disruptions, the landed value for lobster in the Maritimes and Quebec was $1.7 billion, representing 47 percent of the total for all species. Snow crab contributed another $857 million, representing 24 percent of total landed value. While more recent official DFO landings data was not available at the time of writing, there are strong signals that the industry set new earnings records in 2021 as global markets rebounded sharply after a down year in 2020 due to the pandemic.

The current structure of the commercial fishery in the Maritimes and Quebec is evident in the following table. Committed professional harvesters who hold licences for lobster, snow crab, and a few other key commercial species are categorized by DFO as "Core" and "Independent Core" owner-operators.

Table 1.1.1 Numbers of Core Licenses and Lobster and Crab Licenses, Maritime Provinces, and Quebec, 2020

Province	Core and Independent Core Licence Holders	Lobster Licence Holders	Crab Licence Holders
Nova Scotia	3,210	2,969	684
New Brunswick[2]	1,370	1,458	236
PEI	1,273	1,223	134
Quebec[3]	961	583	395
Total	6,814	6,233	1,449

To provide a picture of the economic value of inshore fishing enterprises, the following table provides the average landed value generated by lobster and snow crab licences in each province in 2018.

Table 1.1.2 Average Landed Value Per Lobster and
Snow Crab Licence by Province, 2018

	NS	NB	PEI	QC
Lobster	$238,364	$189,474	$159,743	$198,664
Snow Crab[4]	$256,630	$816,033	$830,550	$424,166

This data would suggest that most lobster and crab enterprises generated good incomes for fish harvesters in 2018. Crew sizes in inshore fleets range from one or two persons on boats that fish lobster close to shore, to three to five on bigger boats that set their traps in deeper offshore waters, to eight or more on midshore crab vessels.

The following table shows the numbers of individuals (captains and crew) who were employed in fish-harvesting jobs and their average fishing incomes in 2018.[5]

Table 1.1.3 Numbers of Individuals Employed in Fish Harvesting,
and Average Fishing Employment Incomes, 2018

	NS	NB	PEI	PQ
Number of Harvesters	11,340	6,000	3,700	4,070
Average Fishing Incomes	$38,300	$34,000	$27,300	$32,000

In 2018, the fishery generated almost $870 million in employment income flowing through fishing communities in the three Maritime provinces and Quebec. The great majority of fishing jobs are seasonal, averaging twenty-six weeks of employment or fewer per year. Over 90 percent of fish harvesters qualify for, and receive, Employment Insurance benefits to supplement their incomes during the non-fishing months of the year.

One more perspective to bear in mind: the inshore fishery is now a dynamic growth sector within the rural coastal economy of Atlantic Canada. The following table shows changes in total harvester incomes, total catch volumes and landed values for all species, and total value of international exports for the three Maritime provinces and Quebec over the 2009 to 2018 period. The dollar figures are adjusted for inflation (constant dollars 2018).

Table 1.1.4 Changes in Catch Volumes, Total Landed Value, Value of Seafood Exports, and Harvester Incomes, Maritime Provinces, and Quebec, 2009 to 2018, in Constant Dollar (2018) Value

	Total Landings (Metric Tonnes)	Total Landed Value ($000s)	Total Value International Exports ($000s)	Total Harvester Incomes ($000s)
2009	485,819	$1,132,612	$1,877,569	$388,637
2018	406,143	$2,382,832	$3,850,673	$869,572
% Change	-16%	+110%	+105%	+ 124%

These data describe an industry that has grown dramatically in economic impact coming out of the Great Recession (2007 to 2009). This growth was not generated by higher production volumes but rather by increases in product values in the marketplace. Overall, the industry is landing fewer fish, but the market value of what is produced has more than doubled over the period, and working harvesters appear to be receiving fair shares of the growth dividends.

The explanations for these trends are numerous—changing consumer tastes in domestic markets, trade agreements providing greater access to countries that consume higher levels of seafood, and surging demand from the expanding middle class in China. Barring geopolitical disruptions or another global recession, these positive economic trends are expected to continue as long as Canadian fish stocks are harvested at biologically sustainable levels.

At this point, we have the fish and we have the markets, but perhaps the most serious limitation on continued growth in today's owner-operator fishery comes from demographic trends. With continuing out-migration and an aging population overall, most fishing communities just don't have enough younger people coming into the fishery to replace the 40 percent of working fish harvesters who are expected to age out of the industry over the current decade.

SUMMING IT UP

The post-*Marshall* push by First Nations to expand their access to commercial fisheries is happening at a unique point in time where major changes are coming together to create new opportunities and risks. While a few key fish stocks are endangered, particularly mackerel and herring, landings in commercially valuable shellfish fisheries are stable if not going up. The fishing economy is booming, and inshore enterprise owners and working harvesters are enjoying income gains that have never been experienced before.

Among other things, this transformation is driving up the value of fishing enterprises at a time when many older owner-operators are looking for good prices for their businesses to support them in retirement. Inflation in licence prices has become a barrier to new entrants and crew workers wanting to become owner-operators and for First Nations wanting to purchase licences to create jobs and incomes in their communities.

However, looming labour shortages across the industry create opportunities for people who haven't grown up in the fishery to get work experience and a toehold in the industry. First Nations communities have many young people looking for access to rewarding careers, and co-operation between Indigenous and non-Indigenous communities to develop mentoring and apprenticeship programs might serve everyone's interests. And many inshore enterprises will change hands over the coming years, providing First Nations with greater access to commercial fishing through conventional market transactions.

An economically robust and sustainable fishery across the Maritimes and Quebec holds potential to help rebuild rural populations and provide jobs and incomes for many young people in First Nations and non-Indigenous communities. There are difficult transitions to be made and competing interests to be balanced, and there have been conflicts among neighbouring communities that need healing. But an industry that is growing and resilient provides a much stronger platform for finding solutions and improving relations.

1.2

DEVELOPMENT of FIRST NATIONS FISHERIES since the *MARSHALL* DECISIONS

by RICK WILLIAMS

T he Supreme Court's seminal decisions on Aboriginal Rights in the 1990s gave First Nations in Canada access to fishing for food, social, and ceremonial purposes. With its 1999 *Marshall* ruling on Treaty Rights, the Court gave First Nations in the Maritimes and Quebec expanding access to the regular commercial fishery. And currently we are seeing the emergence of a third sector for self-regulated small-scale or artisanal fishing for commercial purposes. In the following we describe these three areas of First Nations fisheries development.

I. FOOD, SOCIAL, AND CEREMONIAL FISHING

Fishing for food, social, and ceremonial (FSC) purposes is an inherent "Aboriginal right" as defined by Section 35 in the 1982 Constitution Act and specifically recognized in the Supreme Court's *Sparrow* (1990) decision and subsequent rulings. In the 1996 *Van der Peet* decision,[1] the court defined an Aboriginal right as "a collective right that is an element of a practice, custom, or tradition integral to the distinctive culture of the Indigenous group claiming the right (i.e., fishing for food/social/ceremonial purposes)" and as a "[p]ractice, custom or tradition [that] must have originated before contact with Europeans."

Fisheries and Oceans Canada (DFO) describes its policy for the regulation of FSC fisheries as follows:

> As the right to fish for FSC purposes is communal, the FSC fishing licence is issued to the Indigenous Nation. The Indigenous Nation may then designate some of its members to fish under the communal licence.... Under this type of licence, designated Indigenous harvesters can catch what is needed for themselves and/or their community for FSC purposes. [DFO] evaluates and consults with the Indigenous Nation on any potential changes to these licences.... FSC licence conditions reflect [DFO] regulations as well as management measures and catch monitoring and reporting requirements that promote safe, orderly, and sustainable fishing.[2]

FSC fisheries are well-established and bring significant benefits to First Nations communities in all regions of Canada. The federal government provides funding to First Nations to "build and maintain the technical capacity to manage and exercise their own FSC fisheries, including work by Aboriginal Fishery Guardians, such as monitoring and enforcement, science and technical fieldwork, and community engagement and education."[3]

Continuing development and management of FSC fisheries has been supported by DFO's Aboriginal Fisheries Strategy (AFS) Program. The program was initiated in 1992 and provides for the development of time-limited agreements between DFO and each Nation that set out the amounts that may be fished for FSC purposes by species, area, gear types, seasons, and reporting requirements. These agreements also include commitments to co-operation on stock assessment and enhancement and habitat protection projects. DFO has negotiated AFS agreements with thirty-four Nations in the Maritimes and Quebec, with an annual program investment of approximately $6 million for core operations, capacity building, and conservation projects.

Several *Marshall* First Nations have set up integrated management systems for their FSC and their commercial fishing activities. To take one good example, in 2001 Acadia First Nation in Nova Scotia incorporated a community-owned company, Kespuwick Resources, to manage its Netukulimk (FSC) Fish Harvest Plan[4] and its communal-commercial fishing activities across Southwest Nova Scotia. Their website explains, "The objective of Kespuwick Resources Inc. is to establish a vertically integrated, multi-species, rights-based fishing enterprise that will provide a variety of employment opportunities for Band members while building a positive working relationship with non-Native fishermen and companies."[5]

Kespuwick oversees harvesting with forty-six FSC and communal-commercial licences with lobster being most important, but also including tuna, crab, scallops, gaspereau, and swordfish.[6] For FSC fishing for lobster, each community member over eighteen years of age can fish three traps throughout the year. The rules stipulate that "no more than one-half of the daily allowable catch may be sold, traded or bartered for bait, fishing supplies or other food for the family. For the FSC lobster catch, no more than 20 can be sold per day by any harvester."[7] Kespuwick maintains overall catch data and shares it with DFO to support stock conservation.

As mentioned, First Nations FSC fishing has been underway for some time and is widely accepted and uncontroversial in most fishing regions. However, there have been complaints from non-Indigenous harvester groups in a few regions about FSC fish being sold under the table due to lax enforcement by DFO. As well, some Indigenous leaders across Canada continue to challenge DFO's management of the program as an unjustified incursion on self-determination rights.

2. COMMUNAL-COMMERCIAL FISHERIES

RESPONSE TO *MARSHALL* DECISIONS

The Supreme Court's *Marshall* rulings directed the federal government to expand First Nations access to commercial fisheries but left critical decisions, including the appropriate share of the total commercial fishery and the meaning of "moderate livelihood," to be worked out through negotiation of a new global treaty or treaties. With conflicts breaking out on the water and between communities immediately after the rulings, the government moved quickly on two fronts, as reported by the Canadian Press on February 9, 2001.

> Robert Nault, Minister of Indian Affairs and Northern Development [DIAND], and Herb Dhaliwal, Minister of Fisheries and Oceans [DFO] today announced the launch of the Federal Government's long-term strategy to address the Supreme Court's 1999 *Marshall* decision and build a sustainable treaty relationship with Mi'kmaq and Maliseet communities. In addition, both Ministers named the negotiators they have appointed to represent the federal government in this process.
>
> The long-term strategy will proceed along two complementary tracks. The objective of the process led by DIAND is to reach long-term agreement on issues of Aboriginal and treaty rights. Recognizing that it will take time to reach agreement, a second initiative will be carried out by DFO to negotiate fishing agreements that will provide increased First Nation access to the fishery on an immediate basis. Fishing agreements will be without prejudice to the positions of the federal government or First Nations in any future negotiations.[8]

For DFO, the immediate priority was to fast-track the integration of *Marshall* First Nations within the existing commercial fishery by means of short-term interim agreements. Under these agreements, Nations received DFO-issued licences and quota allocations to fish during regular commercial seasons and subject to DFO regulations and conservation requirements. The one difference with the non-Indigenous fishery is that the access rights are owned communally by First Nations governments rather than by individual enterprise owner-operators. The agreements provided access to a wide range of harvesting activities, from small-scale trapping or netting of river species like eels and gaspereau, to lucrative lobster and snow crab fishing with inshore and midshore vessels, to licences and quota shares in large-scale offshore industrial fisheries (e.g., surf clams, shrimp, offshore lobster).

Some First Nations fish their communal-commercial licences and quotas with captains and crew from their own communities. Others do not have enough community members with the requisite skills and experience, so they generate royalty income flows by leasing some or all their access rights to non-Indigenous crews or to fish processing companies.[9] There has also been success for some communities in employing non-Indigenous captains to operate their vessels and train and mentor community members to learn the trade.

The quotas for offshore industrial fisheries are either leased out or fished under partnership agreements between First Nations and non-Indigenous fishing companies, often with job guarantees for community members as part of the agreements. The 2019 agreement between Clearwater Seafoods and fourteen First Nations to share the offshore surf clam quota is a pertinent example.[10]

DFO policy documents and reports indicate that, in response to the *Marshall* decisions, DFO has invested more than $550 million since 1999 "to increase Indigenous participation in commercial fisheries and contribute to *the pursuit of a moderate livelihood*"[11] (emphasis added).

This effort began with the *Marshall* Response Initiative (MRI) launched immediately after the Supreme Court's rulings to rapidly expand Indigenous access to the commercial fishery. The program provided many of the thirty-two First Nations that participated with their first access to the modern-day industry.[12] DFO investments included $323 million for acquisition of licences, vessels, and gear, and $131 million for fisheries governance, capacity building, harvester training, and at-sea mentoring. According to DFO, annual landed value by *Marshall* First Nations fisheries increased from $3 million in 1999 to $50 million by the conclusion of the MRI in 2006.[13]

This early period also saw two new DFO programs aimed at building First Nations capacity to conduct and manage fisheries: the At-Sea Mentoring Initiative and the Fisheries Operations Management Initiative. These provided over nine thousand days of at-sea training and helped develop First Nations' capacities to plan and conduct their fishing operations and fisheries Guardian programs.

The MRI was followed in 2007 by the Atlantic Integrated Commercial Fisheries Initiative aimed at building capacity in commercial fisheries and aquaculture operations and at providing better-targeted training. All but one of the thirty-five *Marshall* First Nations benefited from the almost $100 million invested by DFO in acquiring licences and vessels, upgrading vessels and gear, and building onshore facilities. The program also delivered 9,500 training days to support Indigenous harvesters and land-based staff in building skills and capacities to operate and maintain 320 fishing vessels.

One other key element in DFO's overall *Marshall* implementation strategy was the banking of fishing licences for future distribution to First Nations through new treaties or other agreements. In the early- to mid-2000s, some 322 licences for lobster, groundfish, herring, and other species were purchased from retiring non-Indigenous enterprise owners and taken out of active use. These are all available now to be transferred to First Nations on a proportional basis as new fishing agreements are put in place. This has proven to be a prudent investment by government because the market value of many of these licences has grown dramatically since their purchase.

RIGHTS RECONCILIATION AGREEMENTS

While real progress was made after the *Marshall* rulings in expanding access to commercial fisheries through short-term agreements with individual Nations, there was little success on the government's second track—negotiation of a "long-term agreement on issues of Aboriginal and treaty rights" with the wider Mi'kmaw and Wolastoqey Nations. To pursue this objective, in 2017 DFO proposed a new type of accord called a Rights Reconciliation Agreement (RRA).[14] Unlike interim agreements under the MRI, RRAS would be negotiated with groups of two or more *Marshall* Nations, would include formal recognition of Treaty Rights, and would support comprehensive fisheries development plans of ten years or more in duration. The agreements would also require commitments to co-operative engagement in fisheries management, conservation, and science research.

To support and provide incentives for this new approach, signatories to new RRAS would have access to a $300-million DFO investment fund and to DFO's bank of licences. The funds would be distributed on a proportional basis among the First Nations covered by *Marshall*, to be used for the acquisition of licences or quota, vessels, and gear. With self-governance rights embedded in the agreements, the Nations could themselves determine how best to utilize newly acquired resources to develop both FSC and commercial fisheries. Additional funds would be available for capacity building to support these expanded self-governance elements.

Up to the time of writing, only three such agreements have been finalized, but they cover three of the largest communities with about 25 percent of the total Indigenous population impacted by the *Marshall* rulings.

In August 2019 the Elsipogtog and Esgenoôpetitj First Nations in New Brunswick together announced a ten-year "Interim Fisheries Implementation Agreement" with DFO to uphold "the Supreme Court of Canada's decision regarding these First Nations' Treaty rights to harvest and sell fish in pursuit of a moderate livelihood."[15] The agreement will expand commercial fisheries capacities in the two communities with funds for more licences, quota, vessels, and gear, and it also committed the parties to a co-operative fisheries management approach with expanded self-regulation. As one part of the agreement, ten of DFO's banked lobster licences from the southern Gulf of St. Lawrence are to be shared between the two Nations.

At the same time, a ten-year renewable "Fisheries Resources Agreement" was signed with Wolastoqiyik of Viger First Nation in Quebec's Gaspé Region. It recognized "the First Nation's Treaty rights to harvest and sell fish in pursuit of a moderate livelihood" and provided funding for the Nation "to acquire more fisheries licences and quota, as well as vessels and gear and [to establish] a process for a collaborative fisheries management approach."[16]

A third Rights Reconciliation Agreement signed in April 2021 between DFO and the Listuguj First Nation, also in the Gaspé, contained similar language on Treaty Rights and commitments to providing more licences, vessels, and gear, and supports for expanded self-governance.[17]

While negotiations are ongoing on specific fisheries development plans, it is our understanding that each of these three agreements involves a core financial commitment by DFO based on proportional access to the $300 million fund and an expansion of rights to regulate how their fisheries are planned and conducted.

It should be noted that, up to the time of writing in early 2022, no additional RRAs with other Nations have been announced, and some First Nations leaders in Nova Scotia have criticized the agreements that have been reached as making unacceptable concessions on Indigenous fishing and self-governance rights.

DIFFERENT APPROACHES

A few examples provide insight into the progress to date in developing First Nations communal-commercial fisheries. There is no one source of up-to-date information on communal-commercial fisheries developments across the First Nations covered by *Marshall*, so the following information is drawn somewhat randomly from the websites of individual Nations and from conversations with fisheries staff.

Eskasoni First Nation in Cape Breton has established its own company, Crane Cove Seafoods, to manage quotas for snow crab and shrimp and to manage a processing plant. Seven community-owned vessels fish for lobster, shrimp, snow crab, and other species and operate out of the ports of Petit-de-Grat and Canso.

Also in Cape Breton, the Membertou Nation likewise organizes and operates its commercial fishery through an incorporated company, First Fishermen Seafoods. According to their website,

> First Fishermen Seafoods is an Aboriginally owned and operated sea-food company.... We emphasize the highest quality seafood products from a fishery rich in history and tradition. First Fishermen Seafoods believes strongly in following the traditional ways passed down from our ancestors, where nature and the environment are respected and appreciated.... Utilizing the fleet of six vessels Membertou's First Fishermen Seafood's Division harvests a variety of ground fish, shellfish and large Pelagic including tuna and swordfish.[18]

In its 2020 financial report, Membertou reported total earnings of $5.6 million from its fishing operations, contributing 11 percent of total band revenues. This figure would not include the employment income earned by working harvesters from the community.

Membertou also led the way in building the consortium of six Nations in Nova Scotia and one in Newfoundland and Labrador that recently purchased 50 percent ownership of Clearwater Seafoods, the largest shellfish processing company in Canada. Membertou holds 36 percent of the First Nations share in the consortium.[19] Premium Brands, a multinational based in Vancouver, BC, owns the remaining 50 percent of Clearwater.

The Fisheries Department of Sipekne'katik First Nation in mainland Nova Scotia manages thirty-three fishing licences for lobster, snow crab, groundfish, and other species, with several of these licences being leased out to non-Indigenous enterprises.[20] This band initiated the recent challenge to DFO policies when it began issuing its own fishing tags to community members to harvest and sell lobster in a self-regulated, moderate livelihood fishery.

In New Brunswick the Ugpi'ganjig (Eel River Bar) First Nation's Fisheries Department oversees the management of offshore fishing for tuna, snow crab, and shrimp and inshore fishing by community members for lobster, herring, smelt, and salmon. The community owns and operates its own midshore vessel, fishing a large snow crab quota.[21]

Elsipogtog First Nation, also in New Brunswick, worked with the early DFO *Marshall* support programs to build up a fleet of more than seventy inshore vessels harvesting lobster, snow crab, and a few other species. The 2021 fishing season was highly successful for the community-owned fleet, with approximately $19 million in lobster landings and $16 million in snow crab. The Nation owns a freezer unit and two fish plants, the second one a state-of-the-art processing facility completed in 2021 at a cost of $25 million. The community also has a boat repair and storage facility and a sawmill to manufacture pallets and boxes. Profits from the fish plant were invested to build the sawmill operation and to construct sixteen new homes in the community. In total, the Elsipogtog fishery employs over 250 band members in fish harvesting and another 30 or more in processing and ancillary activities. Many qualify for Employment Insurance to supplement their seasonal earnings from fish harvesting and processing.

ECONOMIC BENEFITS FROM COMMUNAL-COMMERCIAL FISHERIES

A 2019 report by the Macdonald-Laurier Institute, authored by Ken Coates, provides the following assessment of the benefits generated by the development of First Nations communal-commercial fisheries after the *Marshall* rulings:

> Communities secured licences, boats, and onshore facilities. Hundreds of Mi'kmaq and Maliseet [Wolastoqiyik] individuals received training as boat captains and crew members. Many new businesses opened under First Nations or joint ownership. First Nations that previously secured little financial return from the fishing industry now received substantial

annual payments, typically through community-owned fishing companies and Aboriginal economic development corporations."[22]

The Coates report estimated the total on-reserve economic benefit derived from commercial fisheries to have grown from $3 million in 1999 to $152 million in 2016.

In a report initially published in 2019, DFO identified the following outcomes from its policies and investments to develop communal-commercial fisheries since the Supreme Court's *Marshall* rulings:

- In 1999, the value of Indigenous communal-commercial landings in the Maritimes and Gaspé region was estimated at $3 million. By 2018, the value of these same landings was $140 million. Additionally, in 2018, these fishing enterprises earned $52 million in indirect fisheries-related revenue.
- First Nations' fishing enterprises...employ almost 1,700 people, of which more than 1,300 are fish harvesters and 358 are land-based employees.
- Each First Nation fishing enterprise has developed and maintains a training plan and to date, over 7,730 days of fisheries training have been delivered to more than 3,475 participants.
- Women make up as much as 33 percent of the workforce in the First Nations' fisheries operations, with approximately 10 percent of fish harvesters being women, and up to 50 percent of management positions within their fishing enterprises being held by women.[23]

In terms of employment gains, the Canada Census provides some information on Indigenous participation in fishing. The following table shows changes from 2001 to 2016 in the numbers of Indigenous individuals who identify fishing as a source of employment in provinces with significant commercial fisheries.[24] We include provinces outside the Maritimes for comparison purposes.[25]

Table 1.2.1. Census Canada—Changes in Aboriginal Employment in Fishing, 2001–2016

	Numbers of individuals reporting fish harvesting as source of employment			Aboriginal individuals as percent of total reporting fish harvesting as source of employment	
	2001	2016	% Change	2001	2016
NF	450	690	53%	2%	9%
NS	350	1,370	291%	4%	13%
PEI	60	120	100%	2%	4%
NB	410	820	100%	10%	18%
QC	125	370	196%	5%	14%
BC	885	935	6%	22%	24%

Although this Census data has its limitations, it does point to significant increases in the numbers of Indigenous fish harvesters and growth in their share of the total fish-harvesting labour force over the 2001–2016 period. In the Maritime provinces and Quebec where DFO's post-*Marshall* initiatives were in effect, the rate of growth in employment was relatively more significant than in British Columbia where Indigenous communities have a long history of successful participation in commercial fishing.

NEWS RELEASE BY THE ASSEMBLY OF NOVA SCOTIA MI'KMAW CHIEFS, SEPTEMBER 10, 2020

"We have the right to self-government and that includes our right to govern our fisheries. We are developing our own sustainable livelihood fishery, separate from the commercial fishery as we have a responsibility to protect our affirmed treaty right, and the court ruling. By working together, we will develop sustainable community fishing plans as this is important to our people today and to the sustainability of the resource for future generations.

—Chief Terry Paul, Fisheries Lead for the
Assembly of Nova Scotia Mi'kmaw Chiefs

3. MODERATE LIVELIHOOD FISHING

The fact that no longer-term multipartite treaties between the Crown and the Mi'kmaw and Wolastoqey Nations in the Maritime provinces and Quebec have been arrived at since the 1999 *Marshall* decisions, and that to date only three Rights Reconciliation Agreements have been signed (and none in Nova Scotia), is evidence of continuing disagreements between many of the *Marshall* First Nations and successive federal governments on the interpretation of the Court's rulings. At the heart of these considerations is the application of the Court's language on the right to earn moderate livelihoods from fishing and the extent of First Nations governance over such fishing activities.

This issue came to the forefront in the early fall of 2020 when the Sipekne'katik First Nation in Nova Scotia began issuing its own licences and trap tags to community members to begin harvesting lobster outside the established commercial fishing season. The stated goal was to create a separate and self-regulated sector for limited-scale artisanal fish harvesting to generate "moderate" incomes. In addition to sparking sometimes violent reactions from non-Indigenous industry groups, this action—followed by similar initiatives by the Potlotek and Pictou Landing First Nations in Nova Scotia—forced DFO to take a clearer position on the underlying issue of self-governance.

The legal questions around moderate livelihood are addressed more fully in other chapters. The purpose here is to describe current approaches to moderate livelihood fishing as a sector distinct from the FSC and regular communal-commercial fisheries.

DFO POLICY RESPONSE

The riots and burning of boats and a plant in Southwest Nova Scotia in the early fall of 2020 was followed by a period of confusion and uncertainty about the DFO response. There were sharp criticisms of the government's failure to intervene more quickly to protect Mi'kmaw harvesters, but also concerted pushback from a wide range of non-Indigenous industry groups demanding that DFO enforce a uniform set of rules for seasons and licensing requirements.

In January 2021, then-DFO Minister Bernadette Jordan announced "a new, optional path for First Nations in the Maritimes and the Gaspé region to aid their members in fishing in pursuit of a moderate livelihood."[26] The minister committed the department to

> ...working with interested communities from the Mi'kmaq and Maliseet [Wolastoqiyik] First Nations and the Peskotomuhkati to develop and implement moderate livelihood fishing plans. These fishing plans may be unique to each community and will be licensed by Fisheries and Oceans Canada. They can also be long-term or yearly and can be used ahead of reaching a Rights Reconciliation Agreement. This will enable First Nations to fish and sell their catch in pursuit of a moderate livelihood this season. A key element of these fishing plans is that all moderate livelihood fishing activities will operate within the commercial season. Fishing seasons help ensure that fish species are harvested sustainably and maintain orderly, predictable, and well-managed fisheries.

This announcement made clear that all commercial fishing by *Marshall* First Nations in 2021 would be subject to DFO licensing, seasons, and operational regulations. It was followed by public statements by DFO officials that harvesters fishing out of season or without DFO licences would be taken into custody and their vessels and gear seized. Some arrests and gear seizures did take place in the spring of 2021, but there was no repeat of 2020's open conflicts.

While many First Nations leaders described this position as a betrayal of the commitments to Aboriginal and Treaty Rights, the announcement nevertheless communicated a willingness on the government's part to accommodate small-scale moderate livelihood fishing with unique harvesting plans and enhanced self-governance.

RECENT DEVELOPMENTS

The first break in the apparent impasse came in June 2021 with the announcement that the Potlotek First Nation in Cape Breton, with support from the Assembly of Nova Scotia Mi'kmaw Chiefs and Kwilmu'kw Maw-klusuaqn Negotiation Office (KMKNO), had reached agreement with

DFO on a new fishing plan to allow "the province's first authorized moderate livelihood fishery to go ahead."[27] Potlotek Chief Wilbert Marshall was quoted in a CBC News story saying: "We built a solid plan that laid out our tagging and reporting structures and are developing enforcement protocols with DFO's conservation and protection branch."[28] A DFO announcement described elements of the plan as follows: "As an interim measure, we will be recognizing those harvesters designated under Potlotek's plan to be authorized to fish 700 jakej (lobster) traps without adding additional access and during the established season underway in...Potlotek's identified traditional district.... In acknowledging that this is an interim measure, we are committed to continuing consultations with the community moving forward, including about community concerns on access."[29]

In October 2021 four First Nations in mainland Nova Scotia—Acadia, Annapolis Valley, Bear River, and Glooscap—announced that they also had reached an "interim joint agreement" with DFO for moderate livelihood fisheries based on the Potlotek model. In a CBC News story, Chief Sidney Peters of the Glooscap First Nation explained the purpose of the agreement as follows: "It is important that Mi'kmaw harvesters can exercise their rights without fear of their gear and equipment being seized. That is why we have been open and transparent, sharing our plan with DFO from the onset."[30]

Under their Kespukwitk Netukulimk Livelihood Fisheries Management Plan for lobster, the four Nations will jointly manage 3,500 lobster traps for fishing during commercial seasons with licences transferred from the banked licences held by DFO. The DFO announcement describes the new fishery as follows: "DFO will recognize those harvesters designated under the Kespukwitk Netukulimk Livelihood Fisheries Management Plan to be authorized to fish up to 3,500 jakej (lobster) traps (up to 70 per harvester) during the established seasons in LFAS [Lobster Fishing Areas] 33, 34, and 35—which surround the traditional Kespukwitk District."[31]

These fishing plans for the five Nova Scotia Nations are all short-term and subject to future negotiation. They do include a further expansion of self-governance rights for moderate livelihood fishing with a requirement for co-operative management with DFO.

As of June 2022, new moderate livelihood fishing plans have been approved by DFO for Pictou Landing First Nation,[32] We'koqma'q First Nation in Cape Breton,[33] and Lennox Island First Nation in PEI,[34] and DFO has announced that a quota in the elver (baby eel) fishery has been reallo-cated to First Nations for moderate livelihood purposes.[35]

It remains to be seen whether more *Marshall* First Nations will utilize this approach as a means to exercise the moderate livelihood right set out by the Supreme Court.

LOOKING FORWARD

This limited survey of fisheries development in the thirty-five *Marshall* First Nations suggests a few areas where major changes are underway, and poli-cies and practices will continue to evolve.

It seems clear that food, social, and ceremonial fisheries are not a signifi-cant source of future economic benefits for First Nations, but they are very important for community well-being and for expanding self-governance in fisheries through Guardian programs and stock conservation work. FSC fishing may also provide continuing opportunities to introduce young peo-ple to the fishing occupation through training and practical experience.

The communal-commercial fishery clearly is a dynamic growth sector for many of the *Marshall* First Nations. Several First Nations have already built up substantial fishing businesses with communally owned harvesting and processing operations, and these advances are generating more jobs and revenues for their communities. DFO's $300-million fund for *Marshall* First Nations to acquire more licences, quotas, and vessels through Rights Reconciliation Agreements and the bank of licences available to be distrib-uted as part of the RRAs provide certainty for future growth opportunities.

Until recently DFO did not seem to have envisioned the creation of a dis-tinct moderate livelihood fishing sector to provide opportunities for many more First Nations community members to catch and sell modest quanti-ties of fish. DFO's approach to meeting the Supreme Court's moderate liveli-hood objective has been more focused on integrating First Nations within the existing commercial fishery and expanding the Indigenous share of licences and quotas.

However, since the controversies in the fall of 2020, DFO has demon-strated a clear willingness to negotiate innovative fishing plans to expand access to fishing for moderate livelihoods. The potential benefits include more employment and incomes from fisheries and new pathways for community members to gain access to fishing as a potential career.

After looking at the overall advances in First Nations fisheries since the 1999 *Marshall* rulings, in 2019 John Paul, then Executive Director of the Atlantic Policy Congress of First Nations Chiefs, and Joseph Quesnel, then Program Manager of Macdonald-Laurier Institute's Aboriginal Canada and the Natural Resource Economy (ACNRE) Project, drew the following conclusion:

> All Maritime residents should applaud the impact of the 1999 Marshall ruling. It set the stage for a growing fishing industry for Mi'kmaq and Maliseet [Wolastoqiyik] communities, providing them with more economic prosperity and self-determination, while also leading to increased mutual understanding between Indigenous and non-Indigenous fishing communities.
>
> Twenty years after this seminal decision, First Nation fishing communities in the Maritimes are poised for even more future growth as they seek more autonomy over their fishing sectors.[36]

A HISTORY of EXCLUSION

by FRED WIEN

Mi'kmaw economic history, and indeed that of First Nations more generally, is often depicted in almost idyllic terms in the pre-contact period, followed by a steady decline to poverty and dependence once European and American settlers flooded into their territory. The reality is more complicated and requires understanding different stages in that history, each with its distinctive characteristics, even as the overall narrative is one of dispossession and marginalization. This chapter outlines five stages but pays particular attention to the processes whereby the Mi'kmaq came to be excluded from the fishing sector, which at one time was at the core of their seasonal economy.[1]

EARLY DAYS PRIOR TO 1500

The traditional territory of the Mi'kmaq extended from the southern portion of the Gaspé Region through much of New Brunswick and all of Nova Scotia and Prince Edward Island. Unlike some other First Nations populations, such as the Haudenosaunee, the Mi'kmaw economy did not feature the growing of crops. Rather, it was based on seasonal patterns of hunting, fishing, and gathering.

Food was most readily available in the spring, summer, and fall when the Mi'kmaq would gather in their villages, usually at the mouth of a large river.[2] Fishing was the mainstay during this time, derived from fish spawning runs (e.g., smelt, herring, and salmon) in the early part of the season followed by harvesting species such as shellfish, lobster, crab, eel, and cod.

From July through the fall, berries, nuts, and roots would be gathered. In the fall, hunters moved to the interior with their families, fishing from small inland villages, hunting geese, ducks, and other fowl as well as larger game such as beaver, moose, and caribou.

Like most pre-industrial people, the Mi'kmaq and Wolastoqiyik depended on nature's bounty to provide for themselves. Therefore, the Wolastoqiyik and Mi'kmaq stressed the importance of maintaining close spiritual relationships with all living organisms, and especially fish and animal spirits. Like other Indigenous Peoples, the Wolastoqiyik and Mi'kmaq believed that animals allowed themselves to be killed so that humans could live. However, the continuance of this relationship depended upon respecting the laws that governed the relationship, such as properly disposing of fish and animal bones and not overhunting.[3]

With this kind of a subsistence economy, there was little room for surplus accumulation. Some trading relationships developed, but the emphasis was on just taking sufficient quantities to meet local needs. Indeed, shortages were inevitable, depending on conditions, and certainly people experienced hardship and even starvation.

EARLY EUROPEAN CONTACT AND THE FUR TRADE, 1500–1783

The first regular contact that the Mi'kmaq had was with fishermen who began using the coast for the purpose of drying fish in the 1550s. This led to trade between the parties, with the Mi'kmaq exchanging goods such as furs and handcrafts for items such as iron goods and foodstuffs. A more organized fur trade followed, with the French establishing fur trading stations and ancillary settlements at locations such as Port Royal (1605). During the height of the fur trade between 1580 and 1700, furs from beaver, otter, marten, fisher, mink, bear, muskrat, moose, deer, ermine, and fox were made available by First Nations people. As the British became ascendant, truck houses were established for trading purposes.

For the Mi'kmaq, there were many negative features of the fur trade, such as growing dependence on European food and clothing; the undermining of traditional roles for the hunting family, leaders, and shamen; the depletion of game; and increased intertribal hostilities. However, in contrast to the settler economy that followed, the Mi'kmaq, able to draw on traditional hunting skills, played a valuable role in the economy of the fur trade. They adapted readily to the roles of hunting, preparing hides, and trading. As the fur trade waned, they were able to return to a more balanced and seasonably varied lifestyle, but pressures on their traditional lands increased, as did exhortations to settle and take up farming. The Mi'kmaq were also drawn into the French–English conflicts of the time.

The Mi'kmaq signed a series of treaties of peace and friendship, but not land surrender, with representatives of the British Crown beginning in 1726. As an example, the 1726 treaty brought an end to a three-year war between New England and the Wabenaki alliance (including the Mi'kmaq) that was engaged by New England fishermen pushing vigorously into Nova Scotian coastal waters. The treaty enjoined the British from interfering with the Indigenous communities' fishing, hunting, planting, and other activities. A later treaty, signed in 1752, formalized a commercial relationship between the British and the Mi'kmaq with the establishment of truck houses to facilitate trade. It also affirmed the 1726 provision, saying that "the said Tribe of Indians shall not be hindered from but shall have free liberty of hunting and fishing as usual."[4]

ALMOST EXTINCTION, 1784–1867

The rise of the settler economy represented a much more difficult challenge for the Mi'kmaq, and indeed it almost led to their extermination. Settlers flooded into their territory in large numbers, especially after the American Revolution. Indeed, the population of Nova Scotia tripled in one year in the 1780s. In this context, the Mi'kmaq were pushed aside. Their skills were, for the most part, not desired, they had little to trade, they lost their role as allies as British–French conflicts subsided, and they were no longer needed to help the newcomers survive a harsh environment. Disruption of traditional lifestyles, dietary changes, epidemics such as smallpox and typhus, and genocidal policies such as the offering of bounties for the collection of Mi'kmaw scalps all took their toll.

Virginia Miller, an anthropologist from Dalhousie University, estimates that the original population of the Mi'kmaq was in the order of 26,000, a number that had declined to 10,000 by 1761 and all the way to 1,300 at the lowest point in the 1840s.[5]

The settlers, of course, took the choicest lands—those adjacent to rivers, so that they would have waterpower for saw- and gristmills; those with access to the sea for fishing; and those with the best soils for agriculture. To take fishing as an example, "European settlements pushed the [Mi'kmaq] to more marginal coastal and interior locations. Dams and mills interfered with the seasonal migration of fish, and those people in control of the river mouth were able to net the bulk of the catch before the fish could move upstream to where the [Mi'kmaq] fishermen were now likely to be."[6]

In this context, the Mi'kmaq came to be seen with a mixture of fear and annoyance, as a hindrance to settlement and commerce, and as a population increasingly in need of relief payments. Loss of access to their traditional lands and resources proceeded apace. With respect to fishing, for example, a report from 1847 concludes that "the erection of dams across the rivers have destroyed some of the best salmon and alewife fisheries in the province. The best shore fisheries are occupied by white inhabitants, from which the Indian is sometimes driven by force."[7] Further damage came from the growing mining and lumbering activities of the times.[8] With colonial government policy focused on having the Mi'kmaq end their nomadic ways, they were required to settle down in small communities (reserves) where they were encouraged to take up agricultural pursuits.

Ashley Sutherland points out that most of the reserve lands were located inland, serving to isolate the Mi'kmaq and prevent access to the waterways. "In addition, the land was not suitable to hunt, nor did it provide the necessary resources, such as enough firewood, for survival. So, naturally, the Mi'kmaq continued to practice their traditional transient lifestyle and move from one location to another. As the Mi'kmaq moved from their seasonal camp sites, Settlers encroached on the land."[9]

Despite overwhelming hardship, there are some signs toward the end of this period that a measure of recovery was taking place. The size of the population stabilized, for example, and then began to grow slowly.

MARGINAL EMPLOYMENT, DEPRESSION, AND CENTRALIZATION, 1867–1970

This period can be considered one where the Mi'kmaq became increasingly self-reliant but in precarious positions on the fringes of the non-Indigenous economy and working for minimal returns. On the one hand, the trend noted at the end of the previous section continued. That is, government policy continued to emphasize having a sedentary population engaged in agriculture but provided insufficient land and resources to make it a reality. This period also witnessed the Mi'kmaq serving as a mobile and often seasonal labour force when opportunities arose. Thus, the Mi'kmaq could be found travelling to help with harvesting within Nova Scotia, as well as to Western Canada. They were especially noted for their role in potato and blueberry harvesting in the Eastern United States, and indeed whole families would travel in August to Maine for the blueberry harvest, for example, making it as much a social as an economic occasion.[10]

Other forms of wage labour were in evidence. At Bear River, for example, some Mi'kmaq were employed in a dowel factory. Near Shubenacadie there was work loading lumber at sawmills and in a brickworks. In Cape Breton, men cut timbers to serve as props for coal mines or helped with the construction of the St. Peters Canal. Farther afield, Mi'kmaw families continued to travel to New England, working in shoe and textile factories. With respect to self-employment, Millbrook became known as the centre for masonry work, while in other locations there was coopering (barrels and axe- and pick handles) or handcrafts such as baskets, moccasins, and chair seats, often peddled door to door by Mi'kmaw women and children. Guiding tourists in hunting and fishing expeditions was also a feature of this period.

While one can conclude that the Mi'kmaq were able to establish a reasonable degree of self-sufficiency based on low-income self-employment and wage labour, this period was also notable for some very damaging federal policies and events:

- Confederation in 1867 brought with it the provision of the BNA Act to the effect that the federal government would be responsible for "Indians and lands reserved for Indians." As it played out, the role that was assumed went well beyond organizing relations with First Nations. The government took the additional step of regulating and controlling their internal affairs. Thus the Indian Act is full of provisions setting out how Indian governments should be structured, what cultural practices could no longer be followed, and what approvals would need to be obtained for people to travel or to engage in commerce.

- Beginning in the 1880s, the federal government mandated and funded churches to operate residential schools, requiring Indigenous children to attend, with ruinous consequences to their physical well-being, to the maintenance of culture, and to their prospects for being educated. The intergenerational effects of residential schools are still being felt in the communities.

- The Great Depression proved to be especially damaging to First Nations and other Indigenous Peoples, in part because their toehold in the economy of the time was so tenuous and also because "Indians" were seen to have recourse to the federal government. In 1941, W. S. Arneil wrote in his report on reserves in Nova Scotia, "The local employer, in his endeavour to keep down local unemployment costs, never hesitated to give the preference to the white man. The claims of the Indian for employment, the Indian being a ward of the federal government, he could afford to ignore."[11]

- Faced with unmistakable signs of hardship within the Indigenous population, the federal government made a consequential policy choice. Rather than investing to help rebuild First Nations economies and societies, the government chose to buy off the problem through the provision of welfare. Table 1.3.1 shows how annual expenditures for education, medical relief, and welfare increased in the period 1910–11 through 1939–40, a trend that has continued into recent decades. Indeed, recent data for Nova Scotia reveals that around 50 percent of the adult population living on reserve relied on social assistance for some or all of their income during the year 2015–16.[12]

- One of the most damaging steps taken by the federal government was the decision made in the early 1940s to centralize the many Mi'kmaw communities in the province (of which there were about forty) into two locations, at Eskasoni in Cape Breton and at Shubenacadie on the mainland. A number of reasons were given for this change in direction: administrative efficiency, suggesting that the population would be much easier and cheaper to administer if it were consolidated; economies of scale that could be achieved; and the opportunity for providing better services. There was also a moral and racist argument reminiscent of the rationale for residential schools: "One is forced to the conclusion that the progress of the Nova Scotia Indian at this stage in his development is likely to be determined by his willingness to accept the spiritual guidance extended to him by his Church.... The Indian must be taught to care for his body and to use his hands, and education aimed at this objective will be most effective if closely allied with religious instruction and spiritual guidance."[13]

Table 1.3.1. Annual Expenditure for Administration, Education, Medical Care, and Relief and Welfare, Fiscal Years 1910–11 to 1939–40

Fiscal year	Yearly expenditure in dollars
1910–11	54,779
1915–16	70,308
1920–21	102,249
1925–26	179,674
1930–31	318,091
1935–36	271,986
1939–40	323,352

Source: W. S. Arneil, "Investigation Report on Indian Reserves and Indian Administration, Province of Nova Scotia," Indian Affairs Branch (Ottawa: Department of Mines and Resources, August, 1941)

The centralization policy proved to be a disaster. Mi'kmaq were in many cases forced to move or were induced to move on the basis of misleading promises. Consequently, local economies that had provided a basis for self-sufficiency were abandoned. In the new locations, there was a flurry of activity for a few short years as houses were constructed or nursing facilities and schools were built, but when this phase passed in the 1950s, there were no sources of employment for the expanded population.[14]

In this context, welfare and other income security measures continued to expand, as did direct government employment. The latter took several forms, including "make-work" projects where many Mi'kmaw men became "carpenter's helpers" in the 1960s and 1970s but without entry to properly licensed occupations. Public administration jobs were also created to provide services to the on-reserve population. These jobs were more likely to be held by women than men. Indeed, my data shows that by 1980 about two-thirds of the on-reserve labour force was dependent on public funds of some kind for their employment.[15]

SIGNS OF RESURGENCE: 1971 TO PRESENT

It seems that the 1970s marked a significant turning point for the Mi'kmaq in Nova Scotia as several important developments occurred. First, Mi'kmaw leaders made a determined effort to have the Peace and Friendship Treaties, signed originally at several points in the 1700s, recognized and implemented. They refused to take "no" for an answer, and provisions of the treaties were tested in the courts, resulting in several Supreme Court decisions recognizing the validity of treaty provisions, for example, the right to fish for a moderate livelihood. Other court decisions affirmed the validity of Aboriginal Rights, such as the right to fish for food, social, and ceremonial purposes. Second, great strides were made in establishing and strengthening Mi'kmaw organizations, beginning with the Union of Nova Scotia Indians followed by the Confederacy of Mainland Mi'kmaq and, more recently, the Assembly of Nova Scotia Mi'kmaw Chiefs and its secretariat, Kwilmu'kw Maw-klusuaqn. Organizations in specific service areas, such as education, family and children's services, alcohol and drug counselling, and economic development followed.

While the federal government made many crucially important policy errors in previous decades, it is also worth noting that some policies supportive of the Mi'kmaw rebuilding process have been helpful in the past few decades, pushed along by an impatient Mi'kmaw leadership. The progress made in educational achievement is worth noting, for example, as is a slow but steady approach applied to economic development and health care. An important ingredient in these transitions has been the recognition that increasing levels of self-determination need to be part of the package. Indeed, many of the recent gains in education are credited to the formation of Mi'kmaw Kina'matnewey, the Mi'kmaw education authority that is exercising a significant degree of self-determination in the education field.

Thus, by the 2020s some individual Mi'kmaw communities have made great strides in economic development, self-determination, and the provision of services, to the point where they have not only improved prospects for their own populations, but also serve as regional growth centres for their surrounding areas.[16] What has been responsible for the turnaround? The court decisions mentioned above, recognizing Aboriginal and Treaty Rights, are a significant factor. Analysis also suggests that leadership has been an important factor and, in the early days especially, the capacity to generate own-source revenues from community-owned businesses that could be quickly invested to take advantage of opportunities. For some communities, having a favourable location, for example on a major highway or highway intersection, has been advantageous. Having an urban presence has also helped, given the economic dynamism of urban communities. Indeed, it is worth noting that even if some communities do not have an urban location as their home base, they have taken steps to acquire urban lands through one means or another.

Yet not all Mi'kmaw communities have these advantages, and many are still struggling to break through to a better future. The size of the gap in living standards is still very considerable, as Table 1.3.2, featuring the Sipekne'katik First Nation, illustrates. Given these disparities, one can understand why Mi'kmaw communities are pushing as hard as they can to provide a better future for their members.

Table 1.3.2. Economic Data, First Nations Adults on All Nova Scotia Reserves, First Nations Adults on Reserve at Sipekne'katik, and All Adults Living in Hants County, NS, 2015–16

Indicator	On Reserve in Nova Scotia	Sipekne'katik	Hants County
Percent in labour force	47.3	40.5	62.2
Percent employed	36.8	32.5	56.8
Unemployment rate	22.2	19.7	8.7
Median total annual income	$15,498	$11,483	$32,670

Source: Statistics Canada, 2016 Census, Catalogue 98-510-X2016001 and 98-316-X2016001

CONCLUSION

When looking at the broad sweep of Mi'kmaw history since the arrival of settlers, one can see the broad mechanisms of exclusion from fishing that have been operative. They are as follows:

- Being overwhelmed numerically by settlers, having their traditional lifestyle disrupted, and being pushed away from the ocean and river shores.

- Being settled on reserves with minimal acreage and often limited access to fishing grounds.

- Being forcibly moved to two central locations, neither of which has an ocean harbour, as a result of the centralization policy, although not all communities made the move in the end.

- The consequences of poverty, which include the inability to meet the collateral requirements of provincial and federal lending agencies for the purchase of boats and fishing gear. Because of the Indian Act, on-reserve residents were severely constrained in their ability to put up collateral for loans.

- Not having licences set aside to encourage Mi'kmaq participation once licences began to be required to fish in the late 1960s and through the 1970s. This was a time when larger motorized vessels equipped with mechanical gear became common. Since most Mi'kmaq could not qualify for loans, the number who could actually take advantage of fishing licences declined substantially.

- Other federal policies that have hindered access for the Mi'kmaq, such as restricting the exercise of the Treaty Rights to the reserve land base or making it subject to particular seasons, specifying it is just for personal/community use—not for commercial purposes—and imposing limits to fishing for conservation reasons.

- Courts recognizing Aboriginal and Treaty Rights since the 1970s but setting restrictions on the exercise of the right. For example, a particular right might be recognized only for the First Nation bringing forward the case, or to a particular species of fish, or they might need to establish that a claimed right such as being able to sell fish was an integral part of the culture practised by the First Nation since the time prior to the arrival of Europeans.[17]

As a result, by the time of the *Marshall* decision in 1999, the exclusion of the Mi'kmaq from their most important traditional activity was almost complete. For example, Ken Coates refers to Eskasoni as having "little connection to the East Coast fishery...a license or two at different times.... [P]eople from the community harvested eels but had little presence in the commercial fishery of the region."[18] Indeed, Coates calculates that the return from commercial fishing for First Nations in all of the Maritime region amounted to only $3 million in the year when the *Marshall* decision was handed down. While the situation has improved markedly in the post-*Marshall* period, as described by Coates, the struggle is a long way from being over, especially when it comes to fishing for a moderate livelihood. We can expect that negotiations, court cases, and action on the ground or in the water will be a recurring feature for some time to come.

I.4

The *MARSHALL LEGACY*

by JOHN PAUL and JOSEPH QUESNEL

Note: What follows was originally written in the fall of 2019.[1] The authors note that since then there have been many more discussions to define and implement a moderate livelihood fishery. As was the case when the original Marshall *decision was handed down in 1999, the renewed push for a moderate livelihood fishery has met with considerable conflict, violence, and very strained relations with government and fishers. In spite of this, communities continue to work on the development and implementation of their own regime for a moderate livelihood fishery, each developing their own plans. The First Nations fishery overall continues to produce jobs, revenues, and incomes for communities and fishers. As they continue to develop their interest and capacity, First Nations fishing communities in the Maritimes are poised for even greater future growth as they seek more autonomy over their fishing sectors.*

It has been twenty years since the Supreme Court of Canada delivered the landmark *Marshall* ruling that required the federal government to respect First Nations Treaty Rights within the East Coast commercial fishery and recognized the right of Mi'kmaw, Wolastoqey, and Peskotomuhkati fishers in the Maritime provinces to earn a "moderate livelihood" in that industry.

Fearing the worst, non-Indigenous fishers reacted strongly against the ruling, and tensions ran high between 1999 and 2002.

New Brunswick experienced much of this turbulence during televised confrontations between Esgenoôpetitj (Burnt Church First Nation) and non-Indigenous fisheries. Conflict—often out on the water—occurred between the two communities and was characterized by property damage to the First Nation's fishing equipment.

The federal government had to act quickly to quell the tensions and implement the ruling without depleting fragile ocean fish stocks and disproportionately harming non-Indigenous fishing communities. These communities eventually learned that Indigenous preferential access to the industry was not as much a problem as they assumed, and many non-Indigenous fishers were compensated with buyouts.

Following that turbulent time, the federal government and East Coast First Nations worked on implementing the *Marshall* ruling and negotiated financial and related arrangements. The Mi'kmaq and Wolastoqiyik went from having a marginal role to being significant actors in the expanding Maritime fishing industry.

Mi'kmaw and Wolastoqey communities capitalized on the opportunities generated by the court ruling and government assistance to purchase quotas, vessels, gear, and licences.

A 2019 Macdonald-Laurier Institute report reviewed the impact of the decision, pointing to the impressive First Nations fishing fleets, the dramatic increase in Indigenous workers in the sector, and the substantial financial benefits flowing to these communities. It also documented the growth of onshore processing plants and related value-added businesses.

As the report showed, total on-reserve fishing revenues for the Mi'kmaq and Wolastoqiyik in all Maritime provinces grew from $3 million in 1999 to $122 million in 2016.[2]

Meanwhile, tensions between Indigenous and non-Indigenous communities subsided over time and relations improved. First Nations fishers became more involved in the industry, and governments sought to balance competing rights and interests. The federal government also had to come to terms with increased First Nations independence and legal authority.

The *Marshall* decision came at an important time because the Indigenous population in the region was growing rapidly. The First Nations on-reserve population in New Brunswick grew by 28 percent from 1999 to 2016. Nova Scotia's on-reserve population grew by 34 percent in the same period. Off-reserve populations grew even more dramatically between 1999 and 2016. New Brunswick's off-reserve population was up 77 percent, and Nova Scotia's expanded by 60 percent.

With government help to build capacity at the local level, First Nations populations across the Maritimes (but especially in New Brunswick) took full advantage of opportunities in the sector. Indigenous employment in the fishery spiked upwards, as did economic returns to First Nations communities. Young people entered the industry in large numbers, as did many Indigenous women. The number of seasonal jobs rose, Indigenous engagement in training improved, and First Nations ownership of fisheries-related businesses grew dramatically.

The Indigenous lobster fishery expanded to include snow crab, shrimp, and groundfish, which extended the commercial seasons and improved personal and business income. This allowed First Nations communities in all the Maritime provinces to grow their "own source revenues" to pay for local priorities and expand further economic opportunity.

Based on the federal government's Community Well-Being Index, living standards in Maritime First Nations communities improved significantly between 1999 and 2016. Although *Marshall* was not the only reason, it did play a significant role.

While federal government investment added up to hundreds of millions of dollars over the years, the return on that investment has been substantial. Mi'kmaw and Wolastoqey communities in New Brunswick led the pack with just over $63 million in total fishing revenues in 2016 compared to just $526,933 in 1999. Nova Scotia fishing revenues were not far behind, with just under $52 million in 2016. The East Coast Indigenous fishery has exploded.

In terms of employment generated with the help of the Atlantic Integrated Commercial Fisheries Initiative (AICFI), New Brunswick First Nations again led the way. Total land-based employment in the fisheries in 2018 stood at 154 jobs. There were 691 harvesters overall, bringing the total to 845 people employed in the Mi'kmaw and Wolastoqey communities in New Brunswick.

All Maritime residents should applaud the impact of the 1999 *Marshall* ruling. It set the stage for a growing fishing industry for Mi'kmaw and Wolastoqey communities, providing them with more economic prosperity and self-determination, while also leading to increased mutual understanding between Indigenous and non-Indigenous fishing communities.

Twenty years after this seminal decision, First Nations fishing communities in the Maritimes are poised for even more future growth as they seek more autonomy over their fishing sectors.

II

UNDERSTANDING the LOBSTER FISHERY

UNIQUE CHALLENGES
in the LOBSTER FISHERY

by RICK WILLIAMS

To understand the roots of recent conflicts and the obstacles to finding a peaceful path forward for the development of First Nations fisheries, it's important to understand the unique structure of the all-important lobster fishery and how it is managed and conducted on the water. Most commercial fisheries are managed with total allowable catches (TACS) and percentage catch shares or quotas for each vessel or enterprise. Every year the federal fisheries department (DFO) sets a TAC at an estimated biologically sustainable level for each stock based on scientific advice. If the TAC goes up or down, the harvester's individual quota (IQ) for crab or halibut or shrimp goes up or down as a fixed percentage of the changing TAC. To support all this, DFO scientists do at-sea stock assessment surveys and closely track landings data from vessel logbooks, on-board fisheries observers, and dockside monitors.

In fisheries managed by TACS and IQS, the integration of First Nations can be quite straightforward and often non-controversial. Any Nation or group of Nations can purchase licences and quotas from an existing commercial enterprise and enter the fishery without changing the fleet structure or reducing anyone else's share of the catch. If the decision is made that a First Nation or group of Nations should receive a share of a newly expanding fishery, as may happen soon with the redfish fishery in the Gulf of St. Lawrence, the DFO minister will simply allocate a percentage share of the new TAC to them.[1] In short, except in rare cases when the minister exercises their exclusive authority to change the share structure,[2] a First Nation entering that fishery will not mean that other quota holders have fewer fish to catch.

EFFORT CONTROL MANAGEMENT IN THE LOBSTER FISHERY

None of this describes the management and conduct of the economically dominant lobster fishery. There are no TACs or quota allocations for lobster.[3] The stocks are protected with effort controls (e.g., limited fishing days, limits on numbers of traps allowed, vessel size restrictions) and biological controls (minimum carapace size, bans on harvesting females, escape hatches in traps for small lobsters, etc.). Instead of harvesting a defined quota, every licence holder within each Lobster Fishing Area (LFA) competes with everyone else on their local grounds to catch as many legal-sized lobster as they can, using the same number of traps, for the limited number of fishing days in their season.[4]

A licence holder can only fish within their local LFA, and there are nineteen LFAs that are subject to the *Marshall* rulings, stretching from LFA 38 on the Bay of Fundy to LFA 19 on the Gaspé Peninsula. Map 2.1.1 shows LFAs around the Atlantic coast.

Lobster fishing is intensively co-managed by advisory committees for each LFA. Over many decades these committees have developed regulations and fishing plans tailored to differing ecological, climate, and market factors in their local areas, with variations in seasons, carapace size standards, trap specifications, and other specialized rules. Fish harvesters, processors, First Nations fishing authorities, and environmental groups are all represented on LFA committees, but commercial harvesters make up a majority of members and, along with DFO, have the greatest say in decision making.

Table 2.1.1 shows differences in numbers of licences, in length of seasons, and in trap limits for LFAs on the Atlantic coast of Nova Scotia and in the Bay of Fundy.

LFA 34 in Southwest Nova Scotia has the biggest lobster fishery with 944 "core" (i.e., full-time) licence holders, each able to fish up to 400 traps over a season stretching from late November to the end of May. LFAs in Cape Breton, in contrast, have two-month seasons and fish from 250 to 275 traps.

Map 2.1.1. Fisheries and Oceans Canada Lobster Fishing Areas (LFAS), Maritime Provinces and Quebec

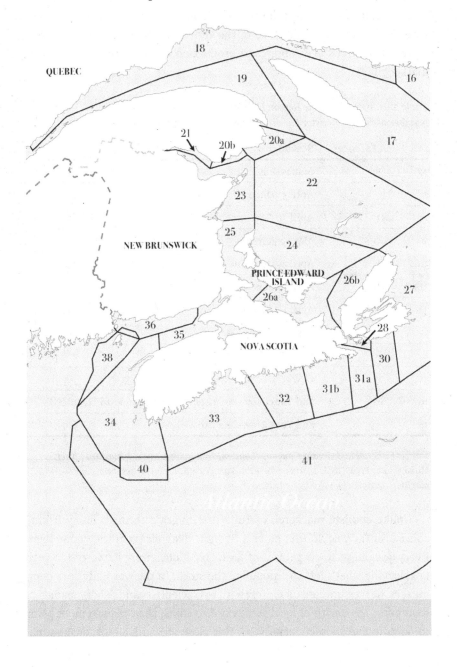

LFAS in the Gulf of St. Lawrence are also in the 250 to 275 range for traps and have relatively short seasons in either late spring or early fall. These differences reflect the size of lobster populations in different areas, seasonal weather factors (e.g., winter ice in the Gulf), and adaptations to different market conditions (i.e., spreading production out over the year to avoid market gluts).

Table 2.1.1. DFO Maritime Region Lobster Fishing Areas
Number of "Core" Lobster Licences, Seasons, and Trap Limits

LFA	# Licences	Season	Trap limit
27	491	May 15–July 15	275
28	7	April 30–June 30	250
29	53	April 30–June 30	250
30	20	May 19–July 20	250
31A	68	April 29–June 30	250
31B	70	April 19–June 20	250
32	147	April 19–June 20	250
33	634	Last Mon. Nov.–May 31	250
34	944	Last Mon. Nov.–May 31	375/400
35	75	Oct. 14–Dec. 31 and Last day Feb.–July 31	300
36	161	2nd Tues. Nov.–Jan. 14 and March 31–June 29	300
38	119	2nd Tues. Nov.–June 29	375

Source: Fisheries and Oceans Canada, "Lobster Fishing Areas 27–38 Integrated Fisheries Management Plan," table 1, https://www.dfo-mpo.gc.ca/fisheries-peches/ifmp-gmp/maritimes/2019/inshore-lobster-eng.html

Unlike codfish, mackerel, or tuna that migrate through many fishing zones over the year, lobster move only short distances over their adult lives. Every season, 50 to 70 percent of legal-sized lobster are harvested in each LFA, leaving what's left to repopulate the stock. In their LFA advisory committees, harvesters consult closely with DFO scientists and fishery managers to monitor the health of local stocks and to adjust their management plans to nurture and protect them. With this close stewardship of local animal populations and habitats, in many respects the lobster fishery is more like a farming operation than a hunt for mobile schools of fish in the open ocean. This helps explain the strong sense of ownership harvesters feel toward their local fishing grounds.

INFORMAL REGULATION OF LOBSTER FISHING

There can be a dozen or more fishing ports in each LFA, and each port can be home to dozens of lobster enterprises. In highly productive areas close to shore, harvesters describe their lines of traps being set literally on top of each other. Over many decades, harvesters have developed strategies and unwritten rules to manage the intense competition for a limited local resource. Boats from each port will typically set their traps on certain grounds based on adjacency and historical fishing patterns. In parts of Cape Breton and along the Northumberland Strait, a tradition evolved where the fishing ground is divided into small sections or "berths" that belong to individual harvesters and are passed on with the licence when an owner-operator retires. It is a widely accepted reality in the lobster fishery that if a harvester sets traps on "someone else's grounds," whether purposefully or not, they may find their lines cut when they come back to retrieve them. Even without racial tensions being a factor, moving licences around and introducing new harvesters into an area will always have challenges. There is a very steep learning curve for new entrants and no established training system to help them learn the ropes.

There are two pathways for First Nations to gain access to lobster licences and fishing opportunities. First, DFO's current program to support the development of Rights Reconciliation Agreements (RRAS) has an investment fund of $300 million available to purchase fishing licences, vessels, and gear.[5] RRAS may also include access to licences currently held in reserve by DFO. In the early 2000s, the department purchased licences from retiring commercial harvesters and "banked" them for this purpose. Prior to recent RRAS being signed, DFO held seventeen lobster licences in Nova Scotia, sixteen in New Brunswick, and one in PEI that were all available for First Nations acquisition.

The second pathway for First Nations is to buy licences from retiring commercial harvesters with the retained earnings and borrowing capacities of their band-owned fishing companies. It might also be possible for Indigenous individuals to raise capital and buy their own lobster enterprises on the open market. However, over the past ten years, licences have risen dramatically in value due to surging global demand for lobster, so this option is more difficult than in the past.

When a First Nation takes ownership of a local licence there is no increase in the number of traps in the water, so the challenge will be one of finding open ground and learning to work within traditional fishing patterns and unwritten rules governing the activities of boats from different ports. However, if a Nation buys a licence from one port and decides to fish it out of a different port within the same LFA, other harvesters in the local area may react to that as an increase in fishing effort (i.e., more traps on their local grounds) and see it as a threat to the sustainability of their "home stock."

So, acquiring licences is an important first step, but there are other management and operational challenges to be overcome in developing successful First Nations lobster fisheries.

ECONOMICS OF LOBSTER FISHING

The lobster fishery is also unique in its economic structure and impacts. The industry in the Maritimes and Quebec comprises some six thousand owner-operated small businesses, each one providing employment for crews of one to four harvesters. The great majority of enterprises generate 50 to 80 percent of their annual fishing revenues during the first four or five weeks of their lobster season. Many harvesters earn half or more of their personal income during these short periods of intense fishing work.

The Employment Insurance (EI) system is an important part of this picture. Over 80 percent of commercial fish harvesters qualify for EI benefits to carry them through the non-fishing winter months. The special Fishers' EI program is unique in that qualifying depends not on number of weeks worked but on the level of fishing income. The more you earn from catching lobster, the bigger your bi-weekly EI cheque through the winter up to a certain maximum. Average fish-harvesting incomes in the Maritimes in 2018 ranged from $27,000 in PEI to $38,000 in Nova Scotia, while EI benefits averaged from $15,000 to $18,000.

While some fish harvesters, particularly owner-operators in Southwest Nova Scotia, earn much higher incomes and don't need EI, many other enterprise owners, and the great majority of crew across the region, earn significantly less on average than workers in the wider economy. For most commercial harvesters in the Maritimes and Quebec, their ability to remain in the fishery and in their communities depends on those limited weeks of lobster fishing each year.

All of this is useful context for understanding the responses of fish harvesters and fishing communities to proposals for new or expanded lobster fisheries, however limited in scale. If such a proposal was aggressively advanced by a non-Indigenous group—e.g., a sports-fishing or scuba-diving association or owners of a coastal tourist resort—the response would also be anxious and hostile. Such proprietary attitudes were evident in the recent militant, harvester-led campaign to block the release of treated effluent from the pulp mill in Pictou, NS, into the Northumberland Strait. In that instance commercial harvester groups were allied closely with First Nations in Nova Scotia and PEI.

OWNER-OPERATOR AND FLEET SEPARATION

In 2019 (before the COVID-19 pandemic) lobster harvesters alone generated $1.6 billion in landed value, representing 45 percent of total landed value in Canadian commercial fisheries for all species. Over 90 percent of that landed value was produced by owner-operated vessels of forty-five feet or fewer in length, fishing out of hundreds of small communities around the Atlantic Coast. It is hard to find any sector of the Canadian economy where small businesses collectively control the production of such a valuable product and where so much wealth is retained in small rural communities.

The single factor that explains this unique industry structure is the federal government's fleet separation and owner-operator policies and regulations. The former blocks fish processing companies from owning and fishing lobster licences themselves, and the latter requires the person who owns the lobster licence to operate the vessel that fishes it. Since their introduction in the 1980s, the combined effect of these two regulatory pillars has been to limit vertical integration in the lobster industry. In introducing regulations in 2019 to give these policies legal force, the DFO minister provided the following rationale in the *Canada Gazette*:

> Fishing remains one of the main industries in rural coastal Eastern Canada generating about $1.7 billion in landed value (inshore fleets only) in 2017 and supporting many fisheries-dependent communities.... The Government of Canada's policy objective is for this wealth to remain in the hands of those individuals that actively fish and for the wealth accumulated to be reinvested and spent in coastal communities, rather than have it concentrated in the hands of a few, wealthy corporations in larger urban centres.
>
> Progressive fisheries policies that prevent vertical integration between the fishing and processing sectors and that prevent the concentration of licences in the hands of a few corporations or individuals have been pivotal in the maintenance of the wealth distribution across the region and small communities. Without these policies, wealth from fishing licences would be concentrated in the hands of ineligible third parties resulting in fewer or lower paying fishing jobs available in rural coastal areas and a decrease of economic benefits being maintained in the coastal communities.[6]

Because of these barriers to vertical integration, the lobster fishery is characterized by dynamic port markets. Instead of harvesters being price takers in an industry dominated by a few large companies (as is the case for many farmers and other primary producers), processors must compete with each other and with independent brokers, small buyers, restaurant owners, and local consumers to maintain the flow of raw material to their plants. This results in a higher proportion of final market value being retained by the primary producer than might otherwise be the case.

Lobster harvesters and their organizations fought long campaigns, with intensive political lobbying and appeals to the Supreme Court, to retain and strengthen these protections. Their reactions to seeing lobster licences acquired and then operated out of vertically integrated companies owned by one or more First Nations, alone or in partnership with non-Indigenous processing companies, are shaped by this history. The recent purchase of Clearwater Seafoods, one of the largest shellfish processing companies in the world, by a multinational company in partnership with seven First Nations has generated just such concerns across inshore fishing fleets.

INTEGRATION OF INDIGENOUS LOBSTER FISHING

Because of the near-shore operations, the high value of the catch, and the manageable costs of small boats and fishing gear, lobster clearly offers the best opportunities for First Nations to develop commercial fisheries and for more community members to enter the fishery and learn the trade.

There are policy and regulatory changes that could help integrate First Nations harvesters into the lobster fishery. In the past, senior DFO officials and some DFO ministers have advanced proposals to manage lobster by TACS and individual quotas in line with snow crab, scallops, and most groundfish. Senator Dan Christmas has suggested a transition to management by TACS and quotas so that an Indigenous share of the catch could be more easily defined and managed.[7] Jim Jones, a former DFO Regional Director General, has suggested an approach based on calculating the average catch per licence each year for each LFA and then assigning that annual average as a quota for each First Nations communal licence. An annual quota, based on the average catch per licence across the LFA, reduces the impacts on other harvesters if Indigenous harvesters fish outside the regular commercial season as they claim they can do under their self-government rights. It might also allow First Nations to develop moderate livelihood fisheries using smaller vessels fishing fewer traps on a year-round basis.

However, it will not be easy to introduce change and innovation into the lobster fishery. Inshore commercial harvesters universally and militantly oppose the introduction of individual quota (IQ) management for lobster. Based on past experiences in several major fisheries, they associate IQ models with government strategies to rationalize fishing fleets by making it easier for bigger enterprises to gobble up the smaller ones. The powerful influence of harvester organizations within DFO's co-management system and their recent success in having the owner-operator and fleet separation policies put into legislation and regulations make it difficult for DFO to attempt change in the current management model for lobster.

The lobster industry is the foundation for a strengthening fishery economy across the Atlantic region and will remain the most critical focus for

First Nations fisheries development. However, the potential for increasing tension and conflict on the water and between communities is inherent in the way the lobster fishery is structured, managed, and conducted. It will be difficult for First Nations to gain a larger share of the lobster fishery in specific areas without improved communications and co-operation with local non-Indigenous harvesters. Creative strategies and wise leadership will be needed on all sides to manage these risks going forward because they are simply not going to go away.

2.2

CONFLICT OVER the MI'KMAW LOBSTER FISHERY
WHO MAKES THE RULES?

by LUCIA FANNING and SHELLEY DENNY

Note: A version of this article was published on October 29, 2020, in The Conversation. *See https://theconversation.com/conflict-over-mikmaw-lobster-fishery-reveals-confusion-over-who-makes-the-rules-148978.*

In October 2020, the Sipekne'katik First Nation and the Potlotek First Nation placed lobster traps in bays at the opposite ends of Nova Scotia. Each community had developed a management plan based on their Treaty Rights to earn a moderate livelihood.

The response to these actions by non-Indigenous fishers led to national and international coverage of the ensuing violence, including damage to property and assault.[1] Both non-Indigenous fishers and the Department of Fisheries and Oceans (DFO) subsequently seized some of the lobster traps.

The conflict largely centred on whether the lobster stock is threatened by out-of-season fishing and on the definition of a "moderate" livelihood. However, this focus misses the root of the Mi'kmaw livelihood issue, namely the question of who has the authority to govern livelihood activities and how it is done.

RESEARCHING THE ISSUE

We're part of a small group that has been examining these very issues since 2014; it includes scholars with expertise in ocean governance and marine policy[2] and colleagues from the Assembly of First Nations. Our research project, Fish-WIKS,[3] aims to understand how Indigenous and Western knowledge systems can be used to improve the sustainability of Canadian fisheries.

The processes that feed into decision making in fisheries in Canada have been primarily influenced by Western, science-based knowledge systems that focus on a reductionist approach to understanding problems. In contrast, Indigenous ways of knowing are based on world views and values that are integrative and holistic, or as Elder Albert Marshall of Eskasoni First Nation once spelled out, "wholistic."

Who would have guessed that our results from examining an alternative governance structure for the livelihood fishery in Nova Scotia through the lens of both knowledge systems, referred to as "two-eyed seeing," would coincide with the conflict playing out in the lobster fishery?

Figure 2.2.1. Conceptual illustration of components of a knowledge system. (From A. Giles, L. Fanning, S. Denny, & T. Paul [2016], "Improving the American eel fishery through the incorporation of indigenous knowledge into policy level decision making in Canada," Human ecology, 44(2), 168.)

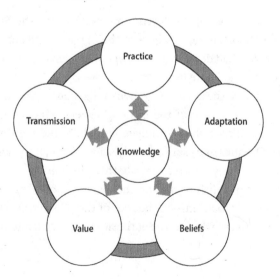

TWO-EYED SEEING

In two-eyed seeing, knowledge is viewed as a system that comprises what is known and how it is known. But a knowledge system, whether Western or Indigenous, is composed of many things.

What we know, how we practise our knowledge, how we adapt to it, and how we transmit and share knowledge are the more familiar elements. But the values and beliefs that underpin these elements, and which actually distinguish one knowledge system from another, are often ignored.

This is a problem because the values and beliefs underpinning one system are often at odds with those of another system, potentially creating a barrier to collaboration. However, the Fish-wiks projects showed there are similarities that can bridge these knowledge systems and lead to greater understanding of the differences.

GOVERNANCE GAPS

Our research identified a number of gaps in governance that have contributed to the lobster fishery situation we have today.

There is still no federal policy to address livelihood fisheries, and the issue of livelihood as a Treaty Right is not mentioned in the Aboriginal Fisheries Strategy,[4] the primary policy guiding the federal response to Indigenous fisheries.

There are also conflicting views on who has the authority to manage fisheries, which stem from the perceived legitimacy of each governing system. Legitimacy influences whether a political action is perceived as right or just by those who are involved, interested, and/or affected by it.

The two sets of rules for fisheries arise from the protection of Aboriginal and Treaty Rights in sections 25 and 35 of the Constitution,[5] complicating the issue of legitimacy. This legal pluralism gives DFO the authority over non-Indigenous commercial fisheries while limiting its capacity to govern Indigenous fisheries.

In addition, Canada must justify any limits it places on the rights of Indigenous people engaged in fishing practices, as determined by the Supreme Court of Canada in R. v. Sparrow[6] in 1990. The court also affirmed Mi'kmaw Treaty Rights in R. v. Simon[7] in 1985 and R. v. Marshall[8] in 1999.

Our research confirms that Mi'kmaq are aware of challenges with the exercise of Treaty Rights and supports the necessity for Mi'kmaq to develop fishery and fishing rules that are legitimate in the eyes of Mi'kmaw fishers, non-Indigenous fishers, and DFO. Some communities have developed such rules, incorporating knowledge from both Western and Indigenous systems.

However, the question remains, does DFO have the justification to intervene with Mi'kmaw lobster livelihood fishing practices if, as Dalhousie University fisheries expert Megan Bailey pointed out,[9] there is no scientific evidence that the current practice of the lobster livelihood fishery threatens the sustainability of the stock?

This needs to be cleared up. The Fisheries Act gives DFO broad regulatory authority, and this may extend to Indigenous fisheries. But the *Marshall* decision narrows that authority to apply only "provided their use to limit the exercise of a treaty right can be justified."[10]

MOVING FORWARD

Canadians need to recognize that the conflict between Indigenous and non-Indigenous fishers represents not only an operational nightmare for DFO, but also a deep-seated governance issue. It requires developing a mechanism by which Mi'kmaq can legitimately contribute to the governance of fisheries as an integrated whole.

Short-term solutions will be identified,[11] but a longer-term solution must address the legal pluralism that exists in Canada and facilitate the adoption of other governance models in which DFO does not have exclusive authority.

The current focus on the lobster livelihood fishery and finding a dollar definition for "moderate" misses the fact that the underlying governance gap is the crux of the issue.

MOVING FORWARD in the LOBSTER FISHERY

by ANTHONY CHARLES

Note: This chapter is adapted from Tony Charles, "Moving forward on lobster fishery means addressing access and conservation," Policy Options, October 28, 2020, https://policyoptions.irpp.org/magazines/october-2020/moving-forward-on-lobster-fishery-means-addressing-access-and-conservation.

Back in 1999, the Supreme Court's *Marshall* decision[1] recognized that Mi'kmaq First Nations have had, and continue to have, a Treaty Right to catch and sell fish. As a result, First Nations have been increasing their presence in the fishery over the past twenty years. Yet all that time, what the Court specified as the Mi'kmaw right to a so-called "moderate livelihood"—for "individual Mi'kmaq families at present-day standards"—was never clearly defined.

Now, more than twenty years later, this remains a stumbling block, as new "moderate livelihood" Indigenous fisheries are emerging. Further, these new fisheries have another crucial angle—First Nations are developing their own fishery management and conservation plans, making this about Indigenous self-governance as well as about catching lobsters. Indeed, what we're seeing unfolding off the coast of Nova Scotia touches on two themes that come up worldwide: who sets the rules for conservation of resources, and who has access to harvesting that resource.

MAKING DECISIONS ON CONSERVATION AND MANAGEMENT

Unlike the cod fishery, which suffered a terrible collapse back in the early 1990s and never really recovered, the lobster fishery has been sustainable and prosperous over the years. The reasons for that revolve around how management works. First, the lobster fishery avoids setting quotas (limits on catches)—anything living underwater is hard to measure, and that makes quota-setting a very risky business. Indeed, the cod collapse was partly a result of poorly set quotas. Instead of catch quotas, the focus in the lobster fishery is on limiting fishing pressure to a sustainable level by only allowing a certain number of lobster traps and limiting when and how intensively those traps are used. The other big advantage in the lobster fishery, a crucial ingredient in successful conservation, is that those doing the fishing also helped set the rules—and were then committed to following them. As a result of all these measures, the lobster fishery has run sustainably for decades.

But when the lobster fishery rules were set, the Mi'kmaq were excluded. It was largely non-Indigenous fishers who were involved in setting the rules. Now this is changing. The new First Nations fisheries are all based on community-developed management plans, ones having many of the ingredients of success described above for the conventional commercial fishery.

These plans are in keeping with a trend around the world toward more local-level (community-based) decision making over natural resources. In Canada, this approach is of interest to both Indigenous and non-Indigenous communities. For example, community forestry flourishes in some places. There is no reason such approaches could not expand in fisheries, though that will require the federal government to accept more local-level management than in the past—perhaps First Nations fisheries will spark progress in that direction.

Another important aspect of the new First Nations fisheries is that they are based on Indigenous wisdom and knowledge. That is reflected in the framing of these fisheries by the Assembly of Nova Scotia Mi'kmaw Chiefs around the Mi'kmaw approach of *Netukulimk*—described by the Unama'ki Institute of Natural Resources as "achieving adequate standards of community nutrition and economic well-being without jeopardizing the integrity, diversity, or productivity of our environment."[2] Non-Indigenous fishers, with their own long-time knowledge and conservation practices, will certainly identify with this approach.

LIMITS ON LOBSTER

A key challenge to the future of the lobster fishery is that, while it is currently sustainable, it is largely fully utilized, without much room to increase lobster catches. There is little spare lobster in the sea. When moderate livelihood Mi'kmaw fisheries are very small compared to the conventional commercial fishery, adding them into the mix does not threaten conservation.[3] However, the other two parts of the lobster fishery, the Indigenous (non-commercial) food fishery and the conventional commercial fishery, each has its own impacts, so ultimately, conservation means limiting the total fishing pressure from all fisheries together.

The same point holds in looking to the future: as moderate livelihood fisheries develop, there will need to be a corresponding decrease in the number of traps used by others, and the extent of that use, to avoid conservation problems. That reduction in fishing by non-Indigenous fishers will require new government funding to make the transition. Meanwhile, as fishing pressure continues to be monitored and controlled, experience shows how important it is to keep catch quotas out of the lobster fishery to avoid another cod collapse.

While a key conservation measure in the fishery is to limit the number of lobster traps used, there are two other important ingredients in fishery decision making—when and where fishing happens.

First, the discussion of lobster "seasons" refers to the dates when fishing can take place each year. In the conventional commercial fishery, these are set for biological and economic reasons—to catch lobsters when they are not reproducing, when they are in the best condition, and when the markets are strong. That makes sense. On the other hand, if for various reasons moderate livelihood fisheries need to operate at other times of the year, that can be sustainable as long as the cumulative fishing pressure over the year, by all parts of the fishery, is kept low enough.

Related to this is the second big issue—where fishing takes place. Too much fishing concentrated in certain small areas can be damaging to conservation, so it is important that fishing be spread out over the ocean.

St. Marys Bay, for example, is a sensitive place on the Nova Scotia coast that can only take so much activity. To understand the limits of fishing in such locations, there are well-established ways of carrying out scientific studies in a fully participatory way.

ACCESS TO THE FISHERY AND RECONCILIATION

As noted above, it is reasonable that Mi'kmaq First Nations—after long being excluded from the commercial fishery and waiting another twenty years after the Supreme Court decision to get to this point—should now be developing new moderate livelihood fisheries. It is notable that the Supreme Court did not restrict who, or how many, in First Nations can earn a moderate livelihood from fishing—nor does it specify this as something for the Canadian government to decide. It can be expected that more First Nations, and more families within them, will enter the fisheries over the coming years.

Given that reality, a corresponding decrease will be needed in the fishing activity of others in the commercial lobster fishery, to avoid conservation problems. That direct impact on non-Indigenous fishers is a consequence not only of the Supreme Court decision, but also of Canada's process of reconciliation. As such, fairness demands that there be federal government funding support to these fishers to make the transition. This needs to be viewed not as a one-time thing but as an adaptive process that will run over several years.

Adjustments to the non-Indigenous fishery could be done through the old method of buying up fishing licences, thereby removing fishery access entirely for some fishers. However, there are other options. One that has received considerable interest is a modest reduction in non-Indigenous trap limits, so everyone fishes a bit less. This may be a route to keep more people in the fishery and minimize damage to coastal communities. It would need to be done carefully, however, with strong scientific effort, so that as Indigenous fishing expands, fishing pressure by others is reduced by just the right amount to ensure conservation to keep the fishery sustainable.

Another avenue for increasing Mi'kmaw access to lobster has been in the corporate offshore lobster fishery. This lesser-known part of the fishery was run until very recently by a single non-Indigenous corporation, fishing relatively far from shore. Now, several First Nations have become new owners, greatly increasing the Mi'kmaw presence in a manner similar to what happened in New Zealand when Maori fishing rights were recognized, leading to Maori involvement in the offshore fishery.

Reconciliation and First Nations Rights are national priorities. In fisheries, that means supporting better fishery access and more self-governance. It also means a federal government role in supporting non-Indigenous fishers who are impacted. What is happening in the fishery also provides lessons for reconciliation more broadly. Beyond the fishery, there is a need for attention to increasing Indigenous involvement in other parts of the economy. While the details will vary, lessons learned in fisheries about improving access and building self-governance, and about the government's role in alleviating impacts of these transitions, can be usefully applied elsewhere. Finally, fisheries highlight the wisdom and knowledge about sustainability that are important in working together, Indigenous and non-Indigenous, to protect local environments and build local economies for the common good.

2.4

ATLANTIC LOBSTER and MODERATE LIVELIHOOD

by JIM JONES

Indigenous communities have harvested lobster for food and trade since long before European settlement. In the seventeenth century, Acadian settlers in the Annapolis Basin reportedly harvested lobster by hand at low tides, undoubtedly having learned how to do it from the Mi'kmaq. Given the historically artisanal nature of lobster fishing, it is little wonder that it has long been important to Indigenous communities as a source of economic benefits and as a focus of their struggles to achieve their Indigenous and Treaty Rights.

Indigenous participation in the lobster industry has expanded significantly over the twenty-three years since the Supreme Court's *Marshall* rulings, but this has almost all been achieved by First Nations acquiring regular commercial licences and conventional inshore vessels with financial and other supports from government. Longstanding Indigenous aspirations to also engage in self-regulated, smaller-scale or artisanal fishing to earn moderate livelihoods became a flashpoint in 2020 in Cape Breton and St. Marys Bay in Nova Scotia. The federal and provincial governments, commercial harvester organizations, and Indigenous communities have since been at a crossroads on how to deal with the fallout from the resulting confrontations, arrests, court challenges, and wider controversy in the national media.

The most pressing challenge today is to find a workable path forward on moderate livelihood fishing for lobster. A quick overview of the lobster fishery and its historical evolution may be helpful for understanding this challenge and some possible ways to address it. I rely here on detailed research by Gordon DeWolf[1] and Scott Parsons.[2]

ATLANTIC LOBSTER: A SHORT HISTORY

The earliest management measures directed at lobster were introduced in the mid-1870s. Rules against the retention of egg-bearing females were introduced to improve stock reproduction, and restrictions on the harvest of soft-shelled lobster and lobster below a minimum weight were brought in to protect the canneries. Closed harvest times and an overall minimum carapace size were introduced in 1874. Most early fishing was by hoop traps, later supplanted by today's box trap with parlours. The number of traps that a single harvester could use was limited by technology until the advent of motorized vessels in the early 1900s made it possible to deploy many more traps over wider areas.

Total landings peaked in the early 1880s at around 40,000 tons, then declined for a period in the late 1880s and continued at a stable level (around 20,000 tons) for the next fifty years. With lower landings, the number of canneries fell markedly, as did overall economic activity.

During this period, government commissioned nine studies on the lobster industry in the Maritimes. Most were focused on conservation, but some also proposed management measures such as licensing. This period saw the emergence of different regulations for different regions and industry sectors. The Bay of Fundy and Southwest Nova Scotia areas were shipping larger live or "market" lobsters to New England, while the Cape Breton and southern Gulf of St. Lawrence fisheries mainly produced smaller "canner" lobsters for processing.

Lobster landings began to pick up after the Second World War, and a modern lobster management regime took shape from the late 1940s to the early 1970s. In 1952, minimum carapace sizes were set at two and a half inches for canner lobsters and three and three-sixteenths inches for markets, the latter based on regulations first introduced in Massachusetts. Regulations on seasonal limits, protections for egg-bearing females, lath spacing to allow smaller lobster to escape the trap, and limits on fishing in more than one zone or Lobster Fishing Area (LFA) were also introduced. The first trap limit, a maximum of 250 traps per licence, was introduced in 1966 in the southern Gulf of St. Lawrence, and by 1968 all LFAs had maximum trap regulations. In 1967 the government put limits on the total number of licences in each LFA, and these have changed little since then.

During the 1960s, the use of the more seaworthy Cape Island vessel become common for lobster fishing with provincial government loan programs and federal subsidies supporting this advance in productive capacity and safety. Many Indigenous harvesters could not make this transition because access to the generous financial assistance offered by fisheries loan boards required borrowers to have collateral, and harvesters who lived on reserves did not own their houses and land. Without the same financial supports, most First Nations harvesters found themselves unable to compete during the commercial season against bigger boats with many more traps. This was a major barrier to continued participation in the lobster fishery as the industry modernized through the 1970s.

Following the 1974 report of its Atlantic Lobster Task Force, DFO fully implemented limited entry licensing and further restricted fishing access rights to committed full-time harvesters. Within this expanded regulatory system, the enforcement of rules by DFO fisheries officers became essential elements in the management and conduct of lobster fishing. The government also invested in a series of licence buyback programs to improve economic viability in inshore fleets.

The harvesting of Atlantic lobster is today the largest commercial fishery in Canada. The modern management system built up over the past forty years has created a robust fishery that supports thousands of enterprises, tens of thousands of jobs, and hundreds of coastal communities across the region. By 1990, new conservation measures had helped Atlantic lobster landings rebound to the 40,000-ton level of the early 1880s. Today, total landings have reached 100,000 tons with a landed value[3] over $1.5 billion and export value of $3.2 billion. Across Atlantic Canada there are nearly nine thousand owner-operated enterprises fishing lobster in forty-one different LFAs. Most inshore lobster boats have been limited to forty-five feet in length since the 1970s, but today's vessels are built with wider beams and bigger engines and utilize advanced navigation and communications technologies to improve carrying capacity, efficiency, and safety. Including captains and crew, there are over twenty thousand harvesters earning livelihoods in this fishery, and many more thousands of Atlantic Canadians are employed in buying and processing lobster.

CURRENT SITUATION

The great success of the lobster fishery is key to understanding current issues. Indigenous participation in the lobster sector has increased significantly over the past thirty years. Some advances were made in the 1990s in both the food, social, and ceremonial (FSC) fishery and the full commercial fishery through DFO's Aboriginal Fisheries Strategy. Following the *Marshall* decisions, the federal government's *Marshall* Response Initiative (MRI) made major investments in additional access and capacity building. To increase Indigenous access to lobster fishing, the MRI supported the purchase of vessels and hundreds of licences from commercial harvesters who voluntarily retired.

Additional programs supported mentoring (the At-Sea Mentoring Initiative), business management (the Fisheries Operations Management Program), and safety training. Indigenous leadership and community support and the involvement of experienced non-Indigenous fishers were integral to the success of these programs.

Over the past fifteen years, the Atlantic Integrated Commercial Fisheries Initiative (AICFI), co-developed and co-delivered by DFO and the Atlantic Policy Congress of First Nations Chiefs and Ulnooweg Development Group, has further expanded Indigenous access. However, the overall level of participation by Indigenous communities is still less than what most communities desire. Access to capital remains a barrier for many communities. DFO's recent Rights Reconciliation initiative has provided more resources to further expand access, but many First Nations view the terms of the program as insufficient and too restrictive to meet all of their needs.

To compete for fish during the regular season requires vessels and traps on par with other commercial harvesters, which requires hundreds of thousands of dollars in capital investment. Fishing a smaller number of traps from smaller vessels outside the season is seen, by some, as the only option for those who have no access to conventional commercial enterprises. To overcome this barrier, some communities moved ahead in 2020 to create their own moderate livelihood fishing plans and began fishing lobster under them.

The non-Indigenous commercial lobster sector has also challenged the federal government on these issues. They argue that any increase in

Indigenous participation could only mean less for their members, and further, they were not consulted on these changes and have no role in the decision making process. The development of moderate livelihood fishing plans for fishing outside the normal commercial season has met with great resistance from various organizations. Non-Indigenous harvesters see any fishing of lobster outside the regular seasons as a threat to stock conservation and to a management system that supported them so well over past decades.

Both Indigenous and non-Indigenous harvesters express concerns about DFO's handling of the fisheries conflicts in 2020. Both question the role of DFO conservation and protection officers, and both criticize DFO's overall approach.

All these issues will need to be addressed if First Nations and non-Indigenous fishing communities are to get past the current impasse. The challenge today is to create new options and compromises that make it possible to meet at least some of the requirements of both Indigenous and non-Indigenous lobster harvesters.

OPTIONS

For any option to address the main concerns of each party, it must allow Indigenous harvesters to see some immediate and incremental increase in their fishing activities while ensuring that conservation is not threatened.

One key factor is the "catchability" of traps outside the season compared to in season. During every commercial season, depending on number of licences and the trap limit in each LFA, there will be thousands or even hundreds of thousands of traps being fished. A large LFA such as LFA 34 in Southwest Nova Scotia may have 350,000 traps fished daily during the season, all targeting the same limited population of legal-sized lobsters.

If, however, a harvester fishes outside the commercial season when there are no other traps to compete with, they would likely land five to seven times the average caught per trap during the season, according to studies undertaken by DFO scientists. Thus, fishing 40 or 50 traps out of season might produce the same catch as 250 to 300 traps in the season.

This was a key issue immediately following the *Marshall* decision when Miramichi Bay became the focus of fishing outside the normal season in 1999 and again in 2000. In late 2000, DFO engaged Dr. John Caddy to work with DFO, Esgenoôpetitj (Burnt Church), and the commercial industry on this issue. Dr. Caddy was a long-time senior fisheries scientist with the Food and Agriculture Organization in Rome and a research fellow at the University of London. In his August 2001 report he focused on the key issue of the catch ratio when fishing outside the commercial season. In the area of Miramichi Bay during the timeframe of the study, he estimated the catch factor for out-of-season fishing as five to six times greater per trap compared to in-season fishing.[4] Some work has also been done in the Baie des Chaleurs by the Quebec Region of DFO to confirm this finding.

In August 2021, DFO and Listuguj Mi'gmaq First Nation reached an agreement on a fall fishery in LFA 21B, which has a spring commercial season. In announcing the agreement, DFO and Listuguj made the following statement to explain how they could conduct a fall fishery without increasing overall fishing effort on the stock: "A catchability factor of seven will be applied to the calculation of the fall fishing effort, which takes into account the fact that lobster is more easily caught in the fall than in the spring. This means that effort deployed in number of trap days in the fall is multiplied by seven and is subsequently deducted from the effort allowed the following spring."[5]

The goal is to conduct fall lobster fishing without increasing total annual fishing effort in LFA 21B. In essence, the agreement provides an option for all licence holders—First Nations and non-Indigenous—to fish outside the regular season without increasing total fishing effort for the year, thereby safeguarding the long-term conservation of the lobster stock. The "catchability" factor will undoubtedly be subject to ongoing review by DFO and Listuguj under the agreement.

A further application of this approach could be to put a fair proportional limit on the amount of lobster that can be harvested for each licence fished for moderate livelihood purposes outside of the regular season. Each LFA has a set number of licences, a maximum number of traps per licence, and a defined season. It is possible to calculate the average catch per licence within a particular LFA and then assign this average as a catch limit or quota for any moderate livelihood fishing outside the regular season.

Under this model, to participate in a moderate livelihood fishery outside the regular commercial season, an Indigenous community would make arrangements with DFO to not fish a certain number of communal-commercial licences during the regular season. DFO would then issue the community a communal-commercial licence to be fished in the same LFA at agreed upon times, and with agreed conditions, including an assigned "catch limit" or quota for each licence it did not fish.

The catch limits would need to be recalculated for each coming year based on the previous season's average catch per licence. This approach would allow First Nations to divide the traps and catch limit for each licence among several harvesters to give more community members opportunities to earn moderate livelihoods. Further, such an option could allow harvesters to use smaller vessels to generate incomes while operating safely within their skill levels. Indeed, many harvesters in First Nations have training, experience, and appropriate vessels and gear to compete on the same basis as non-Indigenous harvesters during the regular commercial season. Fishing remains a dangerous profession, and ongoing training and safety requirements will greatly influence the decisions of Indigenous communities.

For this option to work, Indigenous communities, commercial fishers, and DFO will all need to have full confidence in the calculation of the average catch for commercial licences fished during the season and in the strict enforcement of the assigned catch limit or quota fished outside the regular season.

To build this confidence, DFO, the interested First Nations, and commercial lobster harvesters will need to work closely together to develop the program and agree on how catches are monitored and counted during the regular season and during any moderate livelihood fishery outside the regular season. Both fisheries—in-season commercial and out-of-season moderate livelihood—will need to be more effectively monitored to ensure adherence to the rules. The way catches are monitored is, undoubtedly, a critical element. Most other commercial fisheries in Canada employ a program of independent monitoring at the dockside, but the lobster industry has argued this is not necessary in their sector. Also, the model may not be appropriate for all the forty-one LFAs across Atlantic Canada.

The place to start would be with a pilot project in one or two LFAs where First Nations and commercial harvesters have experience working together and are willing to collaborate to try something new.

III

The
MARSHALL
DECISIONS

3.1

FISHING with DONALD MARSHALL JR.

by L. JANE MCMILLAN

It is a wonderful privilege to be writing here in Mi'kma'ki, the traditional terri-tory of the Mi'kmaq Nation.[1]

TREATIES WITH THE CROWN: THE FIRST THREE HUNDRED YEARS

Due to their proximity to Europe, the Mi'kmaq have endured one of the longest periods of colonial encounter. They have a rich history of engag-ing and negotiating with newcomers to their territories. The Mi'kmaq prac-tised treaty diplomacy, *kisa'muemkewy*,[2] among their own citizens and with allies. They developed conventions of community engagement through *mawiomi*—formal gatherings that included storytelling, ceremonies, and rituals, by which they came to a collective understanding of treaty obliga-tions reflective of their world views.[3] The 1726 treaty with the British Crown laid out protections for the customary rights of the Mi'kmaq, including hunting, fishing, and planting. These understandings were reaffirmed and expanded several times between 1749 and 1778. The treaties of 1760 and 1761 instituted covenants securing the Mi'kmaq rights to both harvest and sell natural resources.

DONALD MARSHALL JR. AND A NATION'S CONSTITUTIONAL REVIVAL

Donald Marshall, a Mi'kmaw man from Nova Scotia, was wrongfully convicted of murder in 1971. Marshall was only seventeen years old. He spent eleven years in prison before he could prove his innocence. It was one of the first miscarriages of justice to gain notoriety in Canada. A Royal Commission of Inquiry into Marshall's wrongful conviction disclosed systemic racism in policing and, more broadly, throughout the justice system. It exposed the unequal treatment of Indigenous Peoples before the law, led to fundamental changes in the law of procedure and evidence, and rightly punctured the Canadian justice system's inflated self-regard. The Commission ultimately tendered eighty-two recommendations to address systemic faults in the administration of justice. In summary, it found that:

> The criminal justice system failed Donald Marshall Jr. at virtually every turn, from his arrest and wrongful conviction for murder in 1971 up to, and even beyond, his acquittal by the Court of Appeal in 1983. The tragedy of the failure is compounded by evidence that this miscarriage of justice could—and should—have been prevented, or at least corrected quickly, if those involved in the system had carried out their duties in a professional and/or competent manner. That they did not is due, in part at least, to the fact that Donald Marshall Jr. is a native.[4]

Donald Marshall's wrongful prosecution, conviction, and denial of his appeals are emblematic of the systemic discrimination and racism experienced by Canadian Indigenous Peoples during the twentieth and now twenty-first centuries.[5]

I shared many wonderful years and many extraordinary experiences with Donald Marshall Jr. My ancestors are from Scotland, Ireland, and the Alsace-Lorraine region and probably arrived in Canada in the early 1800s. I moved to Mi'kma'ki, Mi'kmaw territory, in August 1991. I met Donald Marshall Jr., the eldest son of Grand Chief Donald Marshall Sr. and Kalolin Googoo, and soon became Donald Marshall Jr.'s spouse and fishing partner. Grand Chief Marshall was a highly regarded leader of the seven districts of the Mi'kmaq Nation, a revered Treaty Rights advocate and nation-builder. Donald Marshall Jr., once released from prison, traced his father's footsteps.

Junior loved to fish. He was a grateful harvester and enjoyed cooking what he caught. He embraced the solitude of wandering down the river with his fly rod or jig and the excitement of setting nets in the Bras d'Or Lakes. Junior's passion for fishing led us to catch eels for a living. Eels are an important facet of Mi'kmaw culture, and eel fishing a time-honoured custom. After the catch, we would take out the choice eels, and Junior would spend hours cleaning them to pass to the Elders in the community. He also fished for feasts and important events like Treaty Day and mawiomi (powwows). He embodied the constitutionalism of the L'nu, the Mi'kmaw peoples, respecting the resource and sustaining honour by sharing. Fishing eels is hard, dirty work, but we liked the adventure. Every time there was a heavy rainfall during fishing season, Junior would rub his hands together and say, "Lots of eels tomorrow, baby!" and he was always right.[6]

In fishing and selling eels, Donald Marshall believed he was simply carrying out his Treaty Right to earn a livelihood. Others took a very different view—in particular, the federal government, as successor to the Crown co-signatory to the Peace and Friendship Treaties. In short order, Donald Marshall's comfortable exercise of his traditional Treaty Rights was abruptly interrupted.

On August 24, 1993, we were fishing eel and selling our catch in Welnek (Pomquet Harbour), near Paqtnkek Mi'kmaw Community. We were under surveillance by Fisheries officers. We were later charged with three counts of illegal fishing, and our gear was confiscated. Junior's subsequent prosecution grounded a Treaty test case that ultimately refigured Indigenous and settler resource relations in the Atlantic provinces of Canada. When the Department of Fisheries and Oceans (DFO) officer approached our boat and asked to see our licences, Junior's response was immediate: "I don't need a licence, I have the 1752 Treaty"—just as his father had earlier fought for the Treaty Right to hunt moose. "I don't know anything about a Treaty," said the DFO officer.[7]

It did not cross our minds that fishing slimy, sometimes stinky, but always yummy eels would lead, some six years later, to the transformative Supreme Court of Canada decision of R. v. Marshall. We were just trying to keep food on the table and gas in the boat, and with luck, have a bit left over for beers at the 123 Legion in We'koqma'q. Junior was a Mi'kmaw person whose ancestry is rooted in the land, sea, and air of Mi'kma'ki. He was exercising his livelihood rights as a treaty beneficiary. He was actively shaping the resurgence of his Indigenous identity against the history of its oppression.[8]

Junior quickly understood that his fishing trial had become a crucial test of his Nation's Treaty Rights. He carried the burden with a heavy heart, often looking to his late father's legacy for guidance. The stress of repeatedly returning to court and the lengthy trial and appeals, along with his anxiety over the consequences for Mi'kmaw treaties and livelihood if he lost the case, taxed his already fragile health.

In 1999, in *R. v. Marshall*, the Supreme Court affirmed the Mi'kmaw right to livelihood, as set out in the treaties of 1760–61.[9] The ruling was transformative. It validated the made-in–Nova Scotia reconciliation process initiated in 1997, when the Mi'kmaw Chiefs of Nova Scotia, the Government of Nova Scotia, and the Government of Canada signed the Tripartite Memorandum of Understanding—an agreement between the three parties to discuss issues and "matters of mutual concern." The Tripartite Forum approach was founded on one of the eighty-two recommendations of the Royal Commission on the Donald Marshall, Jr., Prosecution (1989).

The *Marshall* decision triggered a redistribution of access to natural resources, amplifying Mi'kmaw economic development and autonomy. There was now potential to replace historical patterns of dependency and subjugation with sustainable community advancement, through the exercise of affirmed Treaty and Indigenous Rights and through the substantiation of Traditional Knowledge. It marked an unprecedented turn in colonial relations.[10]

As held by the Supreme Court, the Mi'kmaq have the right, pursuant to treaties and Section 35 of the Constitution Act, 1982, to harvest and to sell fish to obtain a moderate livelihood.[11] The Mi'kmaq Nation in Nova Scotia has worked hard to leverage the *Marshall* decision. The Mi'kmaq demand predictable, productive, and respectful consultation and negotiation with settlers and their governments as they implement their livelihood fisheries. However, discussions with the Department of Fisheries and Oceans have failed to generate substantive recognition, changes in fishing regulations, or the implementation of Mi'kmaw livelihood rights management protocols. "Arguably," Anthony Davis wrote in late 2020, "from 1999 to this day, the Mi'kmaq have foregone hundreds of millions of dollars in earnings while waiting for an appropriate resolution."[12]

Impatient with the government's reticence to honour its treaty obligations, some Mi'kmaw communities developed and launched their own
Netukulimk fish-harvesting strategy (see chapters 2.3 and 4.1 for definitions
of Netukulimk). As in the past, Mi'kmaw fishers have been met with threats,
physical assaults, seizure of their gear and harvests, torched boats and stor-
age sheds, and even gunfire. The continuing failure of law enforcement to
protect Mi'kmaw fishers and their families from routine intimidation and
violence only compounds the historical injustice. Tragically and shamefully,
the systemic racism epitomized by Donald Marshall's wrongful conviction
persists. The clashes of the recent lobster wars are only the most recent
example.[13] We are witnessing the inevitable consequences of a colonial regulatory regime that lacks the resolve to decolonize its jurisdiction. The repair
of Nation-to-Nation relationships is a critical first step. The inequities borne
by the Mi'kmaq Nation will continue unless and until the failure to recognize, respect, and honour L'nu governance over livelihood rights are cor-
rected. To address systemic discrimination, we must have systemic change.

Junior Marshall left us far too soon, on August 6, 2009. For close to
thirty years, I have been a student of many generous Mi'kmaw teachers who
patiently shared their stories and experiences with me. I am particularly
grateful to the Marshall family and, of course, for the years I spent with
Junior. Now a legal anthropologist, I am dedicated to sharing these teachings. They instill the values that frame Mi'kmaw legal principles, honour
treaty relationships, and mobilize and respect the rights of the Mi'kmaq
Nation and their sacred relations to the resources in Mi'kma'ki. History
changed that August day on the waters near Paqtnkek, and I am humbled
by the transformative power of eels. I hope that my work honours Junior's
legacy and the Mi'kmaq Nation.

CONCLUSION

We live in an era of aspirational reconciliation. Assessing the distribution
of jurisdiction and the interface between Canadian and Indigenous legal
and constitutional orders is critical to achieving substantive progress.
The Mi'kmaq are critically engaged in decolonizing their legal traditions.
Their cultural resilience grows stronger, as does their confidence to pro-
ductively navigate external and internal pressures. They draw on culturally

entrenched narratives of law to interpret their lives and their relationships. These constructions define their legal consciousness, which in turn legitimates community choices. Netukulimk harvesting strategies are reparative exercises in self-empowerment, autonomy, and legal reification. They exemplify a path forward in which justice, sovereignty, and the right to livelihood and independence may become reality, at last.

THE INDIGENOUS RIGHT
to a MODERATE LIVELIHOOD

by JEFFERY CALLAGHAN, LUCIA WESTIN,
and DAN VANCLIEAF of MCINNES COOPER[1]

The year 2020 was filled with challenges, including in the relationship between Indigenous communities, non-Indigenous communities, and the federal government. Heightened tensions between Indigenous fishers and commercial, non-Indigenous fishers in Nova Scotia in late 2020 highlighted the need for the clarification of Indigenous Treaty Rights to hunt and fish for a moderate livelihood on the Atlantic coast. The Supreme Court of Canada formally recognized a right of Indigenous people in Atlantic Canada to hunt and fish for a moderate livelihood in 1999. Yet decades later, uncertainty persists about what a "moderate livelihood" is and how Indigenous people, including the Mi'kmaq, can exercise their Treaty Rights. Perceived inaction or inadequate implementation of these rights led certain Indigenous communities to establish their own "moderate livelihood fisheries" in the waters off Nova Scotia. To date, the clarification and certainty likely needed to quell tensions and resolve these longstanding issues continues to be elusive, leading more Indigenous communities to express a desire to establish their own fisheries.

Here's a deeper dive into the rights that are at issue and why disputes like those in Nova Scotia and elsewhere across Atlantic Canada have ignited and will likely continue to flare.

THE ORIGIN OF THE RIGHT: PEACE AND FRIENDSHIP

From 1725 to 1780, the British Crown entered into and renewed "Peace and Friendship Treaties" with Indigenous Peoples, including with Mi'kmaw, Wolastoqey, and Peskotomuhkati Indigenous communities in Atlantic Canada. These treaties set out mutual obligations between the Crown and those Indigenous Peoples. Section 35 of the Canadian Constitution Act, 1982 recognizes and affirms the "existing aboriginal and treaty rights of the aboriginal peoples of Canada."[2] Like Aboriginal Rights, Treaty Rights are collective rights and communal in nature. While individuals may enjoy the benefits of these rights, such as hunting and fishing, the rights themselves belong to the community.

THE RIGHT DEFINED: R. V. MARSHALL

The Supreme Court of Canada considered whether the Peace and Friendship Treaties granted a Treaty Right to hunt and fish in the 1999 landmark case of R. v. Marshall.[3]

Donald Marshall Jr., a Mi'kmaw person from Membertou First Nation, was charged under the Fisheries Act for catching, possessing, and selling eels without a licence and doing so outside of the proscribed fishing season. In his defence, Mr. Marshall argued that the Peace and Friendship Treaties enshrined his inherent right to sell the catch of his hunting and fishing, irrespective of modern regulations that may restrict or limit such hunting and fishing.

The Court decided the Peace and Friendship Treaties of 1760–1761 confirmed the right of the Mi'kmaw people to provide for their own sustenance by taking the products of their hunting, fishing, and other gathering activities, and trading for what in 1760 was termed "necessaries." The Court found that the concept of "necessaries" is equivalent in current times to the concept of a "moderate livelihood," and a moderate livelihood includes such basics as "food, clothing, and housing, supplemented by a few amenities."[4] It does not, however, extend to the open-ended accumulation of wealth.

Accordingly, the Court affirmed the Mi'kmaq of Nova Scotia's Treaty Right to fish for a moderate livelihood is validated and protected by the Canadian Constitution. The regulatory prohibitions against fishing and selling eels without a licence infringed Marshall's constitutional rights and were inoperative, unless the Crown could justify the prohibitions—which it could not in this case.

THE SCOPE AND LIMIT OF THE RIGHT: *MARSHALL II*

The *R. v. Marshall* decision caused considerable uncertainty, an escalation in tensions, and, in some locales, even violence. On the one hand, the Court unequivocally recognized a Treaty Right to pursue a moderate livelihood. On the other, a lack of clarity remained as to how the exercise of this Treaty Right would impact stocks and interact with existing regulatory regimes. In the days following the *R. v. Marshall* decision, some Indigenous groups put traps in the water regardless of existing regulations on the basis they didn't constrain the newly confirmed Treaty Right. This led to conflict between Indigenous and non-Indigenous fishers similar to what would occur in 2020. Two months after its decision in *R. v. Marshall*, and in response to the growing tensions, the Supreme Court of Canada issued a subsequent decision in *R. v. Marshall*,[5] known as *Marshall II*, to clarify the scope and implementation of the Treaty Rights in question.

Marshall II clarified that the treaties, and the benefits granted under them, were local in nature and limited to the area traditionally used by the local community with which the treaty was made.

The Court determined that although Treaty Rights could be infringed, the government must produce sufficient evidence demonstrating that the regulation in question is necessary for conservation or other grounds of public importance. Although the Court in *Marshall II* found that the regulations purporting to limit the Treaty Right by imposing a discretionary licensing system and closed season (on eel fishing specifically) were not justified in that context, it left open the possibility that the government could regulate such rights in the future.

The Supreme Court of Canada in the *R. v. Marshall* and *Marshall II* decisions was clear that although the federal government has the right to regulate Aboriginal and Treaty Rights, such regulation must be justified. The burden for proving a justified infringement rests solely with the government. Accordingly, the federal government cannot impose whatever regulation it sees fit.

THE CLARIFICATION OF THE RIGHT: THE MISSING PIECE

There have been some steps taken since the *R. v. Marshall* and *Marshall II* decisions, but significant progress is still needed to ensure a peaceful and mutually acceptable resolution.

In 1999, the Department of Fisheries and Oceans (DFO) launched the *Marshall* Response Initiative, which aimed to increase participation of Indigenous communities in commercial fisheries by providing assets and training. In 2007, DFO implemented the Atlantic Integrated Commercial Fisheries Initiative, which provides funding to Indigenous communities to build the capacity of their communal-commercial fishing enterprises. And in 2019, DFO reached ten-year interim agreements with a few Indigenous communities throughout the region to guide implementation of their Treaty Rights.[6] Criticism, however, has persisted among Indigenous communities that there has been insufficient effort by DFO to ensure the Treaty Rights the Court affirmed in the *Marshall* decisions can be integrated and respected within current regulatory regimes. As a result, Indigenous communities, like the Sipekne'katik First Nation in Nova Scotia, have moved forward with their own self-regulated fisheries. In response, there has again been tension and even violence.

Almost one year after the events involving Sipekne'katik, there have been both signs of progress toward certainty and resolution, and some setbacks.

- On November 29, 2020, the office of the federal fisheries minister proposed a draft memorandum of understanding (MOU) to the Sipekne'katik First Nation Chief. Yet in December 2020, talks again appeared to stall without a resolution.

- In spring 2021, the federal government signed a ten-year Rights Reconciliation Agreement with Listuguj, a Mi'gmaq community in Quebec's Gaspé Region (in addition to agreements signed in 2019 with three communities).

- The House of Commons Standing Committee on Fisheries and Oceans held hearings through late 2020 and early 2021 with respect to the events at Sipekne'katik. In May 2021, the Committee tabled its report on the Implementation of the Mi'kmaw and Maliseet Treaty Right to Fish in Pursuit of a Moderate Livelihood, making forty recommendations.

- During the spring 2021 lobster season, like at Sipekne'katik, another Nova Scotia Mi'kmaw community—Potlotek First Nation—proceeded with its own "moderate livelihood" fishery. But unlike at Sipekne'katik, DFO and Potlotek reached an interim agreement respecting this community's fishery. A promising sign, perhaps.

One thing remains clear: there's further work to do for all parties to agree on just what an Indigenous moderate livelihood looks like and how an Indigenous moderate livelihood fishery can be implemented in Atlantic Canada. These questions will continue to define the relationship between Indigenous communities in Atlantic Canada and the federal government.

3.3

CANADA'S ACTIONS on MI'KMAW FISHERIES

by NAIOMI METALLIC and CONSTANCE MACINTOSH

A cting on the Treaty Right recognized in the Supreme Court of Canada's decision twenty-three years ago in *R v. Marshall*,[1] the Sipekne'katik First Nation launched its moderate livelihood fishery in the waters off Southwest Nova Scotia in early September, 2020. Since the fishery's launch, some have suggested the Canadian government has broad authority to dictate how the Mi'kmaq's treaty-based fisheries can operate.

While the Court in *Marshall* (and in a subsequent, related decision in *Marshall II*[2]) acknowledged Canada could lawfully "regulate" the Treaty Right, regulate does not mean Canada may legislate and limit the Treaty Right in whatever way it sees fit. Far from it. As two law professors who teach Aboriginal law, we have decided to weigh in to provide clarification. Our clear answer is that Canada's actions, thus far, would not meet Constitutional muster.

THE LIMITS ON CROWN REGULATION OF "ABORIGINAL AND TREATY RIGHTS"

Section 35(1) of the Constitution Act, 1982, states that "[t]he existing Aboriginal and treaty rights of the Aboriginal peoples of Canada are hereby recognized and affirmed." Whereas the phrase "Aboriginal rights" refers to the inherent rights of Indigenous Peoples, which are grounded in prior occupation, "treaty rights" refers to rights that were negotiated between Indigenous and non-Indigenous governments and then recorded in legally binding treaties.

In the first Supreme Court of Canada decision interpreting the provision, R. v. Sparrow (1990), the court affirmed that section 35(1) "renounces the old rules of the game"[3] where the Crown had assumed it held unilateral rights to ignore or limit Aboriginal Rights. As a provision of the Constitution, the court found section 35(1) places "a measure of control over government conduct and [creates] a strong check on legislative power." The Supreme Court laid out a two-step test, whereby the government must prove when its laws or actions infringe Aboriginal Rights (for example, where the law or action ignores or denies the right, or places unreasonable limits on its exercise). Failure to meet this test will result in the government's law or action being declared unconstitutional—in other words, illegal.

The first prong of this two-step test asks whether the infringement has a valid objective. The court stated that such objectives would need to be compelling and substantial, and would include those related to conservation and management of a natural resource. The Supreme Court clarified in the 2003 R. v. Powley decision that the government cannot simply assert that it has a valid objective.[4] In that case, the Court said that Ontario could not simply assert conservation as an objective but had to provide actual evidence to support that the particular species in issue (moose) was under threat and that preventative measures were required.

The second prong of the Sparrow test requires the government to follow a process that ensures its treatment of the Aboriginal Right is in line with the honour of the Crown and the government's fiduciary relationship with Indigenous Peoples. To determine if this part of the test is met, the Court said it would look to whether the government ensured the Aboriginal Rights–holder had priority access to the resources after any conservation issues were taken into account; whether the government took steps to ensure that any impact on the Aboriginal Rights–holders were minimized; and whether there had been meaningful consultation with the affected Indigenous group regarding the infringing law or activity and how the infringement would be mitigated. The Court affirmed in R. v. Badger (1996) that this test applies to all Aboriginal Rights, including Treaty Rights,[5] such as those currently being practiced by the Mi'kmaq.

In subsequent decisions, the Supreme Court has built on *Sparrow* and provided specific guidance on commercial Aboriginal Rights. In *R. v. Gladstone* (1996),[6] the Court adapted the requirements in *Sparrow* to situations where the right in question has an expressly commercial dimension (*Sparrow* had involved an Aboriginal Right to fish for food, social, and ceremonial purposes only).

With regard to step 1 in the *Sparrow* test, valid "objectives" for infringing on rights can include addressing economic and regional fairness within an industry, as well as the participation of non-Indigenous groups in an industry. On step 2, the Court clarified that while the government must give priority to the Aboriginal Right, this does not rise to the level of giving *exclusive* priority within a commercial industry after conservation concerns have been addressed but nonetheless does require the Crown to demonstrate recognition of the existence and importance of the Aboriginal interest in the resource. The Court suggested this priority could be shown by according the Aboriginal group a share in the industry that is reflective of both the group's proportional representation and the significance of the resource to the group. The Court also emphasized the importance of consulting with the Aboriginal group affected, as part of assessing what constitutes a priority share.

In *R. v. Adams* (1996),[7] the Court addressed a situation where a statutory licensing regime prohibited fishing without government authorization (a licence). An Indigenous person had been charged for fishing without a licence. The regime was found to be unconstitutional because the licensing regime failed to recognize and accommodate the Aboriginal Right to fish. Drawing directly upon *Adams*, the Court in *Marshall 1* similarly found that the licensing regime in the Federal Fisheries Act and its regulations was unlawful because it failed to recognize or accommodate the Treaty Right to fish. The Court in *Marshall 1* further highlighted that although catch limits could be identified to reflect a "moderate livelihood," the government could not unilaterally impose seasonal limits. Finally, the Court has recognized in numerous decisions that Aboriginal and Treaty Rights belong to the community, including in *Marshall 11*, where the Court noted the moderate livelihood right was to be "exercised by authority of the local community," and so their fishery is to be governed or regulated internally, not by an outside body.

THE LAW AND THE CURRENT DISPUTE

So, what do the law and these legal tests demand of the Crown in the current circumstances?

When the *Marshall* decisions were delivered, the Mi'kmaq were vindicated in a fight for fishing rights recognition they had been waging for seven decades. The Department of Fisheries and Oceans Canada (DFO) finally started negotiations with the Mi'kmaw and Wolastoqey (Maliseet) communities in the Maritimes to support some access to the commercial fishery by issuing licences to the communities and providing them boats and fishing gear. This has been called the *"Marshall* Response Initiative." Canada did not amend the Fisheries Act or regulations to do this. Instead, Canada issued commercial licences under its existing Aboriginal Communal Fishing Licences Regulations.

But there was a twist. While most of the communities signed on to these agreements, DFO negotiators informed the First Nations that these agreements were not intended to be the implementation of their moderate livelihood Treaty Right. The agreements say they are "without prejudice" to the legal positions of DFO or the First Nations with respect to Treaty Rights. Rather, the implementation of the treaty-based moderate livelihood fisheries was to be addressed at another negotiating table (in each Maritime province, there are ongoing tripartite negotiation tables on Aboriginal and Treaty Rights).

The Mi'kmaq and the Wolastoqiyik have been attempting to negotiate for the implementation of their Treaty Rights ever since, but there has been little progress. Driven by frustration over the lack of progress, twelve Nova Scotia Mi'kmaw communities filed a lawsuit in 2013, seeking to require Canada's negotiators to obtain a mandate to negotiate moderate livelihood rights. Communities agreed to put the case on hold after Canada made a commitment to finally negotiate on the fisheries, but seven years later this commitment has still not come to fruition.

Although the commercial fishing agreements offered to Maritime First Nations improved their access to the commercial fishery and have generated economic returns to the communities, the Mi'kmaq would be hard-pressed to say this achieves a moderate livelihood. Communities in the region continue to struggle with intergenerational impacts of residential and day schools and other colonial policies, chronic underfunding of essential services by the Department of Indigenous Services, and racism, all of which contribute to high levels of unemployment and social assistance dependence.

In short, to date, Canada has not implemented a moderate livelihood fishery. Instead, it has provided the communities limited access to the commercial fisheries while failing to deliver on its promise to do more. In our view, this fails to meet the requirements set out by the Supreme Court on several levels. While Canada may be able to identify valid objectives to support limitations of the Treaty Right (step 1 of the *Sparrow* test), Canada must first have established an evidentiary foundation for such objectives (whether this be conservation or historical reliance by other users of the fishery).

We note that independent biologists have studied the situation and concluded that the Mi'kmaw moderate livelihood fishery raises no legitimate conservation issues.[8] If a valid objective is identified and supported by evidence, Canada must prove its treatment of the Treaty Right is in line with the honour of the Crown and the government's fiduciary relationship with Indigenous Peoples (step 2 of the *Sparrow* test). Canada has never actually attempted to implement a moderate livelihood Treaty Right in law. There have been no amendments to the Fisheries Act or its regulations since *Marshall 1*. Nor has Canada attempted to show such rights *any* priority.

The government may argue the *Marshall* Response Initiative accommodated the *Marshall 1* decision and gave some priority to the Treaty Right. However, this is dangerous ground. The DFO negotiators expressly informed the Mi'kmaq and Wolastoqiyik during the *Marshall* Response Initiative negotiations that the commercial agreements *were not* an implementation of a moderate livelihood Treaty Right. Had the First Nations thought these agreements were intended to define how their rights would be practiced and limited, they may not have accepted such agreements. The honour of the Crown requires that its negotiators act in good faith, and there can be no sharp-dealing (making false promises or being misleading, for example). It is highly likely courts will require the Crown to stand by its words.

Even if Canada could rely on the *Marshall* Response Initiative as somehow accommodating some aspects of the Treaty Right, it is very unlikely Canada would be found to have given sufficient *priority* to the Treaty Right—part of the second step in the *Sparrow* test. The commercial licensing regime currently in place treats Mi'kmaq like all other stakeholders and does not accommodate the Mi'kmaw interest in the management of the fisheries. Further, Canada's refusal to consult with the Mi'kmaq in relation to decision making regarding the commercial fishery, or to meaningfully negotiate the implementation of a moderate livelihood fishery, likely fails on the *Sparrow* and *Gladstone* requirements to engage in consultation.

Finally, the Court has been clear that Treaty Rights must remain meaningful and reflect changing circumstances and what it means for technology to evolve. Their practice cannot be undermined. The current situation, where Mi'kmaw fishers fear for their lives and witness their gear being destroyed, undercuts the heart of the *Marshall* decision, which rested on a 250-year-old treaty promise that the Crown would ensure that the Mi'kmaq would "not be hindered from, but have free liberty" to fish, and have "free liberty" to sell their catch.

Our professional assessment is that a court would likely conclude that Canada's current actions to regulate the Mi'kmaw moderate livelihood Treaty Right, actions that were found to be unconstitutional in *Marshall 1*, would still be found to be unconstitutional twenty-three years later.

IV

MI'KMAW VOICES

An **INTERVIEW** with **ALBERT MARSHALL**

by NADINE LEFORT

lbert Marshall is a highly respected and much-loved Elder of the Mi'kmaq Nation. He is from the Moose Clan and lives in the community of Eskasoni in Unama'ki—Cape Breton, NS.

Albert is a fluent speaker of the Mi'kmaw language. A passionate advocate of cross-cultural understandings and healing, and our human responsibilities to care for all creatures and Mother Earth, he is the "designated voice" for Mi'kmaw Elders of Unama'ki with respect to environmental issues.

Albert is a survivor of the Indian Residential School in Shubenacadie, NS. He was profoundly affected by this experience, and it has led him on a lifelong quest to connect with and understand both the culture he was removed from and the culture he was forced into, and to help these cultures find ways to live in mutual respect of each other's strengths and ways.

Albert coined the phrase "Two-Eyed Seeing" (*Etuaptmumk*) to explain the guiding principle and an action-oriented invitation to recognize the strengths that exist within different ways of knowing.

On July 12, 2021, Albert spoke with Nadine Lefort at his house in Eskasoni. Nadine is the manager of communications and outreach with Unama'ki Institute of Natural Resources. She has worked extensively with Albert on Two-Eyed Seeing and has been friends with him and his family for over twenty years.

Nadine Lefort: *What does fishing for a moderate livelihood mean to you? What do you believe it could look like?* ·

Albert Marshall: My key point here is that I don't believe there is such a thing as a moderate livelihood. For me, the concept of Moderate Livelihood is an illusion to distract the public of why the government is denying us equal opportunity to access fisheries.

When taking full consideration for our Treaty and Aboriginal Rights to access resources, how does Moderate Livelihood fit within an economic system, and who does Moderate Livelihood benefit? Most importantly, how does the framework for Moderate Livelihood address and enhance conservation? I believe Moderate Livelihood is a distraction, keeping us from our rightful access to fisheries.

NL: *Is it the terminology of "moderate livelihood" that doesn't work for you?*

AM: The terminology has been crafted in a system that doesn't fully understand the concept of *Netukulimk*. With such vague terminology, it means that we Mi'kmaq are left out.

If we are fishing in moderation, it means we are being held back. Rather, it should be that we are fishing to enable future generations access to a healthy, vibrant ecosystem. Accessing resources should not be about limiting, it should be framed as what we are doing to provide for future generations. We're going about this the wrong way.

Why is someone from outside of my community and culture allowing me access? Why do I need their approval for partial access to our traditional territory when I have Treaty Rights? And why is it my duty to define it within their terminology and mindset? Shouldn't we be defining those boundaries?

If we look at food and ceremonial access, we have an exclusive privilege to access and utilize those gifts from the Creator. We have a duty to uphold our relationships with those species and those ecosystems. It is our honour to do that. But in the Bras d'Or Lakes, so many people have exploited its resources, fishing too much, polluting the water, developing too close to the banks. The water temperature is higher, the salinity is lower, the water is polluted in areas, lands are eroding. People have forgotten (or don't care about) the uniqueness of this ecosystem. The Bras d'Or was always a spawning ground for so many species, but since commercial fishing was allowed in the '80s or so, and dragging was allowed, the ecosystem balance has been off.

Traditionally, people only harvested fish at particular times of year. Nobody fished all year round, and if they fished, it was for sustenance. Herring, mackerel, gaspereau—they were all there in abundance. If someone was particularly gifted in catching one type of species, they shared. Not everyone needed to go fishing, but everyone in the community had access to this aquatic life, this gift, this food. Throughout the year, people would harvest in different areas, so there was never too much of a strain on one area or one species. This helped to maintain the balance of the Bras d'Or's delicate system.

NL: *What does it look like to have rightful access to fisheries?*
AM: Our overarching objective needs to reflect that nature has rights and humans have responsibilities.

In order to manage fisheries properly, it needs to be based primarily on conservation, not on economics. Conservation needs to be our priority in how we each utilize the gifts that nature provides. We each have that responsibility, and collectively, we need to make sure that we are caring for the ecological integrity of our home.

How in the hell can you manage fisheries? It's beyond human capability. From the Aboriginal perspective, you cannot manage something that has living components; that is beyond our capabilities. The only thing that can be managed is the actions of the people.

What I see as our first step in proper management would be an overview of the current state of our environment. I don't know that we can trust government-funded science, because they are biased. We need community-led assessments led by scientists we trust to get a proper picture of the aquatic ecosystem. When we have a true picture of how our species' populations are doing, including the smaller, underutilized species that are bycatch, then we will begin to understand the aspects of our ecosystem that are truly compromised. And then we can determine who can be fishing what, and where.

I believe that Two-Eyed Seeing, the true coming together of ideas and needs, will help each of us understand that our main responsibility is ensuring that no action will create a negative ecological repercussion.

NL: *Can you think of a time when you witnessed Mi'kmaq practicing Treaty Rights freely through fishing?*

AM: When I was young, everyone fished. Well, maybe not everyone, but everyone who wanted to fish fished. Young people fished with their fathers or grandfathers. I fished a little bit of everything with my older brothers and my father. No one was an "expert" in any species. We just went fishing when we needed something to eat.

I don't remember when that changed. Even when we had food stamps, people still fished. I guess that changed in the '80s or so, when people started to feel a bit more nervous if they went fishing. Nowadays, even if people know their rights and are confident they can fish in an area, they still feel nervous that DFO officers will come and check on them. Even if they know they're not doing anything wrong, they are afraid that they'll have to argue it. People shouldn't be made to feel nervous or wrong, or that they have to defend their rights just to go fishing near their home.

Actually, I should say that I don't see fishing as exercising a right. I would not call it a right, I consider it a privilege. The word "Netukulimk" is very much our guiding principle in framing this. The concept of Netukulimk implies our inherent responsibilities in continuing a relationship with species and the entirety of an ecosystem.

You cannot and should not allow any action to compromise the ecological integrity of the area. And Netukulimk reflects not just to the current generation, but acknowledges future generations as well.

We are interconnected and interdependent with all life forms. Each and every time something is taken for our need, we have to show our appreciation by doing a ceremony and thanking the spirit within that species. This ceremony, this thankfulness, keeps that relationship alive and enables us to eat, harvest medicines, survive.

NL: *Can you think of people who embody Netukulimk, now or past?*

AM: Any concept that we have in our worldview requires practice. Netukulimk is practised through acknowledging the spirit of whatever is being harvested, the connection you have with them, and the dependency you have on them. That relationship shapes your action, which you control, making sure that actions don't compromise a particular species and also the entire community presently and in the future.

People didn't philosophize about Netukulimk. No one sat around and discussed it. They lived it. It shaped their world view, the way they lived their lives. This overarching framework of responsibility transcends beyond a particular species or harvest, which helps to explain how we were able to subsist for millennia without policing or DFO restrictions.

In terms of leadership, the Elders of the communities had no official titles, but there was such a respect for that individual that you did not want to break the cultural norms because you would be forced to own up to your responsibilities. You would never know who they would tell, so you had to be responsible to all community members. The respect was so great for community balance that it kept you from doing anything that would put you in front of those Elders and your community members, responsible for your actions. Self-monitoring, self-regulating is very much a part of traditional communities.

NL: *Do those people and those positions exist now?*
AM: Certainly not in a formal way these days. The Chief and Council took all that away when this current system came into place.

I do have a great admiration for people like Ernest Johnson, Kerry Prosper, Joe and Judy Googoo, Danny Paul, Terry Denny, Frank Meuse—these are people who contribute to my medicinal plant and food supplies to maintain my health. At eighty-two, I can't harvest as easily as I wish I could. These are some people who I'm familiar with through my work and life, but I know there are more people throughout Mi'kma'ki.

NL: *How should rightful access be organized or overseen?*
AM: This is not a regional issue, it has to be across the country.

Anyone who is mindful of the current state of the environment needs to be involved. People believe that we have already exhausted the carrying and cleansing capacity of the system. Our last chance of survival is in our oceans and waters. They will not only sustain us with food, but will also sustain our health, because we are now relying on our oceans as our lungs and thermometers. The current approach to fisheries is a full-force assault on this very source of life, and it needs to change.

We know what's best for our environment for now and for the next generations. At this very moment, we need a declaration to determine a true picture of our environment, of all habitats, of all species. We need to truly understand the health of an ecosystem's biodiversity and well-being, and we all need to be committed to working toward it together. A Two-Eyed Seeing approach is necessary. We need the strengths of everyone's knowledge, without the ego that sometimes comes with it.

Governments and Chiefs and Councils need to continue dialogue with organizations like UINR [Unama'ki Institute of Natural Resources], CEPI [Bras d'Or Lakes Collaborative Environmental Planning Initiative], CMM [Confederacy of Mainland Mi'kmaq], KMKNO [Kwilmu'kw Maw-klusuaqn—Mi'kmaq Rights Initiative], and others in New Brunswick and PEI and throughout Mi'kma'ki who have trustworthy goals to protect our water for generations to come.

Government needs to do a lot of reflection and look at the actions of the past. It needs to be held accountable and to recognize that species cannot be removed in such numbers and in such environmentally detri-mental ways. The reflection is not only about blame. By coming together to reflect and to learn, it will help develop our shared ethic of care as we consider best steps forward toward ecosystem health.

NL: *In order to achieve peace on the water and, longer term, a fishery conducted under different principles, how important is it for the Mi'kmaq to engage in dialogue with non-Indigenous fishers and their organizations?*

AM: We need to start the conversation by asking questions like "do you think at this very moment that the fishery is ecologically sustainable?" I think everyone will answer "no." So, we need to develop a management plan that is based on the health and productivity of the ecosystem, and I will be clear that I mean ecologically productive, not economic produc-tivity. Maybe ecology and economy will line up, but ecological value has to take precedence when we're talking about long-term sustainability.

DFO has to actually change not only their language, but also their attitude toward Indigenous fishers. The idea that Indigenous fishers are the main threat to our ecosystems and our fisheries—that is absolutely false, and DFO has a big role in helping to change public opinion on that. Indigenous fishers want to harvest without being subjected to harass-ment, seizure, and incarceration.

NL: *Who should be part of that dialogue, Albert? For example, local, provincial, regional governments? And who should participate with respect to the Mi'kmaq?*
AM: The only people who should be at that table are the federal government and the Mi'kmaq, represented by KMKNO. Everybody else gets in the way.

NL: *Do you have hope that we'll be able to work together toward ecosystem health?*
AM: Yes, I do have hope. In fact, our youth give me hope daily. They seem to have a good understanding that each and every one of us depends upon water, air, soil. I hear youth asking why these fundamentals are not protected with an ecological constitution. Youth need opportunities for their voices to be heard and for their ideas to be put into action.

Let's talk about restoring order. Let's ensure that this will be available for the next seven generations. We have to be very adamant to ensure that anyone who compromises the opportunity for life should be held accountable. And if not, then I think that power should be taken away from people who have been exploiting it. That would give me hope.

We need regular reminding of nature's rights and human responsibilities. Ecosystem health, guided by the principle of Netukulimk, should be our main objective as we move forward in shaping our fisheries. This would change our narrative to focus on maintaining the balance, integrity, and ecological sustainability of the very life on which we all depend.

4.2

An **INTERVIEW** with **KERRY PROSPER**

by L. JANE MCMILLAN

Kerry Prosper is from Paqtnkek Mi'kmaq Nation, located in Eskikewa'kik, one of seven traditional territories in Atlantic Canada established by the Mi'kmaq. Kerry is an avid harvester, a highly regarded spiritual healer, and a leader. He is currently a band councillor and the Knowledge Keeper on Campus for St. Francis Xavier University in Antigonish, NS. Kerry was Chief of Paqtnkek in 1993 when Donald Marshall, Jane McMillan, and Peter Martin were fishing eels in Welnek (Pomquet Harbour) and the events leading to the *Marshall* decision occurred.

Kerry Prosper and Jane McMillan have worked together for close to two decades conducting research on Indigenous resource management, the cultural significance of eels, ethical harvesting, and Treaty Rights implementation. They have obtained research grants, published academic articles, and produced a documentary film with Martha Stiegman called *Seeking Netukulimk*, available on YouTube (https://www.youtube.com/watch?v=jrk3ZI_2Ddo).

On July 25, 2021, Kerry spoke with Jane while driving to the Indigenous Art Exhibit opening at Sherbrooke Village.

L. Jane McMillan: *What was it like for you, learning to provide and earning a livelihood?*

Kerry Prosper: I grew up in a family of thirteen or fourteen, and we did various things in the home. When we grew up, my dad was Chief for some time, and he would travel away for meetings, and my mother brought us up at home. Some of the things we did to survive and make money for clothes or the fall fair or things she needed, we would gather up and go and pick berries. We picked blueberries, raspberries, and strawberries. We would get to town and go door to door selling the berries. My mom would save that money for school clothes and the fall fair in Antigonish. That gave us a small understanding of what the land could provide for you by simply going out and picking berries and selling them.

There was an assumption, we knew we had a Treaty Right, but it was kind of forgotten [by settlers]. Everybody knew we were allowed to go and pick wood on private land and Crown land, there are no real concerns of what we were doing because we were actually contributing to the economy. The one thing we did not really see—we acknowledged we had Treaty Rights, but when it came to hunting and fishing there was a definite disagreement [with settler governments] when it came to whether we had rights or not, to hunting, fishing, and gathering. They [settlers] just assumed that we did not have the right. We grew up knowing that we were expected [by settlers] to buy a licence to hunt or fish and that if we didn't we would get charged.

For some reason the Mi'kmaq refused to buy those licences. Some did, just to be on the safe side and avoid the hassle, but we would like to go fishing before the season because it was a better opportunity for us to get fish before everybody else started fishing in the regular season. We had areas that we usually went to. Our reservation was split up into four pieces of land, and we had to go from one to the other. Sometimes these parcels of land were not known to the wardens [as] pieces of reservation land, and they would hassle us on that spot. A section of the river would go through our reserve, maybe three hundred or four hundred yards of river. We knew where the lines were and we felt safe, but we were unsure, and we certainly did get hassled when we were fishing on reserve lands.

Tom Sylliboy was one of the gentlemen who got charged when he was fishing on reservation land, fishing salmon. We would all work together, five or six of us working a piece of river together, or a pool. We would scare the fish into an area where we could snare them. We would make the snare out of rabbit wire, about four strands, and we would try to get the noose or snare around the salmon about halfway of his body length and hook him either by the tail or by the gills. Once you got the technique you are able to feel the gravel on the snare so you don't touch its belly, and you try to get it around him without scaring him and then you just haul him out of the water. We had people watching the banks for anyone coming up the river that looked suspicious or someone in a green uniform, and oftentimes we would see them coming and we would grab our fish and just disappear into the woods.

When I think of Moderate Livelihood back then, it was an individual practice of a right that was not recognized, and yet it was done in a manner that was like a collective. People would help each other. They would help get raw material and distribute it to the craftspeople. They would get together on a lot of their products and take them to a city or to a fair, someplace where they could sell them. It really helped subsidize their income and bring them to a level that was maybe comparable to what non-Native society was enjoying.

When *Sparrow* came down, it established the Aboriginal Right to fish for food, social, and ceremonial [purposes]. It is like you get a right recognized and all of a sudden, the whole context of that right changes. You went from a discreet use of the resource and a real social sharing of the resource, to almost like having a right that begins to be individualized, and now you are just working for yourself and you become individualized and you are competing with each other. That changed things in a way.

When [James Matthew] Simon got charged with hunting off-reserve and the 1752 treaty was recognized, everybody started hunting everywhere. Of course, you can hunt on Crown land and there is a lot of private land that is not posted and people are catching deer. Of course, the provincial government did not accept us hunting moose at the time, even though we had won the Treaty Right. I guess they thought they could keep us out of the moose hunt and make us enter the draw, the lottery system, to get us to win a licence to hunt moose. We decided to protest that. We put together a protest moose hunt up on Hunter's Mountain. They had their guns confiscated and they got charged. At the same time, the Sylliboy case was going through—the Sylliboy, Denny case. He was getting salmon. He was not selling it. He was criminalized for getting food.

After that the *Marshall* case. We were always wondering what "social" meant after the *Sparrow* case. We could hunt for ceremonial, we could hunt for food, what does it mean to hunt for social? People began to think should we hunt and fish and sell in our own communities? People began pushing that right.

Eventually Donald Marshall, and you, and a bunch of others, started fishing eels for a livelihood. I remember the day that court case came down. We were all up in Halifax and sitting at the World Trade Centre, and there were all these young lawyers who were the soldiers that Bruce [Wildsmith] and Eric [Zscheile] [had] heading up the court case. All these young men and women were fresh out of law school or articling or doing a big research thing. It was really a big research thing about our Treaty Rights for all of us. Everybody researching and diving right into it and finding out about the treaty relationship we had with the British and the French. Whenever I thought about the real negotiations that were held in the background before it was written up, how it involved three languages, the Mi'kmaw, French, and English, I can only imagine how challenging [it was], interpreting all of the discussions and coming out with an end product. Looking at how words can mean two things and that whole process of defining our rights. When that court case came down [on September 17, 1999], I could feel this whole thing in the room for that one moment or hour of "We won!" We could not believe it.

But the amazing thing is that through Charlie Dennis and the Eskasoni Fish and Wildlife, when the charges were laid [in 1993], we began to lay the—I guess, preparing ourselves, just in case we win, let's try to be ready. Over those seven years we established the Mi'kmaq Fish and Wildlife Commission. That's when we had this fellow [Kirk Beatty] from the United States, he told us about the experiences of the Great Lake fishers in Michigan or Wisconsin—they had gone through a similar process of winning a major court case in their fishery—and what their experiences were in implementing their rights. Through that we established the Mi'kmaq Fish and Wildlife Commission. We had developed a fishery during that time before the *Marshall* decision came down from the Supreme Court. We have people fishing in Southwest Nova, and we implemented tags. DFO gave us a quota of crab to implement the Fish and Wildlife Commission that were given up by fishermen in New Brunswick at the time. They gave up a certain percentage of their quota that went toward the Mi'kmaq Fish and Wildlife Commission.

My brother John and another individual named Chris Milley were the main men on the Fish and Wildlife Commission. We had people operating a commercial fishery at that time before the rights came in and DFO was involved. People were fishing in Southwest Nova and making a living, and everything seemed to be going good.

JM: *What are your concerns about livelihood and conservation?*

KP: What surprises me about the fishing and about the regulations and what goes on, everybody knew there was a black-market fishery that people were taking part of in Southwest Nova. A lot of our fishermen were out there fishing, and they would be hauling up all these traps that no one had claimed, and they were being harassed by the non-Native fishermen for hauling these illegal traps. They clued in to what was going on, that there was a fishery that was not being regulated and that DFO was not doing anything about, and we were being hassled for bothering those illegal traps. It really exposed what goes on, and no one really wants to call them out on it because no one knows how deeply implicated people are or who is connected.

We come to find out that everyone knew this happens, and every year there was a raid, but all the fishermen would get a heads-up that there is a raid coming and they would pull up so many traps and everybody was happy and it was a normal thing.

Our fishermen were aware that these traps are not allowed out there, and they complained to the DFO about the traps. That is what happened. So now when *Marshall II* came in and the jurisdiction of conservation fell to the federal government, it changed the relationship. Conservation is a good thing, but it depends how you use it and who bears the brunt of conservation. Is it the non-Native fishery or is it the new implementation of Moderate Livelihood that has to bear it all, or do we sit down and look at a management plan that is for a fully subscribed fishery and say, "Listen, we have to change this whole management plan to include Mi'kmaw Moderate Livelihood. We have to change the whole fishing plan Atlantic-wide." How are we going to have accommodation for the Mi'kmaq, and how are we going to change the management plan so it will suit the new entry of Moderate Livelihood and yet keep the current non-Native fishery and make a sustainable plan that will suit everybody? [That] is the main challenge, I guess.

A lot of Mi'kmaw expressed having an individual right and want to practise that in the fishery and other things, and yet some of the leadership says we have a collective right that has to be managed collectively. We have those struggles within our community and with the thirteen Chiefs and all of the Chiefs in the Maritime provinces. The main thing we have a hard time with is that individual expression of rights and the collective jurisdiction of trying to manage our [Treaty] Right.

When you are deprived from your livelihood for such a long time, you just want to get at it and help yourself. We are going through those pains of trying to manage something that is new. People are entrepreneurs, they want to make money for one reason or another. Some have a knack for it, and some are really jumping ahead of our leadership in keeping it together; [they] are putting together an exclusive management plan for us and joining up with the non-Native management plan and organizing something for everybody. One of the big challenges we have is sitting down with the federal government and sitting down with all the fishing organizations and working. I know there are a number of retired licences through the years and a bank of licences that are available, but there is no indication of Mi'kmaw getting access to those licences or finding a way of releasing them and bringing Mi'kmaw into the fishery and establishing a collective, co-operative management plan for every species.

We are just talking about fishery right now, but we [also] talk about logging and how we have tried to use the *Marshall* case in defining a moderate livelihood in the logging and other resources that Canada has, that the Atlantic has, that the Mi'kmaq should have been able to utilize. ...[We want] to modernize and adapt like every other country and society that learns how to use things they might not have used historically but have found ways of using them, and I think that is fair game for any society. It is how we move forward in that kind of sense and take the pressure off one resource like the fishery to utilize all other resources and spread the impact and increase the sustainability of the resources in Atlantic Canada for the Mi'kmaq.

JM: *What are your concerns about prioritizing your food fisheries?*

KP: The one thing that is subject to all of that, or made subject to that, is our food fishery. We keep losing the presence of the food fishery and its domination over access when it comes to conservation. It applies to every fishery, including ours and our livelihood, our corporate fishery, our individual fisheries, and non-Native fisheries. It has to have priority because food is a priority. A lot of our food today is tied up with the *Marshall* agreements where they are subject to rules and regulations, seasons and quotas, and that kind of protects the commercial fisheries because it harnesses and regulates the food fishery, making it subject to the commercial fishery. It seems to nullify the strength of the [Treaty Right to a] food fishery in the hopes to put it all together. We can see it through the eel fishery and the impact of the commercial fishery on the food fishery. Eels have been labelled a species of concern, and we are still waiting for what DFO is going to do in implementing some kind of strategy to protect them. At the same time, we have these elver fisheries that are popping up. We have established licences and new licences and the new activities that [are] exercised by our Moderate Livelihood people. We have still a commercial fishing of eels through spears, and that is still continuing while the eels are listed as a species of concern. There is no real movement toward doing some kind of altering of the management plan to protect the eels or protect our food fishery. It becomes political when we try to implement those kinds of rules. I don't know what kind of negotiations or talks are going on right now, but the conservation of eels and the protection of our food fishery is our priority in *Sparrow* rights.

The court cases and the treaties are neglected in certain ways. It is tied up in agreements, and some bands have no agreements. To me their *Sparrow* rights are intact, but there is no protection for the food fishery.

JM: *Is Netukulimk an organizing principle for livelihood fisheries?*

KP: People knew kind of what the meaning was, but it began to develop as people began hunting and fishing from *Sparrow*, *Simon*, and *Marshall*. It really took place on treaty in the aftermath of *Simon* [1985], and we really started moose hunting. We had the protest and we started a management plan. Then we began, we had the rules and regulations and the treaty handbook—that was the turning point. People became conscious of Netukulimk, and it started working its way down into the young fishermen and the young hunters, and they started using that in their practices and the little rituals that became part of that.

JM: *Do young people today have a sense of their Treaty Rights? Is there greater rights consciousness today?*

KP: Yes, there is. We have split concerns about Moderate Livelihood when it comes to food. Some people sell moose meat, but a lot of people really frown on that. It is that food thing and sharing. To me, like, forest products are fair to sell, but when it comes to food we are kind of funny about that. We access food to sell, peddle, and trade. But to get rich, a moderate livelihood, when you look at the whole standard of living and what people are trying to develop out of a commercial fishery, a certain kind of living, we are going beyond what is sustainable, for all of us. I do not know how we back that off and come down with what is a good living for everybody. Why should we earn differently? A lot of fishermen are rich, and I don't know why they have to keep fishing, they are millionaires. Why can't you sustain a living with that money you got and let someone else make a living?

JM: *Could a self-governed livelihood fishery establish that protocol?*

KP: When you look at the *Marshall* case and Justice Binnie saying we cannot accumulate wealth, and he mentions on the side, that would be a good thing for everybody. He just kind of mentioned that. It gives you a sense of what he was thinking. I mean, how can you not generate wealth when another part of society is accumulating massive wealth? How can that be sustainable for us, or equitable or sustainable for the fishery itself, for the stocks? Where is the happy medium of what is a livelihood? It is becoming more and more unsustainable, and things are beginning to get out of hand, prices are getting higher and higher. It is like forestry, every individual went out with a chainsaw and cut and made a living, and now an individual can buy a big processor that costs $400,000, and now he is going to have to cut massive amounts of wood to pay for itself and to provide that little livelihood for that individual, so all of that money is going out of the country to buy that processor, but it is having a really big impact on the resource here. It is unsustainable.

JM: *Do you see any hope for a unified fishery authority in Mi'kma'ki?*

KP: I know the Grand Council wants to get some kind of unity and [is] developing one big management plan. I think Paqtnkek would support that. We have to get a feel of what people want. We have individuals who want to make a living and individuals who just want to make a pile of money. We struggle with these different views of how to use the resource and what it means to them.

Our fishermen went through that fishing for food without the protection of *Sparrow* and after with the protection of *Sparrow*, and our fishermen certainly did not want their rights bridled by any agreements. They wanted to continue fishing, not without a management plan but with a management plan within their consciousness. It is not written, but you have a mindset in what you are doing, and they did not want to be hassled or tied to an agreement, a geographic season or a limit.

JM: *Wela'lin, Kerry.*

CHIEFS' POSITIONS on MODERATE LIVELIHOOD

by THE ASSEMBLY OF NOVA SCOTIA MI'KMAW CHIEFS

S tarting in early September 2020, when the moderate livelihood fishing issue became a source of tension and conflict in Southwest Nova Scotia, the Assembly of Nova Scotia Mi'kmaw Chiefs issued a number of media releases about the topic. Here are excerpts from the releases organized by theme or topic. The relevant media releases begin on September 10, 2020, and end on November 30, 2021, and have been slightly modified for the purposes of this book.

I. THE RIGHT TO EARN A MODERATE LIVELIHOOD FROM FISHING AND THE LACK OF PROGRESS

September 10, 2020

Fishing has been a fundamental part of the Mi'kmaw way of life since time immemorial, and in the 1999 *Marshall* decision, the Supreme Court of Canada affirmed the Constitutional Right to earn a moderate livelihood. Twenty-one years later, the federal government has neither established regulations for a moderate livelihood fishery, nor have they engaged the Mi'kmaq in formal consultation on developing regulations.

"We know our people are frustrated that they can't yet earn a moderate livelihood from fishing, despite the right being affirmed by the highest courts in the country," said Chief Terrance Paul, Co-Chair and Fisheries Lead for the Assembly of Nova Scotia Mi'kmaw Chiefs. "We are equally frustrated. We have been at the table for years fighting for movement from the federal government so that our people can have access to the waters and resources."

Despite the lack of movement from the Department of Fisheries and Oceans Canada (DFO), the Mi'kmaq of Nova Scotia are still moving ahead and working together to find solutions that best work for their communities.

II. REQUEST FOR FORMAL CONSULTATION

September 17, 2020

Today marks twenty-one years since the Supreme Court of Canada affirmed the Mi'kmaq's Constitutional Right to hunt, fish, and gather in the pursuit of a moderate livelihood in *R v. Marshall*. Despite our rights being affirmed by the highest courts in the country, exercising these rights continues to bring frustrations, conflict, and hardships to our people.

This week, the Assembly of Nova Scotia Mi'kmaw Chiefs, along with Potlotek's Chief Wilbert Marshall, sent a formal request for consultation under the Terms of Reference (TOR) for a Mi'kmaq–Nova Scotia–Canada Consultation Process to Minister Jordan to inform and discuss Potlotek's Netukulimk Livelihood Fishery Management Plan. Despite the Supreme Court saying the Minister has [the] power to regulate, DFO has never proposed or consulted with the Mi'kmaq on justifiable regulations for our livelihood fishery.

"We have been trying to negotiate a long-term plan with DFO for years," said Chief Terrance Paul, Fisheries Lead for the Assembly of Nova Scotia Mi'kmaw Chiefs. "Through consultation, we hope to find a path forward immediately. Our communities are going fishing, and we want to ensure that they don't have to be fearful of being harassed or charged."

III. THE TREATY RIGHT INCLUDES THE RIGHT TO MANAGE OUR OWN FISHERY

September 10, 2020

"We have the right to self-government, and that includes our right to govern our fisheries. We are developing our own sustainable livelihood fishery, separate from the commercial fishery, as we have a responsibility to protect our affirmed Treaty Right and the court ruling. By working together, we will develop sustainable community fishing plans as this is important to our people today and to the sustainability of the resource for future generations," said Chief Terrance Paul.

IV. POTLOTEK'S EXERCISE OF SELF-GOVERNANCE

September 30, 2020

Tomorrow, on October 1, 2020, Mi'kmaw harvesters from the Potlotek Mi'kmaw Community will be taking to the water, on St. Peter's Bay, to exercise their inherent right to fish for a moderate livelihood under their community's own self-governed fisheries plan. Potlotek harvesters, with support from their leadership and community members, have chosen this significant day to commemorate the annual celebration of Treaty Day, a date to recognize and honour the treaties signed between the Mi'kmaq and the Crown in the 1700s. "Our plan will provide community members with the opportunity to fish under their own guiding principles, all while adhering to the traditional Mi'kmaw practice of *Netukulimk*," said Chief Wilbert Marshall, Potlotek Mi'kmaw Community. "After much engagement with community members, our community-developed plan will provide those in our community, who want to fish, with the opportunity to provide a means of support for themselves and their families through their inherent Treaty Rights."

V. MODERATE LIVELIHOOD IS NOT AN ILLEGAL FISHERY

September 21, 2020

The Chiefs also wanted to make clear to the Ministers, and in turn, the public, that despite what is being incorrectly communicated in mainstream media, Moderate Livelihood is not an illegal fishery. "Our rights were affirmed in the Canadian Constitution, and the right to fish for a moderate livelihood was reaffirmed by the Supreme Court of Canada. While the public may not comprehend a fishery outside the realm of the Department of Fisheries and Oceans, that does not make our fishery illegal. We called on Canada to help educate the public on the truth and to address the systemic racism that has been a major part in denying our ability to exercise our rights," said Chief Terrance Paul.

VI. CONCERNS OVER SAFETY

September 21, 2020

The Assembly of Nova Scotia Mi'kmaw Chiefs met with Minister Bernadette Jordan, Department of Fisheries and Oceans Canada, and Minister Carolyn Bennett, Crown–Indigenous Relations, this morning to discuss what is happening in Nova Scotia in response to Mi'kmaw harvesting for a moderate livelihood. In their discussions, the Assembly also called on the Ministers to publicly speak out against the racism and violence directed toward Mi'kmaw community members and to increase enforcement to ensure the safety of everyone, on and off the water.

"We have Mi'kmaw, which includes Elders, women, children, youth, and men, supporting the rights of the Mi'kmaq," said Chief Terrance Paul, the Assembly's Fishery Lead. "Non-Indigenous fishers and citizens are putting the safety of our people at risk. DFO and the RCMP must address the harassment and illegal activities taken against our people, and they must enforce and charge those who are cutting and stealing our traps, shooting flares at our boats, and threatening the lives of our people."

VII. CONCERN ABOUT FEDERAL GOVERNMENT ACTIONS

October 21, 2020

In recent days, authorized Mi'kmaw community harvesters, from both Potlotek and Eskasoni Mi'kmaw Communities, have had over two hundred legal traps seized by the Department of Fisheries and Oceans' Conservation and Protection Officers in St. Peter's Bay. The seizure of these traps by local officers is without the authorization or authority of their department or the minister. This is unacceptable and unlawful. The Assembly of Nova Scotia Mi'kmaw Chiefs, along with Potlotek and Eskasoni Chiefs and Councils, have demanded the immediate return of seized traps.

VIII. FAILURE OF THE FEDERAL GOVERNMENT TO CONSULT AND NEGOTIATE IN GOOD FAITH

October 19, 2020

The Assembly continues to be firm that DFO needs to justify why the Mi'kmaw communities cannot create our own access to our fisheries and continue to push DFO to come to the table to formally consult the Mi'kmaq.

March 23, 2021

While today, Minister Bernadette Jordan, Department of Fisheries and Oceans Canada (DFO), has recognized our Moderate Livelihood Fishery, she has also made unilateral decisions and asserted a position with DFO having full control over our rights-based fishery. This is unacceptable. The Moderate Livelihood Fishery is a constitutionally protected Mi'kmaw Right and must be Mi'kmaw-led. Twenty years after *Marshall* was decided, DFO continues to take a colonial approach to this matter, and it is time that Canada moves beyond this mindset.

DFO is continuing to impose rules without consultation with, accommodation of, or agreement with, the Assembly. *Marshall II* said that every limitation put on the exercise of our right must be justified and in consultation with the Mi'kmaq. Minister Jordan's announcement is premature to any discussions with the Mi'kmaq, disregards the work and efforts of our communities, and is disrespectful to any attempt at collaboration and reconciliation.

IX. CONSERVATION AND SUSTAINABILITY OF THE RESOURCE

November 18, 2020

Mi'kmaw Community Livelihood Plans are being developed with the philosophy of Netukulimk as a central focus and as a standard, which further supports the Mi'kmaw concerns on the health and well-being of the environment and all living things among it. This is precisely why the Mi'kmaw communities fishing under a Community Netukulimk Management Plan have been very transparent with the Department of Fisheries and Oceans Canada (DFO) on the access the Mi'kmaw harvesters will have to the water.

"We have provided DFO an overview of the number of tags that will be harvested under our Plan and how many of those tags are actively in the water," said Chief Wilbert Marshall, Potlotek First Nation. "In fact, we are fishing fewer traps than what has been authorized in our plans, and any traps in the water that are not properly tagged do not belong to our harvesters."

X. SOME POSITIVE SIGNS

March 28, 2021

Members of the Assembly of Nova Scotia Mi'kmaw Chiefs (Assembly) will be working with their communities to revive traditional and ancient Mi'kmaw customs by looking to our language for guidance. The Assembly is exploring Mi'kmaw concepts found in *Wmɨtkik* and *Nmɨtiknen*.

Wmɨtkik is an old Mi'kmaw word, not commonly used today, that may hold the Mi'kmaw concept of how the lands and waters that we are connected to (the territory we are from and where we live) are to be harvested (through hunting, fishing, and gathering) in a manner that respects the resources and all our relations who live or harvest there (*Msit No'kmaq*). *Nmɨtiknen* holds the concept of territory and the process of how we make decisions together, and much more.

Chiefs in the Kespukwitk District and their respective communities— Acadia, Bear River, and Annapolis Valley First Nations—will begin the development of a Nmɨtiknen approach to the stewardship of the Kespukwitk district of Mi'kma'ki. These three communities will be working together, alongside the Mi'kmaq Grand Council and other Mi'kmaw communities on this important work. Together they will be looking into developing a traditional approach to managing the resources and recognizing conservation and protection of all the resources.

June 3, 2021

Today 196 traps that were seized from Mi'kmaw livelihood harvesters in fall 2020 were finally returned by the Department of Fisheries and Oceans Canada (DFO).

The traps were seized by DFO's Conservation and Protection Branch (C&P) during the fall fishery and belonged to Mi'kmaw harvesters authorized under Community Netukulimk Livelihood Fishery Plans from both Potlotek and Eskasoni First Nations.

While the Netukulimk Livelihood Fishery is managed by the Mi'kmaw communities, most gear, equipment, and supplies were purchased and owned by harvesters who are undertaking and exercising their Supreme Court affirmed Treaty Right. "Seeing the gear be returned today to our community harvesters is a bit of relief," said Chief Leroy Denny, Eskasoni First

Nation. "Our people are fishing to better their lives and the lives of their families—and they have every right to do so. DFO stopping that, instead of working with our communities to support that, is shameful."

June 4, 2021

Since the launch of the Mi'kmaw Treaty Rights–based fishery last fall, many Mi'kmaw harvesters have had First Nation–authorized gear and equipment seized. Tomorrow, that will change for the harvesters from Potlotek First Nation. Potlotek's authorized harvesters, fishing under their community's Netukulimk Livelihood Fisheries Plan, will return to the waters to fish for a moderate livelihood, in the spring 2021 fishery, on Saturday, June 5.

Like many Mi'kmaw communities, Potlotek has been working with community members to develop a Netukulimk Livelihood Fisheries Plan, which outlines and provides community authority and management for their constitutionally protected right to fish for a moderate livelihood. Potlotek's authorized harvesters will be able to fish and sell, pursuant to their right and according to their community plan, with the cooperation of the Department of Fisheries and Oceans Canada (DFO).

"We didn't sign any agreements—I told my community members that we wouldn't. Through talks, we were able to come to an understanding with DFO," said Chief Wilbert Marshall, Potlotek First Nation. "We were open and transparent. We built a solid plan that laid out our tagging and reporting structures and are developing enforcement protocols with DFO's Conservation and Protection branch. We went through all the formal processes and consulted on every part of what our harvesters wanted to do."

September 1, 2021

This morning, Pictou Landing's Netukulimk harvesters loaded their vessels to begin their first day of harvesting of the season. They were immediately approached by Conservation and Protection Officers from the Department of Fisheries and Oceans Canada (DFO) and were advised that any traps set would be seized.

"Our community harvesters are fishing with the full authority of Pictou Landing First Nation, and under a stringent management plan developed by our community to ensure safety and conservation," said Chief Andrea Paul, Pictou Landing First Nation.

"The right to fish and sell fish for a moderate livelihood is a constitutionally protected right, affirmed twice by the Supreme Court of Canada," said Chief Gerald Toney, Fisheries Lead for the Assembly.[1] "We continue to support authorized harvesters who are exercising their Treaty Rights, practicing their culture, and doing so safely and respectfully through community Netukulimk Livelihood Plans. We have created a path forward, but it feels like every time we take a couple steps forward, DFO tries to set us back again."

October 13, 2021

Since the launch of the Mi'kmaw Treaty Rights–based fishery in Nova Scotia, Mi'kmaw communities in the traditional Mi'kmaw district of Kespukwitk—Acadia, Annapolis Valley, Bear River, and Glooscap First Nations—have been working together on a livelihood plan for their shared waters and resources. On October 14, 2021, understanding that not all communities will be launching their fisheries on that date, the Kespukwitk District Netukulimk Livelihood Fisheries Plan will take effect.

The Kespukwitk communities continued the path established by Potlotek First Nation to see their harvesters take to the waters with mutual understandings and cooperation with DFO.

"It is important that Mi'kmaw harvesters can exercise their rights without fear of their gear and equipment being seized. That is why we have been open and transparent, sharing our plan with DFO from the onset," said Chief Sidney Peters, Glooscap First Nation and Assembly Co-Chair.

"Our communities have worked together to build a solid plan, and we took it through all the formal processes, including consultation with Canada. DFO is fully aware of our plans moving forward," said Chief Deborah Robinson, Acadia First Nation and the Assembly's Governance Lead.

For the interim, the Kespukwitk District Collective Fisheries Committee will be testing collective Mi'kmaw self-governance strategies, with the management of 3,500 lobster traps, to support livelihood opportunities fishing lobster in the waters in and around the Kespukwitk District.

November 30, 2021

Today 223 traps seized this fall from Mi'kmaw harvesters authorized under Pictou Landing First Nation's Netukulimk Livelihood Fishery Plan were returned by the Department of Fisheries and Oceans Canada (DFO) Conservation and Protection (C&P) branch.

"Having the harvesters' gear returned today was a welcomed sight," said Chief Andrea Paul, Pictou Landing First Nation. "Our people have the right to fish for a livelihood, and they just want to exercise their Treaty Rights. Having DFO try to stop that is frustrating and completely wrong."

4.4

A MI'KMAW APPROACH to MANAGING FISHERIES

by AMBER GILES, LUCIA FANNING, SHELLEY DENNY, and TYSON PAUL

EDITORS' INTRODUCTION

One of the major issues at the heart of the current dispute over the moderate livelihood fishery is how and by whom it will be managed. The federal Department of Fisheries and Oceans has staked out a position, seeking to set and enforce ground rules that would apply to both First Nations and non-Indigenous fishers. First Nations representatives in the Maritime region have rejected this approach, arguing that their Aboriginal and Treaty Rights, recognized by the Supreme Court, include the right to manage their own fishery. If this is upheld through negotiations or court decisions, how would First Nations go about managing their own fishing effort, and what assurance would there be that the resource would not be depleted? Although there are many differences with fishing for lobster for a moderate livelihood, insights into this question are provided by an examination of how Mi'kmaq harvesting eels have gone about their craft.

The following is excerpted and adapted from Amber Giles, Lucia Fanning, Shelley Denny, and Tyson Paul's 2016 article, "Improving the American Eel Fishery Through the Incorporation of Indigenous Knowledge into Policy Level Decision Making in Canada,"[1] which is based on interviews with thirteen eelers from Eskasoni First Nation.

HOW DID THE ESKASONI EELERS GET STARTED?

Fishers' eeling experience ranged from two to sixty years. The majority began eeling in the summer between the ages of eight and twelve and were taught by family members. The first two or so years of eeling were spent observing others, after which time interviewees spoke of eventually wanting to try for themselves and simply picking up a spear one day. A few of the participants who were not taught to eel by a family member spoke of hearing stories of eeling from family or friends and eventually being offered or seeking a friend to teach them or teaching themselves.

HOW AND WHEN ARE EELS HARVESTED?

Eeling takes place throughout the year. In the summer and fall, eeling is generally done from a boat with a lantern at night, using a summer spear to catch the eels. Some eelers fish from a dock or wade into shallow water. While some mentioned nets, all use spears, although there is variation in spear design. Some of the younger eelers have experimented with new methods of catching eels, such as diving with a spear and flashlight wrapped in a plastic bag, or with a Hawaiian sling (a tiny slingshot speargun).

In the winter, eeling occurs near the shore and is limited by the presence of good ice. Eelers cut a hole in the ice using an axe or chainsaw and methodically circle the hole, searching the unseen muddy bottom with a winter spear.

Eeling trips occur for a variety of reasons but generally are initiated by the need for food and the right weather conditions. One eeler recalled how his father used to go eeling whenever a community member died and would make *Kataqaboul* (eel soup) to bring to the wake. He expressed concern over the loss of this tradition and the implied lack of respect for deceased community members.

EELING PRACTICES AND COMMUNITY VALUES

The connection between practice, values, and beliefs among Indigenous eelers highlights how knowledge is transmitted and adapted over time (see Table 4.4.1). For example, by undertaking a period of observation, eelers show respect for the eel as well as the Oral Tradition. Through this period of observation, the concept of *M'sit No'kamaq* ("all my relations") is expressed, and eelers learn patience, respect for the eel, proper eeling techniques, and how to identify and respect place. The proper eeling technique during summer helps ensure the survival of an escaped eel by targeting the tail, thereby avoiding critical internal organs and fatal injury. The observation period also illustrates how eelers value the transmission of knowledge through Oral Tradition (i.e., stories), observation, and experiential learning.

The values of kinship and generosity are demonstrated in the way eelers transmit knowledge, distribute harvest, and interact during eeling trips. All eelers had either been taught to eel or had been told stories about eeling by a family member. Similar to findings in other Nations,[2] eeling trips were largely initiated by family or community members, including Elders' requests for eels. Nonetheless, demand must be consistent with *Netukulimk* (responsibilities according to Mi'kmaq laws in continuing a respectful and reciprocal relationship with the entire ecosystem), which influences the number of eels harvested. While all eelers spoke of valuing the ability to share eels with Elders, family, or other community members, some of the older eelers spoke of fishing as a time for relaxation and reflection, and to connect with nature.

At the same time, although there is a great deal of respect for eels and place, there is also a great deal of fun and humour. The Mi'kmaq are known for their humour and exhibited this during interviews and eeling trips by telling funny stories of their misadventures and teasing eelers who missed or who mistook a stick for an eel. This humour displayed by eelers demonstrates the depth of camaraderie that takes place during eeling trips and the joy that eelers get from their relationship with the eel, the place, their family, and their community. As in many Indigenous communities, eel fishing in Eskasoni facilitates the transmission of knowledge through Oral Tradition, maintains community bonds, and instills young eelers with social values such as kinship obligations and generosity.

INTERACTIONS WITH PLACE

Mi'kmaw knowledge is place-based, generated with and from their territory.[3] Three categories of use were examined: summer eeling; winter eeling; and place of their first eeling trip.

Table 4.4.1. Various Eskasoni Mi'kmaq Eeling Practices and Associated Community Beliefs and Values

Eeling practice	Community beliefs	Values expressed
Sharing eels with Elders, family, and community members	• Sharing with those who cannot eel for themselves • Showing respect for Elders	• Kinship • Reciprocity • Generosity
Undertaking a period of observation before eelers begin to eel	• Proper skills are needed so eels will not be harmed • Learning how to identify habitat • Patience	• Respect for the eel • Oral Tradition • M'sit No'kamaq
Deciding to leave the commercial eel fishery	• Commercial fishery is hurting eel populations	• 7 Generations • Netukulimk
Using spears over nets	• Nets catch too many eels • Only take what you need	• Respect for the eel • Netukulimk
Keeping all eels caught during winter spearing	• Eels will die if you put them back, it is wasteful	• Respect for the eel • M'sit No'kamaq
Not fishing or only taking enough for the Elders during years of low population	• Not right to eel when population is low • Still want to respect Elders	• 7 Generations
Visiting eeling sites only once in a cycle	• Avoid overexploitation • Avoid too much pressure on the eels	• Netukulimk • Relationship with the territory • Respect for place
Being extremely selective during summer fishing, only taking the "good sized ones"	• Leave the smaller eels to have a chance to grow and reproduce	• Netukulimk • Respect for the eel

Summer eeling was identified in six areas in the Bras d'Or Lakes. Some eelers identified places that had traditional eeling grounds for their family for hundreds of years. Other eelers identified places they had discovered or been shown based on habitats, such as muddy bottoms or eelgrass. Due primarily to more favourable weather, summer eeling has the largest distribution across the Bras d'Or Lakes, with a large amount of activity focused along the shores.

Winter eeling was identified in four areas in the Bras d'Or Lakes. Like summer eeling spots, many areas had been traditional family eeling grounds for hundreds of years. Some potential winter eeling spots were found during summer eeling trips and marked in relation to a unique tree or other landmark.

Only one area in the Bras d'Or Lakes, along the shores of the community, was identified as where eelers experienced eeling for the first time. Three subareas were identified, known to locals as the beaches, John Paul's Lane, and Goat Island and surrounding islands.

The identification of all eeling locations handed down for generations signalled the intergenerational relationship with territory. This awareness facilitates the eelers' ability to detect changes in their environment through observation and to respond to these changes. Eelers felt reciprocity to both eels and to place, and this was reflected in their practice of visiting sites only once within a cycle (see Table 4.4.1). Unlike a fixed closed period, common to governmental management responses, this self-imposed cycle for each eeler was different, generally ranging between one and five years. This response to the decline in eel abundance was rooted in Netukulimk. Eelers, regardless of age or having children, spoke of wanting to make sure that the eels would be around for the next seven generations due to the important lessons eeling can teach about respect and the environment (see Table 4.4.1).

ADAPTATION TO POPULATION DECLINE

Based on an observed decline in their catch from "buckets full" to at most a dozen eels, the majority of respondents stated that there are far fewer eels today than when they started eeling and described eeling as "very much in trouble." Many respondents felt that commercial fishing for eels had caused the decline of populations, and some voiced specific concerns with the elver fishery. Several participants shared their anger and frustration with the non-Indigenous elver fishery and that it is allowed to continue when the eel population is so low. Development was also identified as a potential cause of decline, specifically new roads, bridges, a causeway, and cottages built too near the lakeshore. It was felt that these new developments destroy habitat, act as barriers restricting eel movement, and create stress for the eels that prevents them from settling.

Values are also expressed in the various adaptations eelers have made in technique, technology, and fishing habits. In addition to refining the technological aspects of fishing during different seasons through spear design aimed at minimizing escape once speared, seasonal adaptation to eel management is reflected in the acceptable size of harvest. In the summer, there is generally a set number that is acceptable (a dozen or so per trip), while in the winter it is acceptable to take as many as one can get. Furthermore, in the summer, it is not acceptable to harvest small eels, while in the winter it is an unofficial rule that eelers keep all the eels harvested, regardless of size. These adaptations, based on M'sit No'kamaq, reflect eelers' respect for the eel and a deep understanding of the cycles of their territory.

COMMERCIAL EEL FISHING

Only two respondents indicated that they had been involved in the commercial eel fishery, and both had since chosen to leave because of concerns about the eel population decline. The majority had never been involved in the commercial eel fishery or ever sold eels. Some shared strong moral objections to the commercial fishery, feeling it was disrespectful to sell eels. While they acknowledged commercial eeling takes place within and outside the Bras d'Or Lakes, they noted that commercial fishers are primarily non-Indigenous and target the lucrative elver fishery, which, along with habitat destruction, they consider to be a significant factor influencing the decline of the species and impacting their ability to harvest eels for food, social, and ceremonial purposes.

EXPLORING the RIGHTS and WRONGS of the MODERATE LIVELIHOOD and EAST COAST INDIGENOUS FISHERY

by SENATOR DAN CHRISTMAS

Note: This chapter is based in great part on a speech about the moderate livelihood fishery delivered by Senator Christmas in the Senate Chamber on May 25, 2021.

The name Donald Marshall Jr. is synonymous with the pursuit of upholding Indigenous and justice rights. I was fortunate to know Junior Marshall; we went to school together. Someone also very close to Junior was the man who ultimately became our community's Chief, Terry Paul.

Chief Terry and his allies have been the standard-bearers in leading the fight for the implementation of the Supreme Court of Canada's two decisions in respect of *Marshall* for the twenty-three years since the declaration of the decisions.

The *Marshall* decisions revolved around Treaty Rights and permitting First Nations people to catch and sell fish in respect of the relevant treaties. The Treaty Right was affirmed and established, and Marshall was acquitted.

Yet here we are all these years later, still having to call for the upholding of already Supreme Court–affirmed Mi'kmaw Treaty Rights to a moderate livelihood fishery.

While dealing with moderate livelihood fishing during 2019 Senate hearings around amendments being proposed to the Fisheries Act, Chief Terry testified as an expert witness. When I asked him what he believed Junior Marshall would want us to do, Chief Terry's response was firm and emphatic.

"Keep fishing," was what he said. And it was all that needed saying.

I'd asked him what our friend Junior Marshall might have said he was trying to do by establishing the moderate livelihood fishery, and what his advice to his people, the Mi'kmaq, would have been all these years later.

- Keep fishing—in the same way our people have done for nearly ten thousand years in what is now Atlantic Canada;
- Keep fishing—just as Junior Marshall had been doing when he was initially arrested in August 1993;
- Keep fishing—in the manner prescribed under the Peace and Friendship Treaties signed in 1760 and 1761, and enshrined in section 35 of the Constitution Act, 1982;
- Keep fishing—quietly, with determination, and in full accordance with Mi'kmaw traditions, conservation, and legal systems;
- Keep fishing—and as Herbert Hoover once said, "Be patient and calm—for no one can catch fish in anger."

Yet, here we are as the Mi'kmaq Nation, twenty-three years later, still being told to wait for the implementation of the *Marshall* decisions.

As Chief Terry mused in 2019 at the FOPO [Standing Senate Committee on Fisheries and Oceans] hearings, "One of our problems is that we are a very patient people. So, the government, through the Department of Fisheries and Oceans, came up with interim measures.

"That's what we have been fishing under, since we still fish under the DFO regulations like anyone else. They came up with this interim measure because they had nothing in place to deal with the court decision.

"The court decision was not what had been expected. Nobody in government believed we could win this case."

Chief Terry's words metaphorically describe the current situation in a way that drives home its fundamental reality.

Imagine if, in kindness, you invited a stranger's family into your home and onto your property. As their family grew, you made an agreement to share your land and its resources with them.

In time, they disregarded the agreement and took over your property while forcing you to live in a shack in the backyard.

Then they tell you that you [have] to follow their rules, and you can't use what was once your land, and it is what they now consider to be *their* land and resources.

You go to the courts and the decision says that the original agreement stands and you had a right to use your lands and resources—not to become rich like your neighbours but to make a living.

The family you invited in ignores the court's binding decision and says that you are a threat to the sustainability of the resource even though you represent only 5 percent of the population.

When time comes to harvest on your property, the family refuses to protect you from violence and property destruction perpetrated by their kin. What then do you do?

That question becomes dwarfed by the myriad others that must be considered in examining the 260-year history of the moderate livelihood fishery.

For instance, where was the Department of Fisheries and Oceans when the 1760–61 treaties were signed? Did they even contemplate regulating the moderate livelihood fishery? Were there DFO vessels in the water? Did DFO need to conserve fish stocks and other public interests?

Of course not—the Mi'kmaq had been observing its millennia-old self-management of the resource through the application of Mi'kmaw traditional law called *Netukulimk*.

As defined by the Unama'ki Institute of Natural Resources, "Netukulimk is the use of the natural bounty provided by the Creator for the self-support and well-being of the individual and the community. Netukulimk is achieving adequate standards of community nutrition and economic well-being without jeopardizing the integrity, diversity, or productivity of our environment.

"As Mi'kmaq we have an inherent right to access and use our resources, and we have a responsibility to use those resources in a sustainable way.

The Mi'kmaq way of resource management includes a spiritual element that ties together people, plants, animals, and the environment."[1]

Let us look back and reflect upon the launch of DFO's unilaterally developed "new path" policy.

Hardly a "new path," this policy is an old dirt-road shortcut to colonialism. And it was an unmitigated disaster, likely causing the loss of the DFO minister's seat.

In his final report to the DFO minister, Federal Special Representative Allister Surette said that based on his research, "the root of the conflict in the fishery is the unwillingness of DFO to recognize Indigenous rights and self-determination, and to share any of DFO's jurisdiction with the Indigenous communities."[2]

Another observation one can easily draw from Mr. Surette's report is that the "new path" policy's purpose seems to serve the interests of the commercial industry.

He noted that "the commercial industry generally felt that the [then-] Minister's Statement was a step in the right direction, especially its commitment to enforcing a common fishing season for all, but [they] still have reservations on a number of issues that could affect their industry."

He added, "The Indigenous communities consider this approach to be unacceptable." Who could blame them for thinking so? It's as if the "new path" policy was intentionally designed in the commercial fishers' favour, with Indigenous implications relegated to the bottom of the barrel, if even considered at all.

Questions abound. For starters, with whom did former Minister Jordan consult? Certainly not with the Mi'kmaq—as highlighted in a media statement issued March 4, 2021, by the Assembly of Nova Scotia Mi'kmaw Chiefs in which they declared, "Canada emphasizes a commitment to 'Nation-to-Nation' discussions, yet DFO continues to assert dominance over our Nation—making announcements and decisions, leaving no room for discussion or consultation. This is negligent of promises of working Nation-to-Nation, Rights affirmation, reconciliation and is in complete disregard of our governance and leadership."

There was, it seems, ample consultation with industry—DFO and the Canadian Independent Fish Harvesters Federation collaborated on a series of workshops regarding reconciliation with Indigenous Peoples in the fisheries.

Surette was quick to point out in his final report that "there seems to be general consensus that implementing court decisions regarding treaty rights as they pertain to the fishery is multi-faceted and does not lend itself to easy solutions."

But he was equally prepared to highlight "the Indigenous point of view that the Government of Canada is continuing to take a colonial approach to this matter, disregarding the governance and leadership of the Indigenous communities in the 'Nation-to-Nation' commitment, hence continuing to impose and dictate their rules on the fishery that is outside their scope and mandate."

A further and extremely troubling reality is the very slow pace at which steps were taken to address the growing violence across the communities. It took a full month before the RCMP increased its personnel in Saulnierville, NS.

A CBC News report at the time cited that a top RCMP officer requested help to pay for extra policing costs during the fall 2020 fisheries dispute in Southwest Nova Scotia, but the province's justice minister resisted for two weeks and only agreed after two lobster pounds holding Mi'kmaw catch were vandalized, with one later burned to the ground.

The report also stated that Sipekne'katik Chief Mike Sack said his community tried to work with the RCMP, but there wasn't enough support to ensure people were safe.

He was quoted as saying, "I remember the day we were stranded at the lobster pound. All day they were saying more RCMP are coming, more are coming. And it was just a bunch of lies. There was never more RCMP coming. So much of it could have been prevented.

"Our people were left stranded," Chief Sack said. "For the province to be aware, and just sit back thinking about it, that doesn't sit very well."

Chief Sack concluded by saying, "It just adds to what we went through. The RCMP weren't there for us. There were officers in the area who were great, but overall, they really failed our people."[3]

In the fall of 2020 I spoke with Public Safety Minister Bill Blair after the weeks of confrontations, and I shared my deep concern about the violence. He had only just then received a request from the Province of Nova Scotia to increase deployment. Why did the Province wait so long?

Thankfully, and despite repeated provocation, the Mi'kmaq did not respond to the violence. Why not, you might ask? The answer is simple:

they were respecting the covenant and honouring the Treaty of Peace and Friendship, which lies at the very heart of this matter.

Speaking of timeliness around interventions aimed at defusing the mounting crisis, Senator Brian Francis, MP Jaime Battiste, and I sought, as Canada's Mi'kmaw parliamentarians, to undertake outreach respectively to the federal ministers of Crown–Indigenous Relations, Indigenous Services, and DFO.

We did so with a singular objective in mind: to suggest practical, pragmatic, and innovative remedies to mitigate the impasse that has plagued the Moderate Livelihood for all these years since the rendering of the Supreme Court's decisions in *Marshall*.

We proposed the establishment of a fisheries model that would ensure the fisheries for the future as an Atlantic First Nations Fisheries Authority.

We also advocated that in situations where government intervention may be required in instances where there is an unwillingness to accommodate or respect a moderate livelihood fishery, the government may need to explore the possibility of implementing a quota for lobster or putting a Total Allowable Catch system in place.

This would not only ensure the sustainability of the resource, but also accommodate and respect the rule of law in Canada as well the Mi'kmaw values of Netukulimk.

Sadly, as in so many elements of this issue, our suggested remedies seem to have gone unconsidered, if indeed they were heeded in any way at all.

And yet thankfully, the issue did receive benefit of further consideration by Members in the Other Place.

The House Standing Committee on Fisheries and Oceans studied the moderate livelihood fishery and released its report in May 2021.

Overall, it's my view that the report was a constructive move forward.

I was pleased to note the report's positives.

Thierry Rodon, Associate Professor and Canada Research Chair in Sustainable Northern Development at Université Laval, cited his view that the Government of Canada recognized the inherent right of self-government as an existing Aboriginal Right under section 35 of the Constitution Act, 1982, through its Approach to Implementation of the Inherent Right and the Negotiation of Aboriginal Self-Government policy launched in 1995.

He stated, "The co-management of natural resources allows for the recognition of a dual authority: that of the federal government over the commercial fisheries and that of the Indigenous communities over the management of their resources."[4]

The Committee Report also provided examples of Mi'kmaw harvest management plans designed to ensure the conservation of fishery resources, including rules for conservation, safety, and accountability.

In particular, Chief Darcy Gray said the following about the Listuguj Mi'gmaq Government's lobster fishing management plan:

> We understand the need for a well-regulated fishery. We understand that with rights comes responsibility. After several years of community consultation, we adopted our own law and fishing management plan to govern our lobster fishery.
>
> Our law and plan allow our people to sell their lobster but ensure that fishing efforts remain sustainable.
>
> For the last two falls, we have conducted our own self-regulated fishery. Lobster stocks in our fishing area remain healthy. We have not seen violence like that being witnessed in Nova Scotia. We see our lobster fishery as a self-determination success story. We tried to get here working with DFO. In the end, though, we got here in *spite* of DFO [emphasis added].[5]

I was also *very* encouraged to see the Government of Canada consider alternate governance models that are consistent with treaty and Canadian law that share authority and decision making with Mi'kmaw and Wolastoqey Nations.

So now [in May 2021] we await new government and consideration of a new means of going forward. Our new Parliament and its new Minister of Fisheries and Oceans, once named, will also be dealing with international questions around the state of play in the moderate livelihood fishery regarding the racism and violence Mi'kmaw lobster fishers experienced while they exercised their Treaty Right to fish for a moderate livelihood in Nova Scotia over the last two years.

The UN Committee on the Elimination of Racial Discrimination is now seeking answers from Canada—and the world will be watching as this unfolds—with the future of Canada's lobster industry at stake. But, as Robert F. Kennedy once reminded us, "The future is not a gift. It is an achievement."

As I close, I'm conscious of what the Royal Commission Report on Aboriginal People reminded us of twenty-six years ago: "Canada is a test case for a grand notion that dissimilar peoples can share land, resources, power, and dreams while respecting and sustaining their differences."[6]

The moderate livelihood fishery is a part of this grand notion, and we must all work together to make this nation of ours—the so-called "test case"—a successful one, yielding peaceful and fruitful results both now and into the future.

Senator Dan Christmas
Membertou, NS

V

COMMERCIAL HARVESTER AND COMMUNITY VOICES

PERSPECTIVES from COMMERCIAL HARVESTER ORGANIZATIONS

by RICK WILLIAMS

This chapter surveys the policy positions taken by leaders and organizations representing non-Indigenous fish harvesters across the Maritimes and Quebec. There are many such organizations, some representing particular communities, regions, or provinces, and others representing fleet sectors or fisheries management zones. For the purpose of this book, I rely on public statements made by three umbrella organizations that speak for many of the smaller groups:

- The Unified Fisheries Conservation Alliance is headquartered in Yarmouth, NS, and was set up immediately after the conflict in that area in the late summer of 2020. Its stated objective is to urge the Government of Canada "to establish clear, lasting, responsible, regulatory oversight for all fisheries—commercial, food, social, and ceremonial."[1]

- The Coalition of Atlantic and Quebec Fishing Organizations was also established in the fall of 2020 and is based in Southeast New Brunswick. Their mission is to pursue "peace, reconciliation, and the advancement of conservation, the public interest, and direct dialogue between the Government of Canada, Indigenous Peoples, and fishing organizations for a healthy and sustainable fishery."[2]

- The Canadian Independent Fish Harvesters Federation represents harvester organizations of all types and sizes across Canada and came together in 2010 to advocate for changes to federal fisheries legislation to ensure the independence of owner-operator fishing fleets.[3]

CONTEXT

To help readers better understand the policy positions of harvester organizations, and perhaps the attitudes of many non-Indigenous harvesters at the community level, it will be helpful to first review certain aspects of the structure, governance, and operation of the commercial fishery on Canada's Atlantic coast.

PROFESSIONALIZATION AND LIMITED ENTRY

A recent DFO document describes the evolution of Canada's fisheries licensing system as follows:

> Prior to the 1960s, fisheries on Canada's East Coast were open to anyone who wished to fish, with no restrictions on who could hold a licence, no limitations on the number of licence holders in a fishery, and no significant restrictions on catch levels.... In response to these concerns, DFO developed policies intended to secure the flow of benefits from the resource to independent licence holders and to the *local communities that drew significant cultural and economic value from the fisheries* [emphasis added].
>
> Present day commercial fisheries are largely "limited access" fisheries, which means that a licence is required to access the resource and a limited number of licences are issued for each fishery.... The licence conditions often include, but are not limited to, harvest limits or quotas, assigned fishing areas, gear limits, and/or vessel length restrictions.[4]

The modernization of Canada's fisheries management system in the 1970s and '80s began with limited entry licensing. The goals were to protect fish stocks by strictly limiting the number of fishing enterprises and to "professionalize" the industry by ensuring that committed full-time harvesters would have priority access to those stocks. This approach required a progressive reduction in participation by part-time or occasional harvesters, including many Indigenous people who had long been active in the informal fishing economy. It is important to note that First Nations were not clearly recognized at the time as "communities that drew significant cultural and economic value from the fisheries."

In the all-important lobster fishery, limited entry has meant a net reduction in licences over the past thirty-five years. In 1985 there were 7,005 active lobster licences in the Maritime provinces and Quebec, but by 2020 that number had been reduced by 500 due to the elimination of licences for part-time harvesters and licence buy-back programs to protect depressed stocks in some regions.[5]

In strict legal terms, each licence is a privilege reissued each year by the DFO minister, but DFO policy allows a retiring owner-operator to sell the licence to a qualified new entrant.[6] In practice, and in the minds of working harvesters, the licence is a personal or business asset they own and can sell, with many valuing it as their retirement savings plan. In practice as well, DFO does not take a licence away without compensation, or cancel it, except in cases of gross violation of fishing regulations.

FISHERIES CO-MANAGEMENT

By the late 1990s most DFO fisheries management decisions were being made through consultations and consensus-building processes. For every fishing sector, such as a Lobster Fishing Area (LFA) or a snow crab or groundfish zone, representatives of harvesters, processors, First Nations, provincial governments, and environmental groups come together at least once a year in formal advisory committee meetings where DFO scientists report on the health of fish stocks and advise on total allowable catch levels (TACS) or levels of fishing effort (numbers of traps or days of fishing for lobster, etc.). At these meetings, DFO managers and industry representatives often discuss possible changes to regulations on season opening and closing dates, gear specifications, and other conservation measures. If fish stocks are healthy, representatives of different fleets and jurisdictions often present arguments for receiving larger catch shares.

On a wider regional or national level, major shifts in fisheries policy, legislation, or regulations also require broad stakeholder consultations. Under the Fisheries Act, the DFO minister has the final word on all these matters but rarely exercises this authority without intensive engagement with industry leaders, First Nations, and public interest groups.

In the early days of co-management, the advisory committees were battlegrounds where provinces and fleet sectors argued for bigger shares of the catch, and inshore, midshore, and offshore harvester leaders interacted like bitter enemies. Harvester groups also distrusted environmental advocates and DFO scientists and rejected their research findings and advice on catch limits. But over the three decades since, many parties have learned to work well together most of the time through well-reasoned advocacy, compromise, and consensus building, all in pursuit of common objectives for conservation, orderly management, and growing the fishery economy.

The important point here is that, both in policy and practice, co-management is now widely seen and accepted as the dominant mode of fisheries management decision making at every level and is an integral component of an industry culture.

OWNER-OPERATOR AND FLEET SEPARATION

The current ownership structure and economic viability of the inshore fishing industry across Atlantic Canada is built in large part on two policy foundations.

As explained in an article published in the FFAW-Unifor's *Union Forum Magazine*, "Fleet Separation was established as policy in 1979 and holds that only inshore fish harvesters are authorized to own inshore licenses, and processing companies or other corporate entities are forbidden from doing so. Owner-Operator was established as policy in 1989 and places obligations on inshore harvesters by requiring those who hold a fishing license to be aboard the vessel when the license is fished."[7]

Since their inception these two policies have been heavily contested, with fish processing companies and other external investors trying to find ways to get around or circumvent them, and harvester organizations battling constantly to defend them and strengthen their enforcement. These struggles came to a critical juncture in 2019 when the DFO minister put the two policies into regulations to give them legal force for the first time. The minister justified this major step as follows:

> Progressive fisheries policies that prevent vertical integration between the fishing and processing sectors and that prevent the concentration of licences in the hands of a few corporations have been pivotal in the maintenance of the wealth distribution across the region and small communities. Without these policies, wealth from fishing licences would have concentrated in the hands of fish processors/buyers and/or other investors resulting in fewer or lower paying fishing jobs available in rural coastal areas and in a decrease of economic benefits being maintained in the coastal communities.
>
> DFO's suite of policies that pertain to the inshore and coastal fishery aim to ensure that licence holders remain independent and that the benefits derived from accessing the common property fisheries resources in the inshore fishery flow to licence holders and to their local communities.[8]

After years of studies, consultations, intensive lobbying efforts, and court battles, inshore harvester organizations see the new regulations as an historic achievement but one that will still need to be defended into the future. Every major change in government policy impacting their industry, including the progressive expansion of First Nations commercial fisheries, is now looked at through this lens.

STRONG ECONOMIC GROWTH IN THE FISHERY

As described in chapter 1.1, the fishing industry across Atlantic Canada is experiencing a period of exceptional economic growth. These trends have major benefits but also create new challenges for inshore fisheries. On the positive side, many harvesters who twenty-five years ago could have been described as working poor are now bringing home solid middle-class incomes to support their families and communities. If managed wisely, this new wealth could help to reverse population loss in rural coastal regions and attract much-needed new labour supply to the industry.

On the risk side, however, the rising value of seafood generally is attracting massive outside investment and foreign takeovers in the processing sector and creating new threats to fleet separation as companies pursue new ways to ensure access to raw materials. Most concerning is the dramatic rise in the market value of licences for lobster, crab, and other species, making them unaffordable for many young crew workers in fishing communities who had hoped to become enterprise owners, and perhaps opening new doors to penetration by processor companies and speculative investors.

CONSERVATION MANAGEMENT

Since the catastrophic collapse of Atlantic groundfish stocks in the early 1990s, virtually all industry groups accept conservation as a primary responsibility. Fisheries management is widely seen as a zero-sum game: if new harvesting capacity is introduced in one fleet sector or region, effort must be reduced somewhere else or everyone must take less, to ensure there is no overall increase in pressure on fish stocks. If a depleted fish stock rebuilds to healthy status, the harvesters who previously fished it, accepted reduced landings, and paid for much of the science and protection over many years will feel they should be first in line to reap the growth dividend.

In short, the evolution of a conservation culture across the industry has fostered a sense of proprietary rights and a conviction that harvesters should have a real say in any changes impacting their industry.

PUBLIC POSITIONS ON FIRST NATIONS MODERATE LIVELIHOOD FISHERIES

In late summer 2020 the Sipekne'katik First Nation launched their self-regulated moderate livelihood lobster fishery outside the regular commercial season in St. Marys Bay, NS. When violent conflicts with local non-Indigenous harvesters drew national attention, twelve organizations representing the largest non-Indigenous harvesters in the Atlantic provinces and Quebec issued a joint public statement:

Our leadership is opposed to any violent action on the land or water and is asking, once again, for the Government of Canada to intervene to begin direct talks between the Department of Fisheries, Indigenous Leaders and Fishing Organizations on the long-term management of the fishery," said Martin Mallet, Executive Director of the Maritime Fishermen's Union.

...Historically, the relationships between Indigenous Peoples and fishermen in Atlantic Canada and Quebec have been about friendship, respect and collaboration between communities," said Bernie Berry, President of the Coldwater Lobster Association. "The current difficult situation is a symptom of a flawed process followed by the government and its constant exclusion of the commercial fishermen in the discussions on fisheries management. The government approach is dividing coastal communities that all depend on the fisheries for their living.

There can be no real solution to the long-term management of the fisheries which ignores the views of commercial fishermen. The Coalition believes in the principles of conservation [and] dialogue and that the Department of Fisheries and Oceans is and should always be primarily responsible for the setting and enforcement of rules that apply to both non-Indigenous and Indigenous fishermen.[9]

This brief statement contained core positions—rejection of violence, a demand to have a say, and insistence on a single, unified regulatory system—that have been advocated by most non-Indigenous harvester groups since then. But there are other issues and differences among organizations in how these policy positions are interpreted and acted upon.

THE UNIFIED FISHERIES CONSERVATION ALLIANCE

A month after the above statement was released, all but three of the groups that endorsed it came together to form the Unified Fisheries Conservation Alliance (UFCA). Its member groups include nine organizations representing the great majority of inshore harvesters in Nova Scotia, and one regional association in Southwest New Brunswick. In their statement of purpose, they set out the following positions:

Our members reject all forms of racism, intolerance, and violence, and believe there is a path to move beyond the controversies and heated rhetoric, to a positive outcome for all. The UFCA believes that Indigenous and non-Indigenous fishermen can work side by side like they do today in the commercial fishery. We recognize and acknowledge the importance of cooperation with Indigenous communities, and that Indigenous fishermen have a right to fish for commercial, food, social, and ceremonial purposes.

Just as commercial fisheries operate today, there is room for diversity. There can be differences within allocation structures, administration, and process. However, rules must ultimately and clearly form part of an integrated set of regulations that conserve fishery resources for generations to come and ensure a fair and respectful fishery for all.[10]

The activities of the UFCA include advocacy with federal and provincial government bodies and seeking intervenor status in court cases on Indigenous fisheries rights issues. There are currently four such legal proceedings where the organization has been granted or is seeking status to intervene on behalf of commercial harvesters.

UFCA leaders made appearances before the House of Commons Fisheries and Oceans Committee ("FOPO") in the fall of 2020.[11] In his testimony, UFCA President Colin Sproul attributed the violent events in Southwest Nova Scotia to a history of lax federal enforcement of fishing regulations for Indigenous harvesters in the area and worried about a situation where each *Marshall* First Nation might regulate its own fisheries.

I think it's really the height of folly to think that anyone, no matter how well-intentioned, could manage one lobster resource with thirty-four different sets of management plans as well as the accepted one.... What is evident is how important it is for all people who participate in commercial fisheries to operate under one set of rules.

DFO's failure to enforce the current lobster seasons is what has so angered non-Native fishers and ultimately led to the violence at St. Marys Bay.... That lack of law enforcement is precisely what led to the chaos and the animosity between fishermen who have peacefully coexisted.... [T]he government has good intentions to reach Rights Reconciliation

Agreements with the nations, but the problem is that as a tactic during the negotiations they stopped enforcing the law. That only empowered people to keep fishing outside of regulations. It has obviously been a failed tactic.

Bernie Berry from Coldwater Lobster suggested to the Committee that much had already been done to support the moderate livelihood objective and that a separate moderate livelihood fishery was neither needed nor justified. "Industry believes the Crown has fulfilled its fiduciary responsibility concern in the *Marshall* decision," he said. "Since 1999, almost $600 million has been allocated to buy first nations [*sic*] access into the commercial fishery. Today, another process is under way to negotiate a moderate livelihood fishery that will cost the Crown hundreds of millions of additional dollars."

Peter Connors, president of the Eastern Shore Fisherman's Protective Association, also endorsed the idea that the *Marshall* moderate livelihood goal had largely been achieved and criticized First Nations for not doing more with the fishing rights they already had: "The federal government's response to the *Marshall* decision saw First Nations integrate into the commercial fishery and receive some 10 to 13 percent of a fully subscribed industry," Connors said. "The figures show that there's at least a proportionate amount, and maybe double, the proportionate amount of access to the fishery.... There's access within the bands that could provide a moderate livelihood.... [M]ost of this access is being leased out and fished by people outside of the bands."

Michael Barron, president of another UFCA affiliate, the Cape Breton Fish Harvesters, also addressed the FOPO Committee: "Commercial harvesters quite logically fear that unknown amounts of additional or changed effort, especially if these are concentrated in a few areas, could seriously reduce catches in targeted areas, while leaving others untouched. The big question is that if the government addresses rights and provides more access, where will that leave our small coastal communities?"

To support its advocacy work, the UFCA commissioned Narrative Research to include questions on moderate livelihood fisheries issues in its quarterly panel survey of public attitudes in the fall of 2021. The sample population included 1,100 respondents drawn proportionally across the three Maritime provinces. The findings are summarized as follows:

- 80 percent agreement that representatives from non-Indigenous fishers should be included in any consultations or negotiations between government and Indigenous leaders around changes to fisheries management;
- 73 percent agreement that the established commercial fishing seasons and regulations should be enforced for everyone, including Indigenous and non-Indigenous fishers;
- 69 percent agreement that there should be one set of integrated rules for all Indigenous and non-Indigenous fish harvesters, established by the Department of Fisheries and Oceans Canada.[12]

On October 13, 2021, the UFCA released a statement on the new agreement between DFO and four First Nations in Southwest Nova Scotia for the establishment of moderate livelihood fisheries in that region. "The [UFCA] is supportive of the announcement.... [It] appears to be a cooperative approach toward commercial harvesting that aligns with one management regime for the fishery; specifically, that moderate livelihood fisheries fall under DFO's regulatory authority and science-based rules, follow existing seasons, and do not increase fishing pressure in a given LFA."[13]

UFCA President Colin Sproul is quoted in the press release as follows: "The UFCA has always acknowledged the importance of cooperation with Indigenous communities, and that Indigenous fishermen have a right to fish for commercial, food, social and ceremonial purposes, but we will continue to vigorously defend that science-based rules must ultimately and clearly form part of an integrated set of regulations that effectively conserve fishery resources for generations to come and ensure a fair and respectful fishery for all."

THE COALITION OF ATLANTIC AND QUEBEC FISHING ORGANIZATIONS (CAQFO)

The CAQFO describes itself as a "movement of fishermen committed to dialogue which advances a balance between a sustainable healthy fishery with Indigenous Reconciliation."[14] It comprises the following four organizations representing harvesters in the Gulf of St. Lawrence, from Nova Scotia to Quebec:

- Gulf Nova Scotia Fleet Planning Board (GNSFPB)
- Maritime Fishermen's Union (MFU)
- PEI Fishermen's Association (PEIFA)
- Regroupement des pêcheurs professionnels du sud de la Gaspésie (RPPSG)

The CAQFO's core approach has been to recognize and respect Indigenous fisheries rights and the *Marshall* rulings, but they seek a meaningful voice in decision making on how First Nations fisheries will evolve within the wider commercial fishery. Bobby Jenkins, president of the PEIFA, made the following point to the FOPO Committee: "We currently find ourselves in a situation where, as commercial harvesters, we are not represented in important discussions that impact the resource we all depend on for our livelihood."[15]

Ian MacPherson, executive director of the same organization, underlined this concern: "We were told that the mandate was for Nation-to-Nation negotiations. We were not considered a stakeholder and wouldn't be involved in any of those talks.... Certainly, a few groups, including the PEIFA, have been frustrated that we haven't had direct input."[16]

In May of 2021, the Coalition made a public statement responding to reports from the FOPO Committee and from Allister Surette, a special advisor to the DFO minister on these issues. The CAQFO statement reads in part:

Commercial fishing organizations agree with recommendations that there is a need for more formal, transparent, and open dialogue with all stakeholders....

Until this happens, the [CAQFO] believes the government should immediately pause any negotiations with First Nations on changes to the fisheries that impact the management and conservation of the resource that we all share. The reboot in negotiations would then need to include independent facilitators agreed upon by indigenous [*sic*] groups and fishing organizations and direct discussions between the Government of Canada, Indigenous leaders, and commercial fishing organizations.

Best and most sustainable solutions for the future management of the fishery should be based on peer reviewed science, an equal application of the law to everyone and one set of conservation rules fully enforced by DFO.[17]

In October of 2021, the Coalition wrote to Prime Minister Trudeau to share with him a pledge that had been signed by 7,500 people, including fish harvesters, community leaders, and many elected politicians. The pledge required signatories to make the following commitments:

I recognize and support the rights of Indigenous peoples, parties to the Treaties of 1760-61, to fish both for food, social and ceremonial purposes and in a commercial fishery as set out in the Supreme Court case of R. v Marshall in 1999.

I believe that science, conservation principles, and the public interest should drive decisions on the fisheries. I believe that the Government of Canada has both the right and the obligation under the Marshall decision to manage the fisheries, with conservation of the resource, equality and fairness as "the paramount regulatory objective, for both indigenous and non-indigenous fisheries."

I support the Government of Canada, Indigenous Peoples and fishing organizations having discussions and working directly together to manage sustainable and healthy fisheries in a spirit of reconciliation.

I condemn the use of violence in any form as a means of dealing with conflicts.[18]

THE CANADIAN INDEPENDENT FISH HARVESTER FEDERATION (CIFHF)

As mentioned above, the CIFHF brings together harvester organizations across Canada and is primarily focused on the Fisheries Act and licensing policies and regulations. However, in response to 2020 conflict in Southwest Nova Scotia, it worked with DFO and the federal Departments of Justice, Crown–Indigenous Relations, and Northern Affairs Canada to organize and facilitate seven workshops with some seventy non-Indigenous harvester leaders from across the country. Following the workshops, the Federation released the following public statement:

Over the past decades, commercial fish harvesters and First Nations people have developed strong relationships on both the East and West coasts of Canada.... Our members have worked alongside Indigenous harvesters for decades, in training and mentoring, marketing, species advisory committees, and science and research. It is because of this working relationship that our members understand the need for respectful dialogue between commercial and Indigenous harvesters; and why CIFHF is calling for a joint working group to be established with CIFHF, DFO and Indigenous leaders to review DFO's fisheries reconciliation strategy and governing principles.

"The reconciliation workshops have opened up a dialogue that has helped members understand the complexity of reconciliation. There has been a lot of active listening and deep questioning in these workshops," said Melanie Sonnenberg, President CIFHF.

..."Fisheries bring much more than economic value to our communities. They provide a social and ecological connection to the sea that underpins the cultural fabric of our coast. Our communities need our fisheries to remain sustainable for current and future generations. These workshops—which facilitated meaningful dialogue between fish harvesters and government—are a critical step in developing long-term solutions for a way forward," said Jim McIsaac [CIFHF vice-president for British Columbia]. "Our members want a meaningful role for independent harvester organizations in fisheries reconciliation negotiations. We need the government now to develop solutions that will lead to positive outcomes for all harvesters."[19]

In the FOPO Committee hearings, CIFHF President Melanie Sonnenberg further articulated the heartfelt concerns of non-Indigenous harvesters about how decisions were being made on the moderate livelihood fishery.

"We are told repeatedly that we really don't have a place, that this is government to government.... [W]e have to know where we will fit.... We need to find a place where we can understand what is being discussed about us, yet without us.... Presently, because we don't know any of this, we don't understand what the future holds for us....

"It isn't about denying any rights. It isn't about not acknowledging what has been established by the Supreme Court. It is about making sure that we have a better understanding and that we have some protection. We have an industry that has heavily invested in fishing. We have thousands of fishermen across this country. They've established our coastal communities, as we know them, and we know that the prosperity in these communities has grown as of late. We need to recognize that and figure out a way, collectively, to ensure that everybody is protected, and that we have some sense of community together. This isn't about dividing and conquering; this is about working together for the best of everybody."[20]

OWNER-OPERATOR AND FLEET SEPARATION CONCERNS

As described above, fish harvesters in Atlantic Canada see DFO policies and regulations that exclude corporate interests from owning inshore fishing licences and quotas as essential to their economic survival and future prosperity as small business owner-operators. Their organizations fought for decades to get these protections embedded in law, only succeeding in 2019 with the new Fisheries Act and regulations. There is every expectation among harvester leaders, however, that processing companies will find new ways to avoid the restrictions, and growing concern that partnerships with First Nations are one such workaround.

In the mining, forestry, and energy sectors, collaborative arrangements between corporate interests and First Nations are increasingly used to accommodate Indigenous territorial rights but also to help navigate onerous approval processes and overcome "social licence" challenges. First Nations themselves are sometimes divided over such arrangements, as we have seen lately with pipeline projects in British Columbia.

Such partnerships are now taking shape in the Atlantic fishing industry, the most significant being the recent $1 billion joint purchase of Clearwater Seafoods, perhaps the largest shellfish producer in the world, by a multinational corporation and seven First Nations (six in Nova Scotia and one in Newfoundland and Labrador). The deal is discussed in detail in chapter 6.3. The reaction of one prominent harvester leader was captured in a *Globe and Mail* article:

The acquisition will worsen tensions between Indigenous and non-Indigenous fishermen, and alienate Mi'kmaq [*sic*] bands excluded from the deal, said Colin Sproul, president of the Bay of Fundy Inshore Fishermen's Association.

"There's nobody more hated or viewed as an enemy of lobster fishermen than Clearwater Seafoods, and that's because of the price controls they've exercised over the industry," he said. "The government has just facilitated a deal...that is going to align select First Nations with someone who's despised by inshore fishermen, at a time of historic divisions between our groups. I think it's all pretty irresponsible."

..."This is an attempt to Indigenize something that is not lawful. They're transferring Canada's offshore resources to a multinational conglomerate," Mr. Sproul said.[21]

A related concern among commercial harvester leaders is that licences and quotas that are transferred to or purchased by First Nations are owned communally and are almost all held within Nation-owned, vertically integrated companies rather than by individual owner-operators. Communities like Elsipogtog in New Brunswick and Membertou in Cape Breton are building up large corporate enterprises with integrated harvesting, processing, and marketing operations.

Non-Indigenous harvester leaders see this pattern as advancing the corporate concentration and vertical integration that DFO policies were meant to prevent in the inshore industry. They have fears that First Nations companies, possibly aligned with outside investors, will be buying up more and more lobster, crab, and other licences to fold into their operations. When that happens, they say, non-Indigenous crew workers who want to purchase licences and quotas to become enterprise owners will be at a severe disadvantage in having to bid against large companies with much deeper pockets.

SUMMARY

Seven themes emerge from this brief review of public statements by prominent commercial fisheries leaders and their organizations across the Maritime provinces.

Respect for Indigenous Rights and qualified acceptance of the Marshall rulings

All the groups identified in this discussion have made formal statements recognizing Aboriginal Rights and accepting the Supreme Court's *Marshall* decisions. However, they challenge certain interpretations of the Court's language on moderate livelihoods and self-government rights in fisheries. There is some expectation that further referrals to the Supreme Court may be required to resolve these questions.

Rejection of racism and violence

Leaders of the major harvester organizations have formally distanced themselves from the recent violence in Southwest Nova Scotia and from the racist attitudes that were apparent during those events and on social media. While acknowledging the presence of racism as one factor at the community level, the leaders generally attribute the 2020 conflicts to deeper issues, most notably the perceived weak enforcement of fisheries regulations for food, social, and ceremonial (FSC) fisheries and anxieties over the possible impacts of expanding Indigenous fisheries on their businesses and their communities.

A place at the table

All these groups share frustrations and, at times, anger that major decisions impacting their businesses and their communities may be made through negotiations in which they have no part. Kevin Squires, an MFU leader from Cape Breton, clearly articulated this concern to the FOPO Committee: "We don't feel that we've been heard. We have significant problems with the fact that DFO has failed to figure out a way to include us. We understand the nature of nation-to-nation negotiations, but there has to be a place for commercial harvesters."[22]

These reactions can be explained in part by the simple fact that decision making on Rights Reconciliation Agreements and new moderate livelihood fisheries takes place entirely outside the established co-management processes for decision making and conflict resolution in the fishery. Harvester leaders are experiencing this as a betrayal of long-established co-management principles and practices centred on transparency, consultation with all stakeholders, consensus building, and collaborative problem solving.

Some groups are more accepting than others of the ongoing expansion of First Nations fisheries, but all agree that the planning and decision making on these changes need to be more transparent, and non-Indigenous rights holders need to have some meaningful role in the process.

One regulator

With varying degrees of intensity, all these groups share the view that expanded self-government in First Nations fisheries simply will not work operationally and will generate greater divisions and conflict between communities. Bernie Berry from the Unified Fisheries Conservation Alliance emphasized this view to the FOPO Committee: "There can only be one regulator and one set of rules for all. We cannot entertain any thought of having multiple regulatory regimes. If there are multiple regulators for one fishery it will only lead to confusion, non-compliance, lack of science, lack of enforcement, etc. It simply will not work."[23]

Industry leaders frame this issue in practical terms. In the existing fisheries management system, a total allowable catch (TAC) or trap limit is set for each commercially harvested species based on the DFO science advice, and the TAC or trap limit is then divided up among the different fleet sectors, each operating within its designated fishing zone.[24] In the same way, rules on season and gear specifications are imposed on all fishing enterprises by the central authority, that is, the DFO minister.

Harvester leaders argue that if each First Nation, or a group of Nations, can exercise a right to unilaterally decide how much fish to catch, or how many lobster traps to set, and where and when to fish, there could be chaos. Either total fishing effort will keep ramping up, putting fish populations in danger, or there will be escalating conflicts between communities, fleets, and regions over who will see their shares reduced to maintain sustainable catch levels.

Progress on the Moderate Livelihood Right

First Nations leaders often claim that little if any real progress has been made since the *Marshall* rulings in meeting the Moderate Livelihood Right and that the creation of a separate self-regulated moderate livelihood fishery is therefore needed and fully justified. Non-Indigenous harvesters challenge this view, insisting that the substantial transfers of fishing licences and quotas to First Nations, along with the training programs and other investments, have all contributed significantly to meeting the Supreme Court's requirements and should be counted as such. A few harvesters' representatives go even further to suggest that First Nations now control a fair share of fisheries access rights and that no further expansion is warranted.

Lax enforcement

In a few regions commercial harvesters are convinced that DFO and First Nations fisheries authorities do not uniformly enforce First Nations FSC fisheries regulations and that significant quantities of FSC fish caught outside the regular commercial season are being sold illegally. These perceptions played a part in the violent events in St. Marys Bay in 2020. This is likely to be a continuing source of tension between communities and of harvester mistrust in both DFO and some First Nations fisheries authorities.

Fears about the future

For reasons discussed above, the progressive expansion of First Nations fisheries holds some potential to destabilize the fisheries co-management system and harvester trust in it. Whether fairly and correctly or not, harvesters at the wharf level feel their livelihoods and the sustainability of their communities are threatened. They are putting increasing pressure on their leaders and organizations to advocate for their interests as publicly and aggressively as they see Indigenous leaders advancing their cause and defending their rights.

These feelings of powerlessness and uncertainty about the future are exacerbating the mistrust and polarization between communities and seeding the ground for future conflict. Some new and innovative forms of engagement, dialogue, and negotiation may be needed to relieve these growing pressures.

5.2

AN INTERVIEW with ALLISTER SURETTE

by FRED WIEN and RICK WILLIAMS

A llister Surette has been President and Vice-Chancellor of Université Sainte-Anne since July 1, 2011. A native of West Pubnico, NS, Mr. Surette was elected Member of the Legislative Assembly for the constituency of Argyle in Nova Scotia from 1993 to 1998. He served as special advisor on Acadian and francophone governance within the public school system and as Minister of Human Resources and Minister of Acadian Affairs.

In October 2020, the Government of Canada appointed Mr. Surette as Federal Special Representative, to act as a neutral third party to help rebuild trust between commercial and Indigenous fishers after the unrest and violence in Southwest Nova Scotia (SWNS). He submitted his report, "Implementing the right to fish in pursuit of a moderate livelihood: Rebuilding trust and establishing a constructive path forward," to Minister Bernadette Jordan of the Department of Fisheries and Oceans and Minister Carolyn Bennett of Crown–Indigenous Relations on March 31, 2021.[1]

Question: *In preparing your 2021 report to the federal government, what did you learn about the roots of the conflict between commercial fish harvesters and First Nations in Southwest Nova Scotia (SWNS)?*

Allister Surette: It was quickly apparent that there were deeply entrenched and polarized views among people on different sides of the issues. The reasons for these views seemed to be based on perceptions in some cases, others on misunderstandings, and, of course, some views were based on personal economic or other interests. Furthermore, there were several different issues, and some were quite complex and multifaceted, which led to different interpretations from various groups and individuals. It was clear to me that all could benefit from accessible and timely information, open dialogue, and good communications.

However, good communication is not as simple as one may think. In SWNS, there are several organizations representing different harvester groups, and many independent harvesters who do not belong to any organization. The number of organizations and number of independent harvesters, logistically, makes communication a challenge. There are also challenges in communicating with First Nations and the general public.

Without a well-developed system to inform and consult stakeholders about complex court decisions and government policies, regulations, and enforcement programs, people receive conflicting interpretations of what is going on, especially over social media, and draw conclusions that quickly become entrenched and difficult to change.

And, underlying all of this is a long-standing lack of trust between fish harvesters and DFO, and between First Nations leaders and government. This lack of trust makes progress difficult.

Q: *Briefly speaking, in your advice to the federal government on the possible paths forward to avoid future conflicts, what did you see as the highest priorities?*

AS: The starting point for change must be efficient and effective communication and providing support for dialogue between the different groups. In my opinion, government must provide the leadership to establish new mechanisms to get factual and timely information out to all stakeholders, and mechanisms to facilitate dialogue within stakeholder groups and between stakeholders. I would also suggest that stakeholder leaders and government find ways to use social media and other tools proactively to get out in front of issues before opinions and misinformation get entrenched, fuelling conflicts.

Q: *The situation in SWNS is clearly more complex than is often portrayed in the national media during the events in the fall of 2020. What do you see as the most important things for people in government, the media, and the general public to understand about the conflict and its history?*

AS: As I mentioned, it is a multifaceted and complex situation to begin with, made more difficult when the media focuses so much on the extreme views, extreme events, and individuals with personal agendas. The most extreme events are amplified by the mainstream media and on social media, leading the public and others to think that these are the views of all involved. This makes it more challenging for those acting in good faith to truly resolve issues.

There is some history of commercial fish harvesters and non-Indigenous communities working well with local First Nations. We are neighbours in our communities, we know one another from going to the same schools, same workplaces, and playing sports. I believe that the majority of people in all communities are reasonable and want to see things work out peacefully and fairly, but when extreme events happen, they are less willing to speak out publicly or take on leadership roles.

During my work on this matter, I saw leaders and individuals on both sides making real efforts to try to de-escalate the situation. A few years ago, there was an effective dialogue process with local First Nations and commercial harvester leaders [see chapter 5.3], but unfortunately the conflict in 2020 has made that impossible to continue. As a gesture of goodwill, when some First Nations lobster traps were cut during this conflict, a group of local commercial harvesters from SWNS gathered up traps and gear to replace these cut traps and delivered them to the local First Nation. These are examples that there was and still is goodwill.

Government and others may have underestimated how much misunderstanding and confusion there was in the industry and in our communities and probably could have done a better job at simplifying their messages and working more diligently to get factual information out quickly. Government leadership is required to ensure all involved directly with the fishery, as well as the general public, have a better understanding of court rulings and government decisions, and it is up to government to establish mechanisms to facilitate a path forward.

Q: *What do you see as the main differences in attitudes and approaches among commercial harvesters and First Nations in the area?*

AS: The positions are quite polarized now. Simply said, most independent commercial harvesters and the organizations that represent them say they have no problem with First Nations fisheries as long as there is no increased fishing effort and everyone operates by the same rules and seasons.

First Nations leaders hold firm that the courts gave them access to self-regulated fisheries, and the government and commercial harvesters must accept that and make room for them.

There is no obvious, quick, or easy way to harmonize these two approaches.

Q: *Do you think relations and attitudes in the different communities of SWNS have improved since the violent clashes of September 2020? Is there still potential for conflicts to flare up again in the next fishing season?*

AS: There still is potential for conflict because of the entrenched and polarized views. Even when things seem to be quiet and going well, there needs to be continued effort to communicate and facilitate dialogue. It is also important for commercial harvester groups to keep working with local First Nations to help them develop and manage their fisheries.

The government has recently worked out short-term agreements with four local First Nations for limited-scale moderate livelihood fisheries. This process seems to offer a new way to work on the issues through more effective engagement at the local level. That is very encouraging.

Q: *What do you see as the most important lessons learned from the events of the past two years?*

AS: Because of the complexity of the issues and the polarized attitudes, I believe it's critically important that government take ownership of the situation with strong proactive leadership to facilitate the information sharing, consultations, communications, and dialogue that are needed to establish a path forward. It must continue to work diligently to build trust with First Nations and commercial harvester groups and to encourage more constructive relations among them. The lack of trust in government and the lack of trust in the industry in general gives rise to situations like we saw in 2020.

As I noted in my report to DFO Minister Jordan and Minister Bennett of Crown–Indigenous Relations, it is important for all individuals, either directly or indirectly involved the fishery in the Maritimes and Gaspé Region of Quebec, as well as our coastal communities and society as a whole, that we find a path forward. We need to engage all parties in finding long-term solutions to the implementation of Indigenous Rights in the fishery while ensuring an orderly and productive fishery for all.

The existence of a stable commercial fishery composed of thousands of independent small businesses and First Nations communal enterprises is a huge economic asset for our coastal regions. It is in everyone's interest that we protect and share ocean resources and learn to live and work together to sustain the fishery.

5.3

An EXPERIMENT in DIALOGUE

by FRED WIEN and RICK WILLIAMS

n a March 2021 report to then-DFO Minister Bernadette Jordan, Special Federal Advisor Allister Surette recommended the creation of a "dialogue forum to build trust and relationships" to help reduce tensions over the moderate livelihood fishery issue.[1] In suggesting this approach, he referred to an earlier series of meetings between First Nations and fish harvesters' associations in southwestern Nova Scotia that might serve as a model.

Those meetings were initiated at the suggestion of the local DFO Area Office in Yarmouth, were led by an independent facilitator, and were focused on direct dialogue as opposed to formal consultation, negotiation, or conflict resolution. A public statement, issued with the formal approval of all the participating harvester groups and First Nations, described their purpose as follows: "To establish lines of communication between people who have hands-on working involvement in the lobster fishery in LFAS 33, 34 and 35. The idea is to have a space to meet and talk, building on the good history of collaboration between Indigenous and non-Indigenous fishermen in this area."[2]

The statement identified the starting points for the meetings as "the recognition of fishing rights of the Mi'kmaq people" and a set of shared values, including:

- The responsibility for conservation of the resource for future generations.
- A commitment to sustainable livelihoods in [our] communities.

- A commitment to peace, ensuring that everyone involved in the lobster fishery can fish in a safe and secure manner.

The meeting facilitator, Arthur Bull, identified the main themes that emerged in the discussions as:

- The need for awareness-raising and education about rights-based fisheries.
- Building alliances to address issues that impact the whole lobster fishery.
- Fisheries activities that undermine legitimate fisheries.
- The potential for cooperation on joint science projects.
- A shared interest in increasing access to markets.

The group met fourteen times over two years and included leaders and fisheries officers from five Mi'kmaq First Nations (Acadia, Bear River, Glooscap, Sipekne'katik, and Millbrook) and five harvester groups (Maritime Fishermen's Union, Coldwater Lobster Association, Brazil Rock 33/34 Lobster Association, the Bay of Fundy Inshore Fishermen's Association, and the LFA 34 Lobster Advisory Committee). Representatives of DFO and the RCMP sat in on the meetings to provide liaison with wider support services. Almost all the meetings were hosted by First Nations and by harvester associations in their respective communities.

Bull reported that one of the most successful sessions was a comprehensive presentation by DFO Science on the state of the lobster stocks. In other sessions several Nations also gave detailed presentations on their FSC management plans.

Unfortunately, the meetings came to an end after two years when a few leaders got caught up in higher level policy disagreements. Bull reports that many of the participants at the local level communicated to him an interest in carrying on, but the dramatic buildup in tensions in 2020 around moderate livelihood fisheries closed that door for the time being. However, the experience does provide a model that could be revisited when leaders in the different communities are ready to pursue open-ended dialogue.

5.4

AN INTERVIEW with GILLES THÉRIAULT

by RICK WILLIAMS

illes Thériault has a lifetime of experience in fisheries development. He grew up in Baie Ste. Anne, NB, and as a young community organizer and activist in the Acadian rights movement, he played a lead role in bringing many local fish harvester associations together to form the Maritime Fishermen's Union (MFU) in 1977. He served as Executive Director of the MFU before leaving the organization in 1987 to begin a long and distinguished career in fisheries consulting in Canada and internationally.

With the Supreme Court rulings on *Marshall* in the fall of 1999, tensions between Indigenous and non-Indigenous communities escalated, especially in the Gulf Region of New Brunswick and in Southwest Nova Scotia. A federal negotiator was appointed to develop interim agreements with the Mi'kmaw and Wolostoqey First Nations on access to fishing licences, boats, and other supports. With his strong industry links and deep expertise in fisheries, Thériault was brought on to assist. In 2004 Thériault became lead federal negotiator.

After completing that role in 2007, Thériault began advising First Nations on developing their communal-commercial fisheries. He also worked for the Innu Nations of Quebec on the fisheries component of their treaty negotiations with the Government of Canada. In 2008 he completed a feasibility study for Elsipogtog First Nation leading to the purchase the

McGraw Seafood plant in Tracadie, NB. He helped set up the governance and management structure and sat on the board of directors as an advisor before assuming the role of general manager of the plant from 2015 to 2019. After mentoring a young leader from the community to take over that position, Thériault now serves as business development advisor for McGraw Seafood. In this role he assisted Elsipogtog and McGraw Seafood management in the construction of a $25 million fish processing plant and freezer facility that began operation in 2021.

In an interview with Fred Wien and Rick Williams in November 2021, Thériault shared his views on the development of First Nations fisheries since the *Marshall* decisions.

Question: *In the early years after the Supreme Court's rulings, what approaches were taken to the development of First Nations commercial fisheries?*

Gilles Thériault: In the first few years after *Marshall*, the focus was on getting interim agreements in place as quickly as possible to provide the Mi'kmaw and Wolastoqey First Nations with licences, boats, gear, and training to expand their commercial fishing activities. It was slow going at first because most communities did not have a lot of expertise in managing commercial fisheries and building fishery business models and did not have many experienced fish harvesters with knowledge and skills to succeed on the water. But the First Nations that stuck with it and took advantage of the training and other support programs made real progress in creating jobs and generating revenues for their communities.

The long-term idea was for the government to provide First Nations with a share of the existing commercial fishery by transferring licences and quotas from retiring non-Indigenous fishermen. As I understood it, DFO negotiators and department officials believed that expanding communal-commercial fisheries was the primary pathway for addressing the moderate livelihoods right. Because the licences and quotas would be communally owned and managed within their self-government rights, each community would have a significant say in how best to structure their fishery and distribute the benefits. Some communities might pursue having jobs for increasing numbers of fishing captains and crew and perhaps workers in processing operations. Others might choose to raise living standards for the community as a whole by leasing out licences and quotas and using the royalty revenues to invest in housing, job creation, and social programs. Others chose a mixture of the two. These were decisions the bands were making themselves as things progressed.

Q: *Can you give an example of how one First Nation you worked with developed their fishery?*

GT: After I finished up as a federal negotiator, I began to work with Elsipogtog to help them develop their fisheries plan. Elsipogtog is the largest Mi'kmaq Nation in New Brunswick and is located right on the Gulf Shore where community members maintain a long tradition of engagement in fish harvesting.

After much consideration, the Band Council agreed on a development plan to acquire lobster licences, vessels, and gear and to start building up an inshore fishery. Through their interim agreements with DFO and their own investments, they acquired over sixty lobster licences. While non-Indigenous harvesters in the region fish all of the 250 traps that are permitted by each licence, Elsipogtog adopted a plan for each vessel from the community to fish 25 fewer traps, with the surplus traps used to bring a few more vessels and crews into the fishery.

Today Elsipogtog has over seventy inshore boats fishing lobster with crews of three or four each. Lobster landings and prices have been strong in recent years, so over 280 community members are earning good fishing incomes and qualify for Employment Insurance in the off-season. In 2021 the Elsipogtog lobster fleet generated an estimated $16 million in landed value, with 100 percent of this revenue going to the captains to pay themselves and their crews and to maintain their vessels and gear as would happen in the non-Indigenous fishery.

When Elsipogtog acquired a snow crab quota in 2004, they had to decide how best to distribute the benefits. Snow crab in the Gulf of St. Lawrence is mainly fished by larger midshore boats. If they had chosen to fish their crab with just a few midshore vessels, they would have created only about forty jobs and would have had to go outside their community to find people with the skills needed to operate such vessels. Elsipogtog chose instead to build up better jobs and incomes in their inshore fleet by equipping their lobster vessels to fish their snow crab quota in areas closer to shore. After extensive discussions it was agreed that half their inshore boats would be adapted to harvest the crab quota, creating some 170 jobs for their own harvesters, and the profits would be divided equally between the fishermen and the community. By this formula their inshore fishery was diversified and strengthened, and the entire community saw a direct benefit. In 2021 the landed value for the Elsipogtog snow crab fishery was approximately $15 million.

The same challenge arose again with the purchase of another snow crab quota through the recent Rights Reconciliation Agreement. Having just built a new processing plant, the Band Council decided this time to purchase a midshore vessel to optimize resource supply to the new plant and the revenue flow to the community. Plans are in place to have this vessel fully captained and crewed by members of the community within three years.

Q: *How have relations with non-Indigenous fish harvesters changed as Elsipogtog was developing its fishery?*

GT: When the Supreme Court ruling on the *Marshall* case was announced in the fall of 1999, chaos broke out on the Gulf Shore of New Brunswick. Mi'kmaw harvesters began setting lobster traps outside the regular commercial season, and non-Indigenous harvesters reacted by destroying traps and onshore facilities. Escalating conflicts in the Burnt Church area attracted national attention and heavy police interventions. Relationships between Indigenous and non-Indigenous harvesters and their communities were extremely tense.

I believe that leadership from the Maritime Fishermen's Union played a critically important role in calming the waters with their members in Acadian communities and in building relationships with First Nations leaders and harvesters. There were times when this was strongly opposed by some MFU members. The MFU nevertheless co-operated with DFO licence buyback programs to transfer licences to First Nations fisheries and in arranging for experienced harvesters to serve as trainers and mentors for Indigenous crews. With depressed lobster landings and prices at the time, and the willingness of the government to buy enterprises from owner-operators who freely chose to leave the industry, things mostly settled down after four or five years.

Since then, there have been positive developments in relations between Indigenous and non-Indigenous harvesters in the Gulf Region of New Brunswick. The MFU owns a quota for snow crab, which its members fish with inshore lobster boats. When I was manager of Elsipogtog's crab processing plant, we were able to negotiate an agreement with the MFU that a significant share of the Union's crab quota would be sold to us each year. With this arrangement, McGraw Seafood receives the extra crab supply required by the plant while the MFU gets a guaranteed fair price.

The MFU operates a research and development program for lobster through its Homarus Centre. Fish harvesters from First Nations have been working with the MFU through Homarus in building artificial lobster reefs and conducting other research projects.

One growing challenge for lobster harvesters is acquiring bait for their traps. In 2019 the MFU's Homarus Centre and Elsipogtog's fish plant established a partnership for an R&D project to use waste material from fish processing to manufacture a low-cost bait product. It has taken Homarus several years to find a formula that works well to attract lobster and for McGraw Seafood to develop a processing method to scale up production in their plant. This has been achieved, but fishermen are still reluctant to use this new bait when their traditional bait is still available. I believe that there will be a time soon when harvesters will want to use this innovative, low-cost, and much needed product that was developed through collaboration between Elsipogtog's processing plant and the MFU.

I recently became aware of an interesting innovation that has taken shape with Listuguj First Nation in Quebec. Listuguj harvesters wanted to fish in the fall outside the commercial season and were strongly opposed by non-Indigenous harvesters in their region who can only fish in the spring. As I understand it, Listuguj and DFO have reached an agreement whereby for every lobster trap that Listuguj harvesters deploy in the fall, they have agreed to use seven fewer traps in their spring fishery. In this way, the non-Indigenous harvesters should be reassured that the fall fishery should not be a serious threat to the sustainability of the resource and their lobster catches in the spring. Although non-Indigenous harvesters do not support such an agreement, if it is implemented and enforced properly I think there is a lot of merit in this approach as it recognizes the right to self-government while not impacting landings by other harvesters.

Hopefully it will be possible to keep pursuing such practical innovations, but it is going to be difficult to get non-Indigenous harvesters and their organizations to buy in because of their concerns about inadequate compliance within food, social, and ceremonial fisheries agreements over the years. It will have to be demonstrated concretely that this can work before we will see a change in fishermen's attitudes. That is why this Listuguj project is important.

Q: *In addition to their communal-commercial fisheries, some First Nations have claimed the right under* Marshall *to issue their own licences to community members to conduct small-scale fishing to earn moderate livelihoods. What is your view on the idea of a separate moderate likelihood fishery?*

GT: As I mentioned, I support the view that all forms of fisheries development for First Nations since the *Marshall* decisions are contributing to meeting the moderate livelihood objective to a greater or lesser extent. Because newly acquired licences and quotas are communally owned, individual First Nations have a lot of room within their self-government rights to determine how best to utilize new fishing assets and opportunities to benefit their communities.

Four Nations in Nova Scotia recently negotiated fishing plans with DFO to allow them to reallocate the traps that come with one lobster licence—for example, 375 traps per licence in Southwest Nova Scotia—so that a larger number of harvesters will fish up to 70 traps each with their boats. For this year they agreed to fish during the regular commercial season and to co-operate with DFO on conservation practices and surveillance and enforcement of the rules.

These harvesters will earn less money than a captain and crew in a regular enterprise fishing all the traps that come with one licence, so as they become more skilled and experienced, they may want to keep expanding their operations. This may be a very good way to get young people from the community into the fishery and to build up a skilled labour force. Over time, as harvesters have greater success at fishing, there may be growing pressures to raise the limits on traps to increase the incomes being generated.

However, in my view, the option to use licences for lobster or other species in this way to create more fishing opportunities was already there under the self-governance rights as spelled out in interim agreements and RRAS. As I described, the Elsipogtog fisheries program decided some years ago to reallocate traps from communally owned lobster licences to support more vessels and crews than is normally the case in non-Indigenous fleets.

If a First Nation can set up co-operative management agreements with DFO on fishing seasons, effort controls, and conservation measures, I don't see the need to treat moderate livelihood fishing as distinct or exceptional. The *Marshall* First Nations have latitude now to structure their enterprises and allocate fishing opportunities in innovative ways to grow social and economic benefits and support the long-term development of their fisheries.

It should also be remembered that with the new Fisheries Act, passed in 2019, the DFO minister has the authority to delegate or transfer fisheries management decision making powers to First Nations in recognition of their self-government rights. As Nations reach longer-term agreements with DFO on fisheries development plans and co-operative management and conservation, they will have even greater opportunities to structure, plan, and operate their fisheries to optimize social and economic benefits.

Q: *What do you see as the best pathways to improving relationships between Indigenous and non-Indigenous fish harvesters?*

GT: It seems evident now that Indigenous fisheries in Atlantic Canada will continue to expand, and the application of the Treaty Rights recognized by the *Marshall* decisions will continue to evolve.

With strict limits on the amounts of fish that can be harvested to ensure resource conservation, Indigenous fisheries will advance largely through more licences and quotas being transferred from non-Indigenous harvesters and their communities to First Nations. We will, therefore, be dealing with these changes and difficult relationships for the foreseeable future. There is a lot of work to do to find ways to communicate, to solve problems, and to treat everyone respectfully so we don't have more of the violent conflicts we have seen in the past.

The development of new Rights Reconciliation Agreements, other interim fisheries agreements, and possibly global treaties must all be negotiated on a Nation-to-Nation basis or with bodies representing groups of First Nations. While non-Indigenous harvester leaders recognize that they are not parties to these negotiations, it's a reality that their members and their communities will be significantly impacted by the outcomes. Not having any say in major changes in their industry creates frustration and resistance that can make things more difficult down the road.

If we think of a triangle, two sides are well-defined: First Nations have much better structures and protocols than in the past for negotiating and problem solving with DFO, and organizations representing non-Indigenous harvesters communicate effectively with government, and often exert strong pressures to defend their interests. What is missing is the third side of the triangle, the base perhaps, where Indigenous and non-Indigenous leaders sit together, first to better understand each other's values, goals, and concerns, and then to work on areas of common interest. In the larger picture, there is only one ocean and one fishery resource base, and all the major users need to work together to manage resources sustainably and build a strong fisheries economy to the benefit of everyone.

It is, therefore, critically important over the medium-to-long term that new consultation tables and dialogue processes be created where Indigenous and non-Indigenous leaders can begin to build relationships of trust, mutual understanding, and common purpose.

There is, however, an immediate issue that makes it difficult to build such dialogue processes. Non-Indigenous harvesters in some regions such as Southwest Nova Scotia and the Gulf Region of New Brunswick have long believed that DFO does not adequately monitor and enforce catch limits and rules against the illegal sale of lobster caught in First Nations food, social, and ceremonial (FSC) fisheries. While racist attitudes are often a factor at the local level, the inconsistent enforcement of regulations by DFO officers and First Nations Guardians makes it much more difficult for responsible leaders in non-Indigenous harvester organizations to calm the waters.

By the same token, Indigenous harvesters frequently experience threats and harassment on the wharves and the water with their traps being cut and boats damaged by non-Indigenous harvesters. Indigenous harvesters do not have confidence that DFO and other police forces will protect them when they are fishing alongside non-Indigenous neighbours during the regular season, so that encourages them to pursue fishing outside the season when they feel safer.

It is going to be difficult to get past the current tensions until all sides have greater trust in the enforcement of laws and adherence to the terms of agreements. Indigenous harvesters need to feel safe and accepted on the wharves and while fishing, and non-Indigenous harvesters may become more accepting of the growing First Nations presence in the industry if they believe everyone is following the agreed upon rules.

It will take a long time, a generation perhaps, for First Nations and non-Indigenous fish harvesters to put aside past conflicts and learn to work together and to trust and respect each other. The starting point, I believe, is the effective enforcement of agreements and regulations so fish stocks are protected, harvesters have confidence in the management system, and everyone can conduct their fisheries safely and free from threats and harassment. On that foundation we can build fisheries management structures and processes that bring decision makers from different communities to common tables to share perspectives, work on issues of common concern, and begin building stronger relationships.

Effective fisheries management has always required people from various provinces, fleet sectors, and language groups to overcome significant differences and find common purpose. The issues today may seem more daunting than in the past, but looking back over my years of work in the fisheries, I can say with confidence that these challenges can be overcome with strong leadership, a positive vision for the future, and a commitment to respectful dialogue.

VI

CURRENT ISSUES

6.1

The STATE of the RESOURCE

by SUSANNA FULLER

fforts to reconcile Mi'kmaw, Wolastoqey, and Peskotomuhkati rights to
fish are further complicated by the biological realities of commercially
exploited species, as centuries of industrial fisheries have left many fish
populations severely depleted. Ostensibly, the system of access, licensing, and quota-setting based on stock assessments is designed to limit
overcapacity and overfishing. This system has historically failed some species, the important example being groundfish (e.g., cod and haddock). More
recently, forage fish, including herring and mackerel, are at such levels that
targeted fishing has been closed.

Fisheries are culturally, socially, and economically vital to a significant
number of Atlantic Canadian rural communities—Indigenous and non-
Indigenous alike. While the great majority of fish production is exported,
images of bountiful seafood are often used in marketing the region to visi-
tors. However, there is a long history of fisheries-management decisions
favouring short-term socio-economic benefits over longer-term stock
health and sustainability.

Healthy fish populations are the foundation for successful fisheries and
provide opportunities for increased access. When populations are low, harvesting of any type can reduce chances of stock recovery. It can be argued
that the depletion of fish populations to the level of commercial extinction
is a further barrier to the Indigenous Rights as enshrined in Section 35 of
Canada's Constitution.

As of 2017, Fisheries and Oceans Canada has made its Sustainability Survey for Fisheries publicly available, allowing Canadians to better

understand the population status of 180 major fish stocks and marine mammals. Population status is categorized according to the precautionary approach for fisheries management.[1] The 2020 survey listed seventy-eight stocks as having "uncertain" status, forty-eight in the "healthy zone," and twenty-three in the "cautious zone." There were twenty-three stocks assessed to be in the "critical zone" where fishing is advised to be kept to the lowest possible levels.[2]

When populations are known to have declined significantly (e.g., in the "critical zone"), they are often then assessed by the Committee on the Status for Endangered Wildlife in Canada (COSEWIC). This scientific body provides advice to the DFO minister on whether to list species under the Species At Risk Act (SARA). Once species are listed under SARA, commercial harvest of any type is prohibited. Seventeen commercially harvested species, or species caught as bycatch in targeted fisheries in Atlantic Canada, have been assessed by COSEWIC. These include commercially valuable species such as Atlantic bluefin tuna and American eel (elvers), which COSEWIC has classified as "endangered" and "threatened" respectively. Despite these population assessments, listing commercially harvested species under SARA has never occurred, largely because of the socio-economic consequences of eliminating a valuable commercial harvest.[3] As moderate livelihood fisheries are developed and pressures to recover at-risk populations increase, with species possibly being listed under SARA, there will be further tensions between upholding Indigenous Rights while addressing biodiversity loss. SARA listing is the most powerful tool for legally requiring population rebuilding, but DFO has so far opted to rebuild many of these stocks using its authority under the Fisheries Act.

While many other developed fishing nations have managed to rebuild collapsed fisheries, Canada only adopted legislation requiring rebuilding in 2019 with the modernized Fisheries Act. Regulations on rebuilding were adopted in April 2022,[4] almost three years after being enabled by the Fisheries Act. More than thirty years after the catastrophic collapse of Northern cod stocks, this stock remains well below the level where targeted fishing should be permitted. Yet, at 10,000 metric tonnes of annual catch between 2017 and 2020, it remains one of the larger groundfish fisheries in Canada, albeit well below historic catch levels that peaked at 800,000 metric tonnes in the late 1960s.[5]

Since the early 1990s when almost all groundfish fisheries were closed, fisheries for more lucrative shellfish—notably lobster, crab, shrimp, and scallop—have become economically dominant across the industry. This shift is generally in keeping with a global trend of increasing crustacean fisheries, which have a higher monetary value, lower nutritional value, and higher carbon footprints than groundfish or forage fish.[6] While some groundfish fisheries have been reopened, most remain at low levels or under moratoria where no directed fishing is permitted. Atlantic halibut, caught predominately by bottom hook-and-line gear ("longline"), benefited from the closure of many trawl fisheries as juvenile fish were no longer caught as bycatch.[7] Expanding redfish populations in the Gulf of St. Lawrence have created both an anticipation for resumed fisheries, described by some as a "bonanza," as well as new opportunities for Indigenous access.[8]

Since 2009, Canada has put in place several new policies under the Sustainable Fisheries Framework to better manage fisheries. These include the Precautionary Approach Framework, the Policy to Manage Bycatch, the Policy to Manage the Impacts of Fishing on Sensitive Benthic Areas, the Policy for the Management of New Forage Fisheries, and the Guidance for Rebuilding.[9] Taken all together, these enable better decision making by fisheries managers to protect and rebuild a productive ocean environment into the future. However, the implementation of these policies has been piecemeal at best, with political will being the most important factor influencing their application.

Decision making for fish population assessment and fisheries management takes place at the local, regional, and national levels. For stocks that straddle the two-hundred-mile limit, and for highly migratory stocks such as tuna and swordfish, there are international management bodies. With the modernization of the Fisheries Act, these processes are now required to take Indigenous knowledge systems and values into account. While some species (e.g., lobster) can be managed at a regional or local level, others cannot. There is an opportunity now to incorporate the Mi'kmaw concept of *Netukulimk*, defined as "achieving adequate standards of community nutrition and economic well-being without jeopardizing the integrity, diversity, or productivity of our environment,"[10] into fisheries management decisions at the community level as well as throughout colonial management systems. The 2021 mandate letter for the Minister of Fisheries and Oceans and the Canadian

Coast Guard charges the minister with "working to halt and reverse nature loss by 2030 in Canada, achieve a full recovery for nature by 2050 and champion this goal internationally. You will ensure that this work remains grounded in science, Indigenous knowledge and local perspectives."[11]

Regardless of how fish are being harvested, overall human-induced mortality must be understood and considered when determining how much can be taken while ensuring recovery into the future or maintenance of healthy populations where they now exist. The new Fisheries Act provides a strong basis for sustainable fisheries management with strengthened commitments to the precautionary principle,[12] an ecosystem approach,[13] incorporation of Indigenous and local knowledge, and the requirement to develop rebuilding plans for threatened species. If implemented diligently, this new legislative framework could ensure both the recovery of depleted populations and that mistakes of the past are not repeated. Continued investment in science and knowledge system integration is imperative if we are to have responsible decision making using reliable information on the state of fish stocks. From a Western science perspective, having accurate information on how much fish is harvested through food, social, and ceremonial fisheries, moderate livelihood fisheries, commercial-communal fisheries, and regular commercial fisheries will significantly improve fisheries management decision making. Despite some uncertainty in scientific methods of assessing fish stock abundance, having reliable estimates of spawning stock abundance and of the ability of populations to recover from fishing mortality is the basis for management decisions that will sustain coastal fisheries into the future. The development of new moderate livelihood fisheries and the continuation of commercial fisheries by Indigenous and non-Indigenous harvesters all depend on the health and sustainability of fish populations and habitat.

Further, as moderate livelihood plans are developed by individual communities for specific fisheries, this opportunity should be taken to devolve decision making to communities—a principle of community-based co-management[14] that has yet to be realized for the majority of relevant Canadian fisheries, regardless of who fishes. Enabling co-governance and co-management for moderate livelihood fisheries should be considered a clear and necessary action toward reconciliation as well as an opportunity for the federal government to learn from Indigenous knowledge systems, values, and ethics.

While real progress has been made in improving fisheries science and management decision making, climate change is altering long understood patterns of fish population abundance and creating new conservation challenges. New species are being caught as they move further north, spawning times are changing, and warming waters threaten to alter entire ecosystems. The Gulf of St. Lawrence is warming at one of the fastest rates of any similar body of water in the world.[15] Lobster and shrimp fisheries that once thrived in the Northeast United States are in steep decline.[16]

To date, First Nations moderate livelihood fisheries have focused on species that are both high in value and easily accessible in small boats and near-shore environments. In 2022, lobster at the start of the season was sold for as much as $17.00 per pound at the wharf[17] as compared to $0.73 per pound for cod.[18] Quotas for glass eel or elver fishing have recently been allocated to First Nations for moderate livelihood fisheries, and in 2021 prices were as high as $2,250 per pound.[19]

Most fisheries are managed through quotas that are based on several factors, not the least of which is scientific advice provided by the Department of Fisheries and Oceans (DFO). Lobster fisheries are managed through effort controls including limits on the number of traps and fishing seasons. One of the impacts of the dramatic growth of lobster and crab fisheries has been increased pressure on mackerel and herring stocks, the historically dominant source of bait. While there are limited estimates of bait use, one study suggests that 1.9 pounds of bait is used for every pound of lobster harvested.[20] The use of low-cost and formerly high-volume fisheries to support high-revenue fisheries may make sense at the wharf, but the growth of the lobster fishery has meant significant pressures on bait fisheries to the point where those populations are at very low levels. After more than a decade of declining populations, in 2022 DFO closed the fisheries for Atlantic mackerel and Gulf of St. Lawrence spring-spawning herring,[21] and local bait markets are shifting to international imports.

Deep concerns about the sustainability of American eel populations and unsustainable fisheries have led to shutdowns of commercial harvesting in the state of Maine[22] and increased scrutiny on hydroelectric dams in Ontario.[23] The DFO minister must soon make a decision on the listing of American eel under SARA, given its current assessment as "threatened." American eel is considered one large population with an extensive species range from Venezuela to Greenland, and attempts to assess its overall population size have been largely unsuccessful. With redistributions of commercial quota underway to allow increased Indigenous access, assessment and management at the river level will likely continue.

As Indigenous Rights are upheld and as decisions are made about who fishes what species, with what fishing gear, and in what areas, careful consideration must be given to the impacts on future generations in Indigenous and non-Indigenous rural communities. These considerations will vary depending on the population status of the targeted species, the scale of the fishery, and the ability to account for all fishing mortality. Improved communications between Indigenous fisheries authorities and colonial management science and management decision makers will be imperative. Regardless of who is fishing, the impacts on the stocks is the same. Marine ecosystems are under increasing threats while struggling to rebuild after past abuses.

Fisheries are being reshaped to accommodate expanding Indigenous participation, but even greater changes may be happening in marine ecosystems. An industry once dominated by cod, one of the largest biomasses of any living species in the world, has been transformed in just a few decades by collapse of the stock and the continuing weak recovery. Such a radical shift could take place again as species vulnerable to climate change, such as lobster, shrimp, and crab, are impacted by a changing environment. As First Nations moderate livelihood fisheries expand, a rigorous focus on ensuring the overall sustainability of the wild populations is imperative if current and future generations are to benefit.

6.2

STRATEGIES for OVERCOMING RACISM

by FRED WIEN and JEFF DENIS

INTRODUCTION: UNDERSTANDING RACISM
AGAINST FIRST NATIONS PEOPLES HISTORICALLY

The Mi'kmaq are no strangers to experiencing racism, and in fact it has been pervasive throughout their history over the last several centuries. To address its manifestations in the current context of seeking to obtain access to fishing for a moderate livelihood, it is essential to understand the nature of the phenomenon.

Discussions of racism have typically focused on prejudice and discrimination that seizes on people's distinctive physical characteristics, such as skin colour.[1] Mi'kmaw and other First Nations people in the region have certainly experienced this type of racism, which takes the form of things like being followed in stores on the presumption that shoplifting will occur, or encountering racist graffiti in high schools, or being refused access to services. Indeed, according to a 2015–16 survey, some 15 percent of Mi'kmaw adults living on reserve in Nova Scotia said that they had personally experienced racism in the prior year.[2]

The antidote to racism that is frequently advanced is to engage people in educational and experiential initiatives to modify attitudes and behaviour. The focus of these efforts is largely at the individual level. What this model ignores is the extent to which racism directed to First Nations people has its roots in colonial history and that it has a very important collective and institutional component. It is historical in nature because incoming settlers and their governments brought with them an ideology that defined First Nations and other Indigenous Peoples as being inferior, perhaps as a way of justifying the actions that were taken to limit, control, and marginalize them, including, as we saw in a previous chapter, pushing them away from fishing as a source of livelihood. In the colonial period and even today, there are many examples of institutional racism,[3] ranging from acts of genocide by colonial authorities (e.g., putting a bounty on Mi'kmaw scalps); putting in place the Indian Act with all its impositions and controls; forcing children into residential schools; attempting to centralize Nova Scotia Mi'kmaw communities into two locations; or inequitably funding services such as education and child welfare.

With respect to fisheries, a July 2022 Senate committee report cited examples of continuing systemic racism in the federal government.[4] It describes DFO officers seizing traps and not adequately protecting Mi'kmaq harvesters during moderate livelihood fishing. A key example was the DFO minister imposing regulations on moderate livelihood fisheries without providing justification or meeting the consultation standard.

For First Nations communities, breaking out of this historically defined straitjacket is an enormous challenge. It is not surprising that their attempts to change the historical picture of inferiority and marginalization by confronting the established order lead to conflict.

UNDERSTANDING RACISM IN THE CURRENT FISHING CONTEXT

While Mi'kmaw, Wolastoqey, and other First Nations people have experienced individual acts of discrimination or racism, what was in evidence in Southwest Nova Scotia in fall 2020 was of a different order of magnitude. It was collective action, and it was violent as groups of non-Indigenous fishers blocked access on the wharves and in the water, cut traps, screamed racist insults not only to fishers but to Mi'kmaw Elders and others who had gathered in support, and trashed a fish plant.[5] In concert, local processors refused to provide bait for traps or to purchase lobster caught by the Mi'kmaq. While collective and violent, it was also not unprecedented, as similar reactions were seen on the wharves and on the waters in the immediate aftermath of the 1999 *Marshall* decision.[6] What lies behind these actions? We offer several observations.

Case study and survey data have found that support for Indigenous people is there in the Canadian public, but it doesn't go very deep, especially when more fundamental issues such as Treaty and Aboriginal Rights and their implications are brought into the picture.[7] There is ample evidence from Southwest Nova Scotia and elsewhere in the region that the issue is about this deeper level. That is, First Nations in the region, in light of the *Marshall* decision, are pushing for the implementation of their right to fish for a moderate livelihood, and non-Indigenous fishers are resisting. They are defining the issue in zero-sum terms—more access for First Nations to the resource means less for them—and they see their future being threatened if, for example, First Nations communities are allowed to be self-determining when it comes to managing their involvement in the moderate livelihood fishery.

In this context, underlying tensions are brought to the surface when a critical incident arises, such as the Sipekne'katik fishers pushing their way into St. Marys Bay in Southwest Nova Scotia. The response can quickly take a racist direction as race becomes a tool in the struggle, used by some non-Indigenous fishers to denigrate and demean those whom they see as the enemy. In that context, it doesn't matter so much who the people are—they could just be a group defined by wiggly ears—but they will be denigrated in the process as a way of excusing the actions that are taken against them. And it is an arena where the extremists take the floor, their voices amplified by the media. It doesn't help that there is fragmentation in the organizations representing non-Indigenous fishers and they are not strongly organized, meaning that it is hard for them to keep renegades under control even as some organizations have accepted in principle the *Marshall* decisions and the idea of having more Indigenous participation in the industry.

WHAT TO DO ABOUT IT

Wherever acts of racist violence occur, whether in the Maritimes, the rest of Canada, or elsewhere, there is no escaping the need for industry and community leaders to speak out against it and to control such action, wherever possible.

Another option for resolving intergroup conflicts of this nature, and one that is very popular, is to advocate for cross-cultural education, bringing people together from both groups and working on mutual understanding. Indeed, as we have seen in chapter 5.3, there are examples of this strategy being implemented and having some impact on the participants. The question is, is it enough? We submit that it is not, because they reach only a few people, and we have seen how quickly these efforts are overridden in a context where group positions and interests are at stake. It may well be that persons who were part of these cross-cultural initiatives were not themselves swept away as extremists took over, but nevertheless they were not able to mobilize an effective impediment to the racist violence that occurred.

This suggests that an effective anti-racism strategy must come to grips with the underlying tensions and issues. The fundamental issue is one of a group legitimately seeking greater participation in accessing a limited resource where exiting interests are entrenched and the struggle is defined in zero-sum terms. Strategies need to be pursued that involve measures such as making room for First Nations fishers in such a way that the livelihoods of non-Indigenous fishers are taken into consideration (e.g., government purchasing of existing licences). It also involves clarifying and obtaining acceptance of the ground rules for the fishing effort, how the moderate livelihood fishery will be managed and by whom, and how sustainability of the resource will be ensured. The answers to at least some of these questions can be addressed in higher level negotiations between federal representatives of the Crown and First Nations in the region to set the parameters,[8] but they also need to filter down and be accepted at the individual and organizational level. In short, the outstanding questions need to be answered, and trust and confidence need to be built. This means that a lot of work needs to be done at the local and regional levels through tables that bring the two sides together.

Overcoming racism also requires shifting attention from competing interests to common interests. Perhaps the most important common interest is the shared environment where both groups wish to promote conservation and deal with climate change. There are other common interests. As we have written elsewhere, for example, many owner-operator and crew workers in the inshore fishery are reaching retirement age, so expansion of First Nations involvement can help meet labour supply and intergenerational succession challenges.[9]

A focus on common interests might also lead to the realization that welcoming First Nations participation in the industry through moderate livelihood fishing has the potential to benefit the industry as a whole, rather than being seen as a threat. This has played out in a small way when First Nations fishers have joined non-Indigenous fishers who share the same wharf in making common cause against threats to their lobster. It has played out in a larger way when First Nations that become successful economically, such as Membertou, become a major source of employment and economic growth in the region of which they are a part, despite initial resistance from merchants and others who believed they would be damaged by unfair competition. This kind of dynamic is in fact a major driver of attitudinal change over time, as First Nations leadership and accomplishments become widely appreciated.

Even with an emphasis on common interests, there will still be some non-Indigenous people who feel threatened by First Nations' success and continue to perceive Treaty Rights as an unfair advantage, but not everyone needs to be convinced. If the norm shifts so that most Nova Scotians recognize the common interests and respect First Nations, it will be harder for the hard-core extremists to mobilize support for racist activities.

6.3

The CLEARWATER PURCHASE

by RYAN STACK

The purchase of Clearwater Seafoods Incorporated (Clearwater) was officially announced on November 9, 2020, causing a stir in local,[1] national,[2] and international news. The purchase involved two equal partners, each contributing 50 percent of the required money. The first partner is a First Nations coalition that includes seven Mi'kmaw communities, led by Membertou. The other participating communities are Miawpukek, Potlotek, Pictou Landing, Paqtnkek, Sipekne'katik, and We'koqma'q, who came together to form FNC Holdings Limited Partnership (FNC Holdings). The second partner is Premium Brands Holdings Corporation (Premium Brands), which owns a broad range of food brands and services more than 22,000 customers with operations throughout Canada and the United States.[3]

Under the deal, which Clearwater shareholders accepted on January 7, 2021, a company called 12385104 Canada Inc. purchased all outstanding shares of Clearwater for approximately $500 million and the company's debt, in a deal with a value of $1 billion. FNC Holdings and Premium Brands formed this company to hold the shares of Clearwater. A share acquisition allows a change in ownership while maintaining Clearwater's corporate structure and allowing continuity of operations. Existing assets, including Clearwater's fleet of ships, processing plants, licences, and technological patents, are still owned by the company, as are existing subsidiaries. Some one thousand employees continue with the company.[4] Figure 6.3.1 is a diagram showing the ownership structure. Each existing Clearwater shareholder got $8.25 per share, a 15 percent premium over the share price on the day the agreement was announced.[5]

Figure 6.3.1. Clearwater's new ownership structure

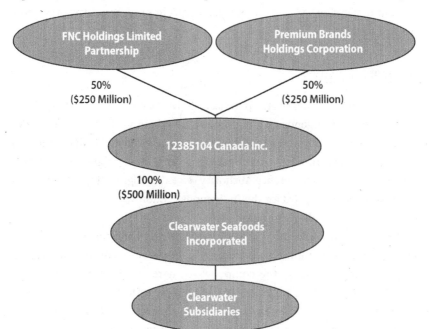

The $250 million Mi'kmaw portion of the deal was financed through a loan from the First Nations Finance Authority, a non-profit First Nations institution dedicated to the economic and social development of First Nations communities.[6] This loan was available in part due to the robust governance and strong financial and business record of Membertou since Chief Terry Paul became chief in 1984.[7] Conversely, Premium Brands raised its $250 million using existing credit, which it made available by issuing new shares to interested buyers.[8]

A key consideration for the participating Mi'kmaw communities was a desire to have a "clear pathway" to sole ownership of Clearwater.[9] Chief Terry Paul noted that several potential deals, including prior discussions with Premium Brands, had fallen apart over this issue.[10] However, the parties reached an agreement based on a shared vision for the company and the fishing industry's future in Nova Scotia. Premium Brands wanted to grow the value of Clearwater over a long time, and the stated intention of Chief Terry and the Mi'kmaq was "[to be] here to fish...until the rest of time."[11]

Under their agreement, Premium Brands and the Mi'kmaq each retained 50 percent ownership of Clearwater, with first right of refusal if the other ever wanted to sell.

IMPACT OF PURCHASE

The impact of the Clearwater purchase for the participating communities, and indeed for Indigenous communities throughout Canada and the world, is difficult to overstate. The entities involved in the deal all hailed it as a groundbreaking, transformative deal whose impact would be felt for generations.[12] First Nations Finance Authority (FNFA) recognized the purchase as "an historic step forward for the Indigenous economy,"[13] a sentiment shared by Clearwater CEO Ian Smith.[14]

Since the announcement that Clearwater was considering a sale, several Mi'kmaw communities, including Membertou, were very interested in purchasing. Likewise, the company's owners had been eager to make the Mi'kmaq a part of any sale. The communities forming FNC Holdings had worked successfully with Clearwater in the past. In 2019, for example, Clearwater signed a fifty-year partnership agreement regarding the surf clam fishery with fourteen First Nations communities in what was hailed as a "historic agreement."[15] A subsequent groundbreaking agreement was reached in September of 2020, when Clearwater sold two of its eight licences for Lobster Fishing Area (LFA) 41 to Membertou First Nation for $25 million.[16] This deal also gave Membertou access to Clearwater best practices, usage of Clearwater's sole lobster ship in LFA 41, and usage of the company's value chain to sell the catch. Through the purchase of Clearwater, the Mi'kmaw coalition would now retain the remaining six licences in the lucrative year-round fishing ground.

Critically, the Clearwater acquisition offers the opportunity to grow Indigenous employment and prosperity for the participating communities and for them to participate at a high level in the world seafood market.[17] This is evidenced through discussion of plans for lucrative licences to be migrated to the control of FNC Holdings, which would allow for commercial fishing separate from the activities of Clearwater.[18] The details of such plans remain unknown, as they are considered confidential to the three concerned parties. Although many of the communities, and Membertou in particular,[19] had many successful business ventures, the value of this acquisition and the size and complexity of Clearwater is far beyond any of their existing ventures. In their communication to Membertou, Chief Terry and the Council stressed that the acquisition was separate from normal financial operations of the community and would offer financial diversification and years of wealth for the community.[20] However, not all observers were so optimistic about the transaction, with some suggesting that the long-term debt and terms of acquisition were "totally unfair to [First Nations partners]"[21] since it may take decades before they see free cash flow from the transaction.

Although it gives them access to greater resources, infrastructure, and capabilities, it was also recognized that any Clearwater acquisitions were separate and distinct from Mi'kmaw involvement with either the inshore or treaty-based moderate livelihood fishery.[22] However, the role of Clearwater as a buyer and processor of catch from inshore fishing also provides the opportunity to buy from inshore Mi'kmaw fishers. It remains to be seen how the participating communities' relationship with Clearwater might function with rules restricting "controlling agreements" between companies and fishers.

Finally, the acquisition serves as an example for other First Nations groups to follow toward economic prosperity. Chief Terry and the other community partners expressed the desire to help other First Nations follow the same path to become major participants in the commercial economy.[23] It is the vision of Chief Terry and the other partners to see Mi'kmaq at every level of the company, "from the decks of the ships and the floor of the factory, all the way up to the boardroom."[24]

A MI'KMAQ NATION APPROACH
CONVERSATIONS WITH MI'KMAW LEADERS

~~

by L. JANE MCMILLAN and FRED WIEN

O n October 25, 2021, Jane McMillan and Fred Wien had a virtual conversation with Senator Dan Christmas and Assembly of First Nations Regional Vice-Chief P. J. Prosper about possible directions for going forward with the Treaty Right to fish for a moderate livelihood. Grand Chief Norman Sylliboy also took in the conversation and subsequently issued a statement on behalf of the Mi'kmaq Grand Council summarizing its position. This statement is reproduced below.

Jane McMillan also spoke with Jaime Battiste, the Member of Parliament for Sydney-Victoria. The leaders made clear that they were not speaking for their organizations or for the elected Chiefs. Rather, they were giving their own views, many of which had already been made public. The exception to this is Grand Chief Norman Sylliboy's address, which has been approved by the Mi'kmaq Grand Council.

One of the ideas that has been put forward by Senator Dan Christmas (from Nova Scotia), Senator Brian Francis (from PEI), and Nova Scotia MP Jaime Battiste has to do with the possible creation of an Atlantic First Nations Fishing Authority. We begin with this, followed by a discussion of whether the time was right for establishing one or more dialogue tables with non-Indigenous fishers and their organizations as a way to increase understanding and reduce tensions. An additional segment deals with the purchase of Clearwater by a consortium of First Nations from the region. We conclude with the statement from the Grand Chief.

THE IDEA OF AN ATLANTIC FIRST NATION FISHING AUTHORITY

Dan Christmas: A major concern we have with the current situation is that the way things are going, we would probably end up abiding by all of DFO's laws and regulations, subject to their Conservation and Protection Division (C&P). Our conclusion is that the oppression will go on. They already have that control over commercial licences in that a number of Mi'kmaw communities have communal or commercial licences that fall under their control. We have the food ceremonial fishery that's already regulated by DFO. It falls under C&P. And if all things were allowed to continue to go in that direction, then the moderate livelihood fishery would fall in that same path and DFO would take 100 percent of the governance and management. Of course, a question we asked ourselves is, is that where we want to go as Mi'kmaq, is that consistent with Mi'kmaq Aboriginal and Treaty Rights?

DFO strongly believes that recent court decisions give them the ultimate governance and control and management of any Indigenous fishery in Canada. Of course, that's in total contradiction to what we believe. So, we began throwing out this idea of how Mi'kmaq can begin to exercise governance over their own fishery, be it food/social/ceremonial, or communal-commercial, or moderate livelihood. And the example that popped to mind is Mi'kmaw Kina'matnewey, a kind of Mi'kmaw school board or education authority for Nova Scotia. Back in 1997, I think it was, there were nine First Nations from Nova Scotia who signed a self-government education agreement with the Government of Canada. I think the Province of Nova Scotia was also part of it. And the organization was formed and here we are, some twenty-five years later. And I think all of us can say that the results of that self-government agreement have been beyond expectations; they've been phenomenal.

We went from 25 percent graduation rate from high school back in the mid-'90s, and now we're into the 90 percent range. I think we're even exceeding the provincial graduation rates. That governance control primarily over our schools in our communities has had a dramatic impact. Now we're having the first two generations come out of that system, and they have flooded our universities and community colleges, and many of them have gone on to be professionals and are having an impact. So it was that example that really, for us, became the model. We say, well yes, if Mi'kmaq are given the tools and the responsibilities to govern ourselves in a particular sector, we've usually found success. And so we began thinking, how can we apply that to the fishery be it food/social/ceremonial, communal-commercial, or moderate livelihood?

And around the same time as we were talking about this, the Atlantic Policy Congress announced that they were creating an Atlantic First Nations Water Authority. With examples such as these, we finally came up with the idea that maybe the best way to go forward collectively is to seek the full exercise of our Aboriginal Right, our inherent right to govern ourselves, especially in an area such as fishing where it's very clear that we've done it since pre-colonial times. And so we brought forward the idea to both federal ministers of forming the Atlantic First Nations Fishing Authority.

Question: *What would the Fishing Authority do?*

DC: I think the biggest need at that time, it may still be, was the need to create fishing plans. And the capacity within the Mi'kmaq to do that, or the Maliseet [Wolastoqiyik] for that matter, was somewhat limited. We had a few people that could do it but not enough. And so we thought that the first main responsibility was to work with all Mi'kmaw and Maliseet [Wolastoqey] First Nations to help develop and grow the capacity of doing moderate livelihood fishing plans. The second need, of course, was that once the plans were developed, you would need to discuss and perhaps negotiate them with government. We needed people to interface with Fisheries and Oceans and other parts of government.

Thirdly, assuming that the plans are approved by everybody, once people begin to go out on the water, we would need to be able to verify that the plans are being upheld. So we started thinking, yes, we probably need fish monitors and vessels and need to make sure that the catches are done according to the Mi'kmaw principle of *Netukulimk*. We would have fish monitors to ensure that principle was being followed.

And then the last idea, of course, was the need for protection. At the time, the incidents themselves were very fresh in our minds, when our vessels were going out on the water basically without any protection either from C&P [DFO's Conservation and Protection Officers], from DFO, or even the RCMP. They were basically sent out at the mercy of those who saw them as vulnerable and were willing to cut their traps and burn their vessels and other things.

So, we introduced the notion of having our own Mi'kmaw protectors on board vessels, and this would be the parallel to today's Guardians or DFO's fisheries officers, but we saw them as basically protectors for the Mi'kmaq. So that's how we began to put together the initial concept of an Atlantic First Nations Fishing Authority.

Q: *How has the idea of a First Nations Fishing Authority been received?*

DC: We explained the concept to both the Minister of Indigenous Services and the Minister for Crown–Indigenous Relations. I think they saw a couple of benefits. For one, I think they saw that, for once, the government didn't have to be involved in day-to-day micromanagement of our vessels and our crews and our catches and our fish. This would be done by an arm's-length organization, by the Mi'kmaq. I think they saw that as a positive because they knew that the risk and the threat of violence between DFO and Mi'kmaq and between non-Indigenous fishers and the Mi'kmaq was quite high. This would provide another level of governance that would deal directly with the Mi'kmaq.

They also liked the idea, of course, of doing excellent harvesting plans and to have the expertise within the Mi'kmaw community to be able to do that. We argued that this is the next level beyond *Marshall*. *Marshall* was a Treaty Right to trade fish. And now we're talking about an inherent Aboriginal Right to govern the management of the fishery. This was a whole different box, and it fell within the box of Crown–Indigenous Relations [CIRNA], not DFO. How we left it was that if other First Nations Chiefs felt this was something to be considered, and if there were resolutions, if there were motions from the various organizations in PEI, Nova Scotia, New Brunswick, and Quebec, if they supported the idea, and that was the big if, then DFO and CIRNA would definitely consider it.

But then we got short-circuited. You may remember back in March 2021, DFO announced without any warning that they were introducing a "new path" policy, and once that happened, then this whole topic of the Atlantic First Nations [Fishing] Authority was basically superseded and set aside. So, we haven't talked about it since, but I still believe that once we get over this current bump of Moderate Livelihood, we still basically have the same problems.

One is basically a problem of capacity; one is basically an issue of communities wanting and desiring and needing to manage their own harvesting activities; and we still need some kind of method of dealing with government and non-Indigenous fishers. So, I still think the idea is valid. I still think the idea is worth discussing. And I think the government is still interested. But it's pretty clear now that the ball is in the First Nations' court, and we haven't pushed it very much further.

J. P. Prosper: I always admire people wanting to be innovative and solution-oriented and to take brave steps. What I find, though, is that anybody who takes a step involving the fishery—whether it's food, social, ceremonial, or moderate livelihood—it is a brave step because the environment is always shifting and volatile at times.

Because there is little movement at the negotiating table, you do have, you know, bands taking the initiative. Look at Potlotek, for example, one of the first to take the bull by the horns and say, "Well, we're going to develop our own fish management plan with the support of KMKNO [Kwilmu'kw Maw-klusuaqn Negotiation Office] and administer this fishery ourselves." You look at Sipekne'katik, you look at Listuguj, you look at the consortium of bands within Kespukwitk who have come out with their district plan, and you have a mixture of various approaches that have been developed.

I like the idea of the authority. I think there's a distinct need to have a role in terms of bringing people together—First Nations Mi'kmaw groups, Wolastoqey groups within the region—to just bring information together and share that information and try to look for common ground. Also, there are benefits to non-Mi'kmaw fishers and government as well.

THE IDEA OF ESTABLISHING DIALOGUE TABLES

Another issue that we asked the leaders to address is the extent to which there should be communication with the non-Indigenous fishing sector. This would not involve sitting down at a dialogue table to negotiate rights or establish seasons, which are matters for a Crown–Indigenous Relations table. Rather, it would be a forum basically for understanding where different people are coming from; how the Mi'kmaq understand Moderate Livelihood; the history of the two communities, which are often misunderstood; or what the experts have to say about the sustainability of the resource. It might be a way of diffusing tensions, because at the end of the day, people are by and large fishing from the same harbours, they're in the same waters, and their children often go to the same schools. We have seen how quickly tensions can flare up even when there have been many years of effort to create understanding.

DC: That [i.e., dialogue tables] was an important topic when Allister Surette, the Special Federal Representative, issued his report, and he certainly recommended that. But I think one of the drawbacks from the Surette Report is that he had very little discussion with First Nations leaders. It was the perception that really Allister Surette was representing the non-Indigenous fishers. But it's an interesting—at least, this is my point of view—it's an interesting power imbalance that's happening. And it strikes me that the Mi'kmaq and Maliseet [Wolastoqiyik] have the upper hand. They have a court case in their favour, they have a Treaty Right, and they have a claim on the fishery that no one else has. And on top of that the government is working directly with them, and that's their mandate. They have negotiators working out plans, you know, be it FSC [food, social, ceremonial], or be it communal-commercial, or be it moderate livelihood.

There's a direct link between the federal government and Mi'kmaq and Maliseet [Wolastoqiyik], and I think that has created a lot of animosity with the fishermen's group. They don't like being left out. They say this is their livelihood too, and they don't know what's going on. They don't hear from the government, and they definitely don't hear from the Mi'kmaq and Maliseet [Wolastoqiyik], so they feel they're definitely in the dark.

And of course, when that happens you have a situation where they can basically generate their own truth or beliefs about what's happening. And so, I think the lack of information has really put non-Indigenous fishers, especially their representative organizations, in a tough spot. They are supposed to represent them, yet they have to tell their membership, "We don't know. We don't know what's going on at the government table. And we don't know what the First Nations fishers are thinking."

All they know is what they see in social media or the paper or from news media. So, we have a situation now that's strange, really. You have a federal–First Nations relationship that's obviously been active, and it has produced some results, and you have non-Indigenous fishers and their organizations working with the federal government. More recently, the federal government [DFO] has put on a series of workshops, which in part attempted to explain the treaties and Moderate Livelihood. So, you've had that happening from the government to non-Indigenous fishers, but you had very little between non-Indigenous and Mi'kmaw fishers. On the Mi'kmaw side, I think they would prefer if they can get the treaty-related issues resolved with government first before they talk to non-Indigenous fishers.

Some non-Indigenous fishers want to have a role in prescribing the Treaty Right, which they have no right to do—for instance, the whole issue of fishing out of season. Non-Indigenous fishers have drawn a line in the sand, basically saying they will not accept any out-of-season fishery. Of course, the Mi'kmaq always questioned that. So we're stuck in a knot, and how you untie the knot is the question. I think the first trick is to get some agreement with DFO. The district approach outlined by First Nations in Kespukwitk may be a great opportunity. Once the agreement is in place, maybe there's a model to be followed down the South Shore, one which non-Indigenous fishing organizations have spoken about in positive terms.

Once agreements are made between representatives of First Nations and the Crown, then, yes, I think those First Nations would turn their attention to their neighbours and say, well, how do we implement this without having boats burned, traps cut, and things like that? So, I think the agreements have to come first, and then secondly, maybe then the tables with the non-Indigenous sector will happen. There is still a long way to go. I can tell you from the Mi'kmaw side, when they look at non-Indigenous fishers, the first ones they see are the radicals, right? And there's a few really, I mean, hothead, redneck radicals who are always in the media, that always capture the media's attention, which just inflames the situation. There are some chiefs that will not meet with certain non-Indigenous fishers' organizations. They just will not, and there's good reason for that—they are so racist or so violent that there's no hope of dealing with them.

But that doesn't describe the whole fishery, and I've come across a number of non-Indigenous fishers who have worked a long time with First Nations, like those that worked with Elsipogtog or those who worked with the ones in PEI, and they have great relations. They respect the fishery, they respect the [Aboriginal] Right, and those relationships are intact. There are some who are more moderate, who are more open-minded, who are willing to talk about things, even the difficult things. And then there are some who are even willing to say that their non-Indigenous brothers have really messed things up, and they're willing to come to the table with some ideas on how to change that. So, there are some people who I think can work well in a dialogue table, and there are others who cannot.

And so I think to go forward is to meet with the moderates when the time is right, once we've gotten over the mountain with DFO and government. And then once we have some agreements, then meet with the non-Indigenous fisheries about that.

THE CLEARWATER PURCHASE

DC: Now there's a second big problem, nothing to do with moderate livelihood fishery, it deals with Clearwater. And for the longest time the small inshore fishermen, the lobster fishermen, have always viewed big industry as trying to buy up all of the inshore fishery and trying to control all the licences, all the quotas, and basically put them out of business. This is sometimes referred to as vertical integration. And there's good reason to believe that. I mean there are so many ghost agreements and so on. To address this concern, some years ago the government developed a policy called PIIFCAF—I forget now what that acronym means—but it's basically designed to introduce a firewall between big industry and the small inshore fishermen. It's intended to support the independence of the inshore fishermen with respect to their quotas and their catches and their sales, and to make sure big industry never buys-out inshore.

A couple of years ago this policy became part of the Fisheries Act, and the inshore industry was really pleased with that, that they finally had laws and protection for any potential takeover or buyout or any underhanded agreement to take over their livelihood on the inshore. The one big villain in all this, of course, was Clearwater. They figured Clearwater was still a big threat to the inshore even with PIIFCAF, even with the amendments to the Fisheries Act. And then some First Nations [bought] Clearwater, and the industry went crazy. Non-Indigenous tried to interfere and stop the transfer process, making it really difficult and painful. They said, "Well for sure now big industry is going to take over the inshore because now the Mi'kmaq run it."

So that's the other big issue that we have at play. Basically First Nations own Clearwater, and once again they view First Nations as the de facto enemy for the future of their industry. So it's not just Moderate Livelihood, it's now who manages and controls the main commercial fishing industry in the Atlantic. And I can tell you, those fisherman organizations are really afraid, are really worried about their futures.

A CONVERSATION WITH JAIME BATTISTE, MEMBER OF PARLIAMENT

Jane McMillan spoke with Member of Parliament Jaime Battiste on October 27, 2021, and offers the following summary of his comments:

He spoke positively about the emergence of regional or district fishing agreements, suggesting that they could be a step in the direction of establishing a First Nations Fishing Authority. He also mentioned the number of younger Mi'kmaq who are interested in taking part in the lobster fishery, but there are significant obstacles facing them, not the least being the rising price of gear, vessels, and licences. Communities are also facing challenges in developing and being able to enforce moderate livelihood fishing plans. One area of tension is between those who see the Treaty Right as an individual right, as opposed to those who deem it to be a collective right. Opposition from non-Indigenous fishing associations is also an issue, with some refusing to recognize the Treaty Right, or promoting misinformation

about it. He believes either that the Mi'kmaq need to develop their own fishing associations or have an equal and respected place in existing associations. And if dialogue is to be promoted across the divide, it would be better
if it were coordinated from a university, rather than a government, setting.

An Address to all Ul'nu's (Mi'kmaq) from the Mi'kmaq Grand Chief, Kji-
Saqmaw Norman Sylliboy, and the Grand Council, Santé Mawiomi, repre-
senting the seven districts of Mi'kma'ki, Land of the Mi'kmaq

As you know, the Grand Council encompasses seven districts in Atlantic
Canada, all of Mi'kma'ki. We want to see a unified plan that would serve
all of our districts. These plans have to respect our inherent rights to
fishing and trade as protected in the treaties with King George. The big
issue we see concerning the plan is to ensure that any plan does not put a
price tag or limit on the Mi'kmaw fishing effort, as pricing in the fishing
industry fluctuates. And the other big issue is that we don't want to see a
timeline around the development and implementation of the plan. Time
frames have to withstand the test of time. And we want our plan to be
safe and very conservative for everybody.

And this plan has to be the best one available at this time; it has to be
better. As you know, any Mi'kmaw plan will be micromanaged by all the
government levels. And this is what we said as Mi'kmaq, that we'd been
denied our way of life for over five hundred years, and now our oppres-
sors want to regulate still our way to exercise our rights to fish. It is the
Grand Council's position that we do it our way, developing our plans and
self-determining. Because of years of divide and conquer, the biggest
challenge we have is that everything is divided by province, whereas the
Grand Council seeks to speak for all seven districts of families of the
Mi'kmaw Nation.

This plan is going to be a very big challenge for the government
because they're not structured like the Grand Council. We were the

Grand Council before the arrival of Europeans; we still have the same territory. And the sad thing is that in the middle of the COVID-19 pandemic, no one was able to meet. A lot of communities and families were suffering; the government was trying to fragment our constitutional right to fish and focus on regulating or buying into the Moderate Livelihood issue by offering some money when the communities were not making any money, nothing was coming in. That was a very challenging time in Mi'kma'ki.

It's going to be challenging to come to a unified position as, right now, the Government of Canada is not unified or attempting to reconcile with our constitutional right to fish. The provincial laws regulating the fisheries are not unified or consistent with our constitutional rights or the rule of law. The Mi'kmaw Chiefs are not unified across all the districts. The Chiefs and their administration on reserves do not have jurisdiction over the off-reserve natural resources. They have jurisdiction over the reserves but not Mi'kmaq on the rivers and ocean. The Mi'kmaw jurisdiction over the treaty fishery is vested in Grand Council, but Canada and the provinces keep denying and avoiding these jurisdictional issues. Our attempts at Treaty Day events to pull them together are tricky. I want our Nation to be strong and unified. And that's the challenge I face.

Wela'lioq,
Kji-Saqmaw Norman Sylliboy Sr.

CONCLUSION
FLASHPOINTS AND POSSIBLE PATHWAYS

by FRED WIEN and RICK WILLIAMS

The idea for this collection of articles took shape in the immediate aftermath of the events in Southwest Nova Scotia in the fall of 2020, when Mi'kmaw harvesters began a push for greater access to the lobster fishery under the *Marshall* decision pertaining to the Treaty Right to fish for a moderate livelihood. They were met with strong resistance, which, in the extreme cases, took the form of violence and racism that garnered national headlines. As we spoke with community leaders and ordinary Nova Scotians, a need for public education and for strategies to address the deeper issues became evident. As the book took shape, our goals were to describe the development of First Nations fisheries in the Maritimes following the Supreme Court's 1999 *Marshall* decisions; to provide wider contextual information on the commercial fishery in the region; and to share a wide range of perspectives from First Nations, commercial fish harvester groups, and other informed observers regarding current fishing rights challenges. We also hoped that some ideas would emerge about how the issues might be resolved with peace and justice.

Below we draw out what we see as the important themes, the unresolved flashpoints, and possible future directions from the different perspectives and interests that have been represented in the book.

A DEEP DIVIDE

In situations where groups, communities, or even nations disagree, the parties most often are contesting a clearly defined issue or competing for control of the same asset or resource. It is easy to frame the implementation of the *Marshall* rulings as this kind of dispute, to eventually be resolved by some new sharing arrangement for the fishery that is acceptable to all sides. In the early years after the Supreme Court's decisions, the Department of Fisheries and Oceans (DFO) took just this approach, with the fast-track negotiation of interim agreements and the investment of hundreds of millions of dollars to transfer licences and quota and build fishing capacity in First Nations communities. The goal was to give First Nations communities some agreed upon "fair share" of the existing commercial fishery, while negotiations would continue on a separate track to clarify and implement self-government rights and the practical interpretation of "moderate livelihoods." Those negotiations have not advanced, while significant progress has been made in developing communal-commercial fisheries as described in chapter 1.2.

Leaders representing non-Indigenous harvesters followed the DFO approach, expressing an openness to First Nations receiving more commercial fishing licences and quota up to some proportion reflective of the regional population. Many expect that at some point in the future there will be a Supreme Court ruling that will definitively establish the practical meaning and limits of moderate livelihood and self-government rights, or that the government will impose a clear ruling on matters such as these that will survive court challenges.

Close attention to the Indigenous voices and perspectives shared in this book, however, reveals that First Nations communities aspire to more than some notionally fair share of the existing commercial fishery and a stronger voice in a management system in which they are just one group of stakeholders. While they acknowledge the significant benefits derived from recently acquired licences and quotas and from training and capacity-building programs, it is not their only or ultimate goal to be integrated into a commercial fishery in which their future development will always depend on the agreement or perhaps charity of the non-Indigenous majority, subject to fishing parameters defined by DFO.

Rather, First Nations leaders have long interpreted their Aboriginal and Treaty Rights to mean they should have and control their own fishery under self-government. This vision of a rights-based fishery is holistic and self-defining. As it evolves it will include a governance system to set rules and oversee management planning; capacities to integrate scientific evidence with Traditional Knowledge to guide fishing plans; their own Guardians to monitor fisheries and enforce rules; and vessels, gear, and fishing methods that are affordable and easily adapted to community capacities and lifestyles.

STATEMENT BY ASSEMBLY OF NOVA SCOTIA MI'KMAW CHIEFS

Canada emphasizes a commitment to "Nation-to-Nation" discussions, yet DFO continues to assert dominance over our Nation, making announcements and decisions, leaving no room for discussion or consultation. This is negligent of promises of working Nation-to-Nation, rights affirmation, reconciliation, and is in complete disregard of our governance and leadership.

—March 4, 2021

The disagreement is fundamental. Commercial harvester groups are saying, "You are welcome to participate in the fishery as long as you fish in our seasons, follow our rules, and are policed by our officials" and "We welcome you to send representatives to participate in the governance of the fishery at our advisory committee." First Nations voices reply, "We may make accommodations for now, but we will never accept your right to limit our access to the fishery or regulate our fishing activities."

This clash over aspirations and rights creates legal, political, and policy challenges for government. The *Marshall* First Nations have constitutional and legal leverage to expand their self-government rights and fisheries access through Nation-to-Nation negotiations, while commercial fisheries groups are powerful partners in the existing management system and have local political influence as evidenced in the 2021 federal election when the then-Minister of Fisheries and Oceans, Bernadette Jordan, lost her seat in Southwest Nova Scotia because of these issues. Over the past few years, we see the federal government, with or without extensive consultations, coming down sometimes on one side and sometimes the other, and relying on short- to medium-term interim agreements with First Nations to defuse situations and manage the pressures.

FUTURE CHALLENGES

Given the current impasse, there is significant potential for tensions to continue to escalate as First Nations communities build capacities and push for greater access under expanded self-government, and non-Indigenous groups react with increasing anxiety to changes in which they feel they have had no say and to perceived threats to their livelihoods and communities.

> **TESTIMONY TO HOUSE OF COMMONS FISHERIES COMMITTEE**
>
> *We are told repeatedly that we really don't have a place, that this is government to government.... [W]e have to know where we will fit.... We need to find a place where we can understand what is being discussed about us, yet without us.... Presently, because we don't know any of this, we don't understand what the future holds for us.*
> —Melanie Sonnenberg, President, Canadian
> Independent Fish Harvesters Federation

We encourage readers to think carefully about the risks for everyone as this situation evolves. A progressive escalation of tensions between Indigenous and non-Indigenous communities could threaten two huge assets that everyone depends on: a fragile fisheries resource base and the pristine brand of our seafood products in global markets.

The fall of 2020 saw the beginnings of an industry-wide crisis driven by a national media narrative centred on greedy non-Indigenous fish harvesters and racial violence. This spurred serious talk of international boycotts of Nova Scotia lobster. Commentators recalled the violent upheavals in the Miramichi and Burnt Church area twenty years earlier to convey how bad things could get. We should ask whether it serves anyone's interest to risk having our fishery gain an international reputation for resource battles and racial acrimony.

There may be people on both sides who are prepared to take these risks, thinking perhaps they can somehow, someday, prevail as clear winners. They should consider how unlikely it is that either community will ever passively accept a surrender of their rights or the loss of their place in the fishery, or that government will ever put itself in the position of picking out-right winners and losers. We again must ask whether escalating controversy and the resulting economic instability are to anyone's advantage.

We should also bear in mind that across the region, Indigenous and non-Indigenous communities live side by side along the coast: children go to the same schools, people work and play sports together, and fish harvesters sail out of the same ports to fish adjacent grounds. These everyday interactions are not always convivial, and racial friction is an ever-present risk, but are people in all these communities really prepared to see these tensions amplified and everyone's everyday life made even more difficult and stressful?

Escalating conflict must not be the only possible future. We believe that, with wise leadership and appropriate government supports, these diverse communities can find ways to live with their differences, manage conflicts, build strong and sustainable fishing economies, and make meaningful prog-ress toward genuine reconciliation.

CRITICAL ISSUES AND FAULT LINES

Leaders from the different communities who set out to lower tensions and work together on solutions will face serious challenges. We briefly describe here the critical flashpoints that will need to be managed or mitigated if conflict is to be avoided and progress is to be made toward reconciliation and building a fishery that is stronger for everyone.

Interpretation of the Moderate Livelihood Right

A critical area of disagreement between *Marshall* First Nations and non-Indigenous harvester groups is the interpretation of the Supreme Court's language on the right to a moderate livelihood fishery. In its first ruling, the Court affirmed that "the Mi'kmaq, Wolastoqey, and Peskotomuhkati of Atlantic Canada have a treaty right to hunt, fish, and gather to earn a moderate livelihood." Under pressure to further clarify these rights, the Court issued a second ruling with the following language:

> The federal and provincial governments have the authority within their respective legislative fields to regulate the exercise of a treaty right where justified on conservation *or other grounds*.... The paramount regulatory objective is conservation and responsibility for it is placed squarely on the minister responsible and not on the aboriginal or nonaboriginal users of the resource. The regulatory authority extends to other *compelling and substantial public objectives which may include economic and regional fairness, and recognition of the historical reliance upon, and participation in, the fishery by non-aboriginal groups.* Aboriginal people are entitled to be consulted about limitations on the exercise of treaty and aboriginal rights. The Minister has available for regulatory purposes the full range of resource management tools and techniques, provided their use to limit the exercise of a treaty right can be justified on *conservation or other grounds* [emphasis added].[1]

This and other language in the rulings left room for divergent interpretations. Within the wider context of constitutional provisions and Court rulings on Aboriginal and Treaty Rights, the *Marshall* First Nations claim the right to develop self-regulated moderate livelihood fisheries independent of existing commercial fisheries. Indigenous leaders argue that advances in the development of communal-commercial fisheries are important but do not take the place of, or satisfy the requirements for, a self-regulated moderate livelihood fishery in which many more of their community members can participate on their own terms.

In contrast, leaders in the commercial fishery, along with DFO ministers and senior DFO officials, see the rapid development of communal-commercial fisheries since 1999 as directly addressing the moderate livelihood right through the generation of jobs, incomes, and revenue flows to raise community living standards. Commercial harvesters also argue that "compelling substantial public objectives" require the federal government to maintain a single, integrated regulatory system to protect a common resource and maintain orderly fisheries management. The lack of clarity on self-governance rights, they argue, could generate chaos with thirty-five

Marshall First Nations potentially each having its own fisheries management regime with different seasons and regulatory standards.

In their review of the Supreme Court's *Marshall* rulings in chapter 3.2, the McInnes-Cooper lawyers Jeffery Callaghan, Lucia Westin, and Dan Vanclieaf conclude with the following comment: "One thing remains clear: there's further work to do for all parties to agree on just what an Indigenous moderate livelihood looks like and how an Indigenous moderate livelihood fishery can be implemented in Atlantic Canada. These questions will continue to define the relationship between Indigenous communities in Atlantic Canada and the federal government."

Consultation rights

Supreme Court rulings on Aboriginal Rights and the *Marshall* case have determined that the continuing development of First Nations fisheries will be pursued through Nation-to-Nation negotiations. Aboriginal and Treaty Rights are, by their nature, bilateral links between the Crown and Indigenous Peoples, and court rulings and the honour of the Crown place the onus on government to bring non-Indigenous interests into conformity with Nation-to-Nation agreements.

As described in chapter 3.3, Supreme Court decisions require government to provide clear justifications for actions that infringe on Treaty Rights and impose on government a duty to consult before making any such decisions.[2] First Nations leaders in the region maintain that DFO officials have a blind spot and act as though they are not subject to the rules as set out in *Sparrow* (1991), *Badger* (1996), and other Supreme Court judgments. A case in point was DFO Minister Jordan's unilateral "new path" proclamation in March of 2021 setting out new rules on how First Nations moderate livelihood fishing would be regulated.[3] There was no consultation with First Nations leaders nor any attempt to justify the infringements that were imposed.

For commercial harvesters, this runs counter to the collaborative culture that has evolved within DFO's co-management regime over the past forty years. The federal government has always consulted the fishing industry on international agreements, environmental and climate policies, and resource management policy and regulatory changes that affect their livelihoods and the industry as a whole. To not be consulted on Indigenous fisheries issues that could impact their businesses and communities, and not have transparency in such decision making, runs counter to established practices and expectations.

This is a dynamic situation that holds potential for constant tension and policy gridlock. While commercial harvesters may fear they have no say in such decisions, we have seen them exercise significant leverage over fisheries management and political decision making in the recent past. This has led First Nations leaders to criticize DFO for not meeting the duty-to-consult standard when making decisions that they see as concessions to non-Indigenous interests.

Enforcement issues

The lack of trust in the effectiveness and fairness of DFO fisheries officers and First Nations Guardians in enforcing fisheries regulations is a critical issue for both Indigenous and non-Indigenous fish harvesters.

Indigenous harvesters accuse DFO fisheries officers of not working in collaboration with their communities, not protecting them from harassment by non-Indigenous harvesters on the wharves and at sea, and applying different standards in their treatment of different harvester groups.

Non-Indigenous harvesters in some regions are convinced that neither DFO officers nor First Nations Guardians are effectively enforcing fisheries agreements and regulations in First Nations fisheries. The major concern is the food, social, and ceremonial fishery where commercial harvesters believe significant amounts of lobster, eels, salmon, and perhaps other FSC fish are being caught and sold illegally.

Until ways are found to build greater trust in all fisheries surveillance and enforcement systems in both commercial and FSC fisheries, it will be very difficult to develop collaborative relations and innovative solutions.

Scale and ease of access to fish harvesting

As discussed in other chapters, DFO fisheries managers and non-Indigenous harvester groups have approached the development of First Nations fisheries largely in terms of expanded participation in commercial fisheries under the existing policy and regulatory regime. Along with rights issues, however, there are other reasons why First Nations leaders are now choosing to develop separate moderate livelihood fisheries. In many First Nations there are more community members who want to be able to catch and sell fish from local waters than the licences held in their current communal-commercial fisheries can accommodate.

Many community members may want to fish but do not have the skills and experience to "jump in the deep end" of fishing with larger vessels using complex and costly fishing gear. However, fishing for lobster, salmon, and eels can be done in sheltered coastal waters and rivers with relatively simple equipment and limited capital costs while generating strong financial returns. Small-scale and occasional fishing activities could make it possible for more Indigenous individuals to get involved in fishing at affordable costs and in ways that accord with lifestyles and limited knowledge and skills. This level of fishing activity may also provide entry points to careers as professional fish harvesters within communal-commercial or regular commercial fisheries.

Non-Indigenous harvester groups see such proposals for informal, small-scale harvesting as contrary to the existing management culture in which all fishing activity is subject to effort controls, limited seasons, training standards, and other regulations. Even sports fishing in freshwater lakes and streams is subject to government licensing, catch limits, and catch-and-release rules. The idea of free and open fishing by First Nations communities throughout the year will almost certainly raise concerns about stock conservation and orderly management and be a source of interpersonal friction in local communities.

Special challenges in the lobster fishery

As discussed in chapter 2.1, the lobster fishery is the dominant sector within the fishery economy and is the most important source of employment, incomes, and enterprise viability for both non-Indigenous harvesters and First Nations. It is also perhaps the fishery where new entrants can most readily gain a foothold in the industry because it can be conducted in safer near-shore waters with relatively affordable vessels and gear.

However, the unique ways the lobster fishery is regulated and conducted create significant barriers for Indigenous new entrants. In an open competitive fishery without individual quota shares, any new entrants on any local fishing ground create more competition for the limited population of legal-sized lobsters that can be sustainably harvested each season. Even if a First

Nation purchases a licence and fishes it out of the same community, they must navigate the unwritten rules, built up over generations, that govern how harvesters regulate their competition on the water.

Even without any issue of racial enmity, the integration of new-entrant Indigenous harvesters into the lobster fishery will inevitably be complex and difficult. A lack of respectful communication and collaboration between communities and harvester groups compounds these challenges significantly.

Leadership constraints

Efforts to build relations among Indigenous and non-Indigenous fisheries interests and to plan and implement coherent strategies and binding agreements are complicated in parts of the Maritimes by the fragmentation of leadership structures and capacities.

In the lobster fishery in Southwest Nova Scotia, there are several small organizations representing commercial harvesters. However, unlike harvesters in four other regions of the province, none are certified under provincial legislation and therefore cannot collect mandatory dues from the three thousand or more captains and crew they claim to represent, nor can they sign agreements that would be legally binding on their members. The lobster industry in that region generated some $700 million in landed value in 2021, and yet there is no formally constituted body that can speak for and make agreements on behalf of the sector.[4] The same is generally true for commercial harvesters at the provincial level in Nova Scotia and New Brunswick.[5] In New Brunswick the Maritime Fishermen's Union is certified under provincial legislation to represent enterprise owners in the northeast and southeast regions, while the southwest region has voluntary local associations. Only PEI has a province-wide organization set up under provincial legislation to represent inshore harvesters.

For First Nations there are provincial and regional organizations and ad hoc groups representing different clusters of Nations on different issues in different contexts. On a regional basis the Atlantic Policy Congress (APC) of First Nations Chiefs has significant capacities to support fisheries development and has been a leading First Nations voice in developing fishing capacity in the two decades since *Marshall* (see chapter 1.4 by John Paul and Joseph Quesnel). As it says on its website, "The APC Fisheries and

Integrated Resources Department is responsible for research, analysis, and development of policy alternatives and programs for all aspects of fisheries for our member communities.... Our work includes supporting the commercial communal fisheries operations of member communities and fostering long-term collaboration and management with communities and First Nation organizations on fisheries issues."[6]

The Ulnooweg Development Group is another Atlantic region Indigenous organization that is active on fisheries matters. Ulnooweg's Fisheries Development Business Team works with the APC to support business development in the fisheries field, and the two organizations partnered with DFO to develop and implement the Atlantic Integrated Commercial Fisheries Initiative as described in chapter 1.2.

The Kwilmu'kw Maw-klusuaqn, known by the abbreviation KMK, works to support consultations and negotiations with the federal government on the recognition and implementation of Aboriginal and Treaty Rights and other matters.[7] It has helped develop fisheries agreements between DFO and individual Nations and also groups of Nations. It acts on behalf of Mi'kmaw communities whose Chiefs form the Assembly of Nova Scotia Mi'kmaw Chiefs and brings together the fisheries directors from those communities. However, not all Mi'kmaw communities in Nova Scotia are members of the Assembly or KMK, making it more difficult to achieve coordinated action.

There are umbrella organizations representing First Nations in each province—sometimes more than one—and these are often active on fisheries issues with special committees and working groups. However, none of these organizations has authority to speak for, or negotiate on behalf of, individual Nations unless specifically mandated to do so. Most interim agreements with DFO are reached bilaterally with individual Nations, although a recent Rights Reconciliation Agreement was developed with two large communities, Elsipogtog and Esgenoôpetitj in New Brunswick, and in Nova Scotia the 2021 Kespukwitk Netukulimk Livelihood Fisheries Plan was set up with four Nations in Southwest Nova Scotia.

In general, however, it can be said that, for both commercial harvesters and First Nations, the lack of lead organizations with clear mandates to represent their communities in broader, longer-term planning and consultation processes makes it more difficult to develop First Nations fisheries in harmony with other sectors. This lack of clearly delineated governance is also a drawback if immediate action is needed in a crisis management situation.

Racism

All the major organizations representing non-Indigenous commercial harvesters have made strong statements condemning racist attitudes and behaviour. To our knowledge, however, few have taken direct and practical action to challenge racism as an issue among their grassroots members and in their communities.

For First Nations, racism is a deep and longstanding concern that shapes their relations with surrounding communities and their practical approaches to developing their fisheries. Many Indigenous harvesters report being harassed on the wharves and the water and having their fishing gear damaged or lost. Particularly for young harvesters just entering the fishery, the push for rights to fish outside the established commercial season is motivated in part by the need to be safe from threats and harassment. If Indigenous harvesters experience abuse and mistrust despite conforming to rules and local fishing traditions, they see less reason to respect a management system that does not respect them.

The simple reality is that racist attitudes and behaviour are toxic influences that seriously impede efforts by responsible leaders on all sides to solve problems and build relations of trust.

Communications challenges

During the conflicts in Southwest Nova Scotia in the fall of 2020, it became apparent that social media was playing an expanding role in spreading misinformation and inflaming tensions. In the absence of an authoritative source of clear and up-to-date information, the vacuum was immediately filled with rumours, falsehoods, and speculation that raised anxieties across the Maritimes. What was a very localized conflict rapidly morphed into a traumatic event for First Nations and non-Indigenous fishing communities across the region and beyond.

The impacts of social media on public attitudes and behaviour are a growing concern in many areas of modern society, but the fishery is a unique social environment with special challenges. In often-remote coastal regions, fishing communities have less access to more conventional and diverse information flows, and social media channels tend to create silos and echo chambers where users rarely encounter ideas and factual information to counter misunderstandings and prejudices.

Given the complexity of the issues involved in the continuing development of First Nations rights-based fisheries, the current lack of trusted and influential sources of information to bridge between communities and encourage mutual understanding and dialogue is a serious constraint that will need to be addressed.

Clearwater

The Clearwater Seafoods deal is a new and potentially significant source of misunderstanding and mistrust between First Nations and non-Indigenous fisheries groups.

For Indigenous leaders and communities, the 50-percent ownership of Clearwater by seven First Nations, with the multinational corporation Premium Brands owning the other half, is a huge advance that opens possibilities for building an integrated industry with Indigenous leadership and control. Along with profit revenues, First Nations hope to benefit from many new employment opportunities and having a ready buyer to process and market their catches.

However, the Clearwater purchase has taken shape at a time when huge investments from multinational corporations and foreign interests are flowing into the fish processing industry across Atlantic Canada. DFO's owner-operator and fleet separation regulations normally bar processing companies from owning licences and operating fishing vessels in the critical lobster and snow crab sectors, but commercial harvesters worry that new corporate investors are using partnerships with First Nations to get control of fishing licences and quotas to secure raw material supplies for their plants. They fear that Clearwater, the dominant company in the lobster industry, will now be able to buy up many more lobster licences and manage them under First Nations communal-commercial title. For inshore harvesters this a setback in their long struggle to strengthen owner-operator and fleet separation protections as barriers to vertical integration and greater corporate control over lobster prices across the industry.

NEW PATHWAYS

While not suggesting large-scale and easily achieved solutions, the various contributors to this collection provide insights into possible ways to overcome the barriers and flashpoints identified above to make possible a more positive future.

Building trust in enforcement systems

As discussed above, the lack of trust in the enforcement of agreements and fisheries regulations is a major concern and a barrier to trust building for both Indigenous and non-Indigenous fish harvesters and their respective communities. There is no simple solution to this problem, and DFO is not in a strong position itself to find or impose solutions unilaterally. It will likely require significant increases in government spending on surveillance and enforcement services—both DFO's own programs and First Nations' Guardian programs—but the priority should first be on building some higher level of agreement about the nature and scale of the problem, the potential benefits of improving current systems, and how this might be achieved.

The most effective way to address this challenge might be with an independent task force or commission to define the issues and identify possible solutions. To be successful, such a body would need to have strong representation for Indigenous and non-Indigenous interests along with technical and legal expertise, and would need to consult intensively with First Nations authorities and commercial industry groups. An appropriate mandate might include directions to study and advise on fisheries surveillance and enforcement policies and services generally across all commercial and communal-commercial fisheries and in food, social, and ceremonial fisheries.

Again, this is not an easy challenge to take on, but the evidence suggests that greatly strengthened and more widely trusted surveillance and enforcement systems would contribute significantly to reducing tensions between fleets and communities and could open new pathways for innovative moderate livelihood fisheries.

Artisanal livelihood fisheries

First Nations leaders have recently begun to pursue the development of smaller-scale or artisanal fishing activities as a new pathway for more community members to engage in commercial fishing. Fishing on a less intensive basis with smaller vessels and limited gear also may make fishing more compatible with certain lifestyles and more accessible financially. In many respects this moderate livelihood fishery model is a direct adaptation of existing food, social, and ceremonial fisheries except that the catch can be sold for income.

The potential benefits of small-scale commercial fishing by First Nations community members are clear—sharing the fisheries wealth with more people and providing opportunities for young new entrants to develop skills and interest in the fishery as a career. The challenge is to find ways to develop and manage such fisheries without negatively impacting conservation and other rights holders in the commercial fishery.

There are, in fact, many such examples of small-scale artisanal fisheries that are well managed and fully integrated with dominant commercial fisheries without risking conservation or economic outcomes. The FSC fishery in many First Nations is well-managed and uncontroversial, as are the operations of eighty-two lobster "B" licence holders in the Maritimes who fish part-time with one-third the regular number of traps.[8] In Newfoundland and Labrador there is a local food and recreation fishery in which members of outport communities can catch up to five groundfish a day over a limited season. In Maine, high school students are given small allotments of lobster traps to spark interest in fishing as a career, and coastal residents can set a few traps off their properties. In Alaska and Norway there are special fish quotas set aside for small-scale fishing to get new entrants started in the fishery, and in Iceland every citizen is allowed a daily catch of small quantities of fish from a community quota to consume or sell.

For First Nations fishing to develop on a similar artisanal scale in this region, the critical issue will be to build effective and transparent management capacities to ensure consistent and full adherence to fishing plans and regulations. That will require transparency and collaborative management practices as are already in place for most FSC fisheries.

At the end of the day, like so many other aspects of this situation, it will all depend on building relationships of trust between First Nations and commercial harvester leaders and communities, and trust in the rigour, consistency, and fairness of fisheries management and rules enforcement systems.

Opening First Nations access to the lobster fishery

The lobster fishery is foundational to the continuing development of First Nations fisheries. Due, however, to its surging economic value, unique structure, and operational culture, it is not easy or straightforward for Indigenous harvesters to acquire licences and integrate on local fishing grounds.

To date, *Marshall* Nations have acquired new lobster licences through interim agreements and Rights and Reconciliation Agreements with DFO, and there is potential to further expand both communal-commercial and moderate livelihood fisheries this way. These licences were first acquired from non-Indigenous harvesters through DFO's voluntary buy-back programs. It is also possible for Nations to buy licences themselves in the open market.

It's also possible for the DFO minister to expropriate licences and reallocate them to First Nations, as happened recently in the east coast baby eel (elver) fishery and in the crab fishery in British Columbia. In this vein, some First Nations representatives have proposed that DFO impose moderate cuts in the number of traps per licence in each Lobster Fishing Area (LFA) and reallocate the freed-up traps to First Nations.[9] However, non-Indigenous harvester leaders strongly oppose expropriation and are urging the government to focus on "willing seller–willing buyer" options.

As an alternative to expropriation, it has been suggested by First Nations representatives that, in the spirit of reconciliation, non-Indigenous harvesters might voluntarily give up 5 to 10 traps from the 250 to 375 traps per licence in different LFAs to be used by First Nations for moderate livelihood fishing. Such an option might be feasible within a wider give-and-take process where concerns of non-Indigenous harvester were also being addressed.

There may be other ways to reduce barriers to Indigenous access and facilitate acceptance of new moderate livelihood fisheries. Seven Nova Scotia First Nations have recently developed innovative ways to conduct lobster fishing for moderate livelihoods, allowing one licence to support more harvesters, and specifying when fishing can occur and how the activity will be monitored. Three of these plans were devised by individual communities, while in another case four communities are working together within a region. These models have thus far been well accepted by non-Indigenous harvester organizations.

First Nations fishing for moderate livelihoods outside regular commercial seasons has been a critical flashpoint. The Listuguj First Nation in Quebec has initiated a lobster fishery where they give up traps in the spring commercial fishery in exchange for a much smaller number fished outside the season in the fall, when the catch rate per trap is much higher with fewer people fishing. In chapter 2.4, former senior DFO official Jim Jones proposes an approach where First Nations lobster licences each have a quota based on average lobster landings per licence across the LFA in previous seasons. With this model there could be a defined limit on the total moderate livelihood catch, regardless of time of year.

Pursuing such innovations could be facilitated by the creation of joint planning committees at the Lobster Fishing Area– or community level to involve First Nations and non-Indigenous fisheries leaders in planning and facilitating the integration of Indigenous harvesters into local fisheries. Training programs with non-Indigenous mentors worked well in the earlier development of communal-commercial lobster fishing and could help again in improving skills and operational practices for future development of moderate livelihood fisheries.

Given how the lobster fishery is structured, regulated, and conducted, the bottom-line issue here is that it will continue to be difficult to grow First Nations lobster fisheries unless leaders in First Nations and non-Indigenous communities find ways to work together on fishing plans and management models to make it happen.

Dialogue tables

In chapter 5.3, we describe an effort by Indigenous and non-Indigenous fisheries leaders in Southwest Nova Scotia to carry on a process "focused on direct dialogue as opposed to formal consultation, negotiation, or conflict resolution."[10] Leaders from the major harvester organizations and several First Nations met regularly over a two-year period simply to hear each other's views on pertinent issues and to build trust. Over the course of their meetings, they held information sessions on rights-based fisheries, explored new ways to protect and develop the lobster industry, and planned joint science projects. The process broke down due to higher-level conflicts among certain leaders, but it was successful within its own terms and many participants wanted it to continue.

Allister Surette, the special advisor appointed by DFO Minister Jordan after the 2020 conflict in Southwest Nova Scotia, referred to this example in his report when he recommended the creation of "a dialogue forum to build trust and relationships...between Indigenous and non-Indigenous parties (excluding governments)."[11] Surette reported that during his consultations with commercial harvesters and First Nations representatives, "Many expressed the need for 'real' discussions and for parties to discuss in good faith. Many also expressed the need for an approach of 'we are all in this together' for safe and prosperous fisheries and safe and prosperous communities. No one I spoke to wants to see the emotions, tensions, and violence of last summer and fall."[12]

In his interview in chapter 5.4, fisheries consultant Gilles Thériault describes fisheries governance as a triangle. Nation-to-Nation negotiation is one side, and the DFO co-management system makes up another. Relations between First Nations and commercial harvesters make the third side of the triangle, and perhaps its base. Commercial harvesters are not party to Nation-to-Nation processes that may impact them, so they use their strong positions at DFO management tables to try to influence government positions at the Nation-to-Nation tables. The lack of direct and constructive communications between Indigenous and non-Indigenous leaders makes the governance structure unstable and unnecessarily contentious. Thériault makes the argument that "In the larger picture, there is only one ocean and one fishery resource base, and all the major users need to work together to manage resources sustainably and build a strong fisheries economy to the benefit of everyone."

Leadership structures

As discussed, the absence of formally certified and well-funded organizations with formal mandates to represent commercial harvesters across the Maritimes region, and the parallel lack of umbrella organizations with authority to collectively act and speak for First Nations, makes communications, collaboration, and problem solving much more difficult than it might otherwise be.

There are efforts on both sides to address this issue. Three prominent Mi'kmaw leaders, Senator Brian Francis, Member of Parliament Jaime Battiste, and Senator Dan Christmas have proposed the establishment of a regional fisheries governance model, the Atlantic First Nations Fisheries Authority, to unify Indigenous leadership in fisheries development (see chapter 6.4). And, as outlined in chapter 5.1, commercial harvester organizations across the Maritimes and Quebec have recently formed two new umbrella organizations to address Indigenous fisheries development concerns, and many of the associations in both groups belong to the Canadian Independent Fish Harvesters Federation.

Government has a role to play in creating stronger incentives for smaller entities to work together, as they are attempting with the Rights Reconciliation Agreement strategy. DFO has also been working since its 2004 Atlantic Fisheries Policy Review on criteria to limit participation in fisheries advisory committees and other consultation tables to formally constituted and democratic harvester organizations. Advances in these efforts could create new energies and leadership capacities to address reconciliation objectives in the region.

Leadership in communications

When asked what he saw as the most important lesson learned from his study of the 2020 conflicts in his home region, Allister Surette pointed to the need for new and well-resourced capacities to proactively share accurate and up-to-date information to affected communities and stakeholder groups. In his report he suggested the idea of an information clearing house to be "easily accessible on a national, regional, and local basis by all stakeholders and rights holders directly involved in the fishery. It must also be capable of accommodating real-time communication for matters requiring a prompt response. The clearing house can take various forms, such as a centralized website, including social media and other electronic mechanisms. An authorized agency, such as DFO, should take on responsibility for the ownership and the management of these mechanisms and should make maintaining them a priority."[13]

Meeting this need will require a significant investment of financial resources and expertise, and Surette recommends that DFO take on this role. However, given the department's often-strained relations with First Nations and commercial harvester groups, an alternative would be to establish an arm's-length agency to carry out this function. It should have representation of First Nations and commercial harvesters in its governance structure and could, for example, be centred in one or more universities.

And further, we have noted the role possibly played by social media in exacerbating tensions during the conflicts in Southwest Nova Scotia in the fall of 2020. It could be useful and strategically important for appropriate experts in government, the media, or perhaps academic settings to undertake research and consultations on the nature and scale of this challenge and possible mitigations.

Addressing racism

In chapter 6.2, authors Wien and Denis make the point that racism is a complex phenomenon with multiple causes and no simple solutions. It may have long historic roots, passed down from one generation to the next, fortified by what is taught (and what is omitted) in educational systems and manifested through the racism inherent in public policies such as those that for centuries denied First Nations access to commercial fishing in waters adjacent to their communities.

Racist attitudes that may be latent in any community can come to the surface and be expressed even in violent terms in certain situations. The circumstances that triggered expressions of racism in Southwest Nova Scotia in the fall of 2020 had to do with a Mi'kmaq Nation pushing to regain its historic and treaty-defined place in the inshore fishery by licensing its own harvesters and setting their own seasons. The lobster fishery to which it sought to regain entry was defined in zero-sum terms: that is, an expanded Mi'kmaw fishery would directly reduce catches for the non-Indigenous harvesters and possibly threaten their livelihoods. While one can debate the size of this impact on the resource, and this was exaggerated in the rhetoric of the time, it is clear that the threat was perceived in this way, and some non-Indigenous fishers responded accordingly.[14] Wien and Denis suggest that racism was used as a tool in this conflict to demean First Nations harvesters and to mobilize support in the non-Indigenous community. The unique ways in which the lobster fishery is regulated and conducted, as described in chapter 2.1, clearly exacerbate the problem.

It follows that these more blatant and violent expressions of racism can and should be addressed, in the first instance, through the kinds of measures described above that assure Mi'kmaw access to the fishery while taking into account the interests of non-Indigenous harvesters and their communities. More specifically, this will require new and innovative measures that address the unique challenges of the lobster fishery, and more effective enforcement in all fisheries. All of this can only happen with more effective leadership, dialogue, and communication than has been the case in the recent past.

Walking the Talk

In a situation where bigger and more lasting solutions are not readily at hand, small steps become very important. Symbolic gestures and practical actions to acknowledge and then address the concerns of diverse groups can help reduce tensions, strengthen relationships, and lay foundations for future progress.

It might lower tensions significantly, for example, if leaders in commercial harvester organizations made public statements confirming the reality of harassment of Indigenous harvesters in fishing ports and on the water and committed to reducing such behaviour. This could include grassroots anti-racism education programs among their members and in their communities. By this we do not mean just pointing fingers and accusing people of bad attitudes. The priority should be on information sharing about the history of Indigenous communities in the region, their treaties, and the various court decisions on fisheries rights issues. After a series of workshops in the fall of 2020 where various federal agencies provided some fifty Canadian commercial harvester leaders with this kind of background information, Melanie Sonnenberg, President of the Canadian Independent Fish Harvesters Federation, offered the following comment: "The reconciliation workshops have opened up a dialogue that has helped members understand the complexity of reconciliation. There has been a lot of active listening and deep questioning in these workshops."[5]

That is an important start, not necessarily in solving big problems but at least in changing the way leaders understand and talk about those problems. There is a role for government to play in providing resources and financial support for commercial harvester organizations to undertake these kinds of educational programs among their grassroots members and in their communities.

On the other side of the table, while not compromising their rights or altering their fisheries development strategies, First Nations leaders could help reduce mistrust and anxiety levels among non-Indigenous harvester communities by, for example, acknowledging concerns about the Clearwater deal and its possible impacts on owner-operator protections. It might open an important door if First Nations leaders expressed an interest in knowing more about the roots of these concerns and a willingness to consult on the issue.

As leaders in many other sectors across Canada are doing, and as is common in almost all fisheries meetings in British Columbia, non-Indigenous commercial fisheries leaders might also develop habits and establish protocols for acknowledging their presence in unceded Indigenous territories and for affirming their recognition and respect for Aboriginal and Treaty Rights, in their public statements.

Similarly, First Nations leaders could help defuse tensions and encourage dialogue by openly acknowledging the reality that Indigenous fisheries developments, including the Clearwater acquisition, have significant impacts on the commercial fishery and that the concerns of commercial harvesters and their communities about these impacts are understandable and legitimate.

These are the kinds of small steps that build the trust and mutual respect needed for more lasting solutions to be found in future.

LAST WORDS

It is our belief that the fishery holds huge potential to support much needed economic and social development for First Nations communities across our region, and that First Nations have fundamental Aboriginal and Treaty Rights to develop their fisheries as a source of new employment and income generation and for food, social, and ceremonial purposes. It is important to note that all the individuals and interest groups whose views are represented in the book have recognized and affirmed these rights, albeit with differing views on their scope and application.

Beyond the court rulings and legal arguments there is also a compelling human need to right historical wrongs. The simple fact that at the close of the twentieth century coastal First Nations had only a tiny share of the huge commercial fishery in Atlantic waters is stark proof of a history of systemic racism and exclusion. As recently as the 1980s the Government of Canada imposed a limited entry licensing regime on previously open-access fisheries without allocating any meaningful share to First Nations. Access to commercial fisheries was also blocked by the persistent failures of provincial loan boards to help finance acquisition of vessels and gear by First Nations harvesters as the industry modernized after the Second World War. This is the fertile ground in which the frustration and mistrust so often expressed by First Nations leaders took root and still flourish in their communities.

The challenge we address in this book is the need to find ways for the many different communities that depend on fisheries to learn to live and work together as First Nations continue to develop their fisheries in accordance with their Aboriginal and Treaty Rights. Certain trends in the fishery, we believe, may help to make this possible. Growth in the fishery economy is strong, and important commercial fish stocks are stable or, for the all-important lobster industry, strengthening. We believe the healthy state of the fishing industry overall creates space and opportunity to develop First Nations fisheries while maintaining the viability of non-Indigenous commercial fleets and the coastal communities that depend on them. And everyone shares responsibilities to manage the resource sustainably and to build the economic value of fisheries and defend our regional brand in world markets.

If there ever has been a time when it is both necessary and feasible to find a constructive path to reconciliation in Atlantic fisheries it may be now. The fishery economy and our marine resource provide the means to get there. It is up to leaders in all our communities to find new ways forward in peace and friendship.

ABOUT THE CONTRIBUTORS

The **Assembly of Nova Scotia Mi'kmaw Chiefs** comprises eleven Mi'kmaw Chiefs in Nova Scotia and two ex-officio members, the Grand Chief and Grand Captain of the Mi'kmaq Grand Council. The Assembly is the highest level of decision making in the Rights Implementation and Consultation processes for the Mi'kmaq of Nova Scotia.

Jaime Battiste was first elected as the Member of Parliament for Sydney–Victoria in 2019. He is the first Mi'kmaq to be elected to Parliament. Since he was first elected, Mr. Battiste has served on various parliamentary committees, including the House of Commons Standing Committee on Indigenous and Northern Affairs, where he helped review, examine, and report on the issues affecting First Nations, Inuit, and Métis peoples, and Northerners. He previously held positions as a university professor, Treaty Education Lead, and Assembly of First Nations (AFN) Regional Chief. He holds a Juris Doctor from the Schulich School of Law at Dalhousie University and an undergraduate degree in Mi'kmaq Studies from Cape Breton University.

Jeffery Callaghan is a commercial lawyer with McInnes Cooper, focused on energy and natural resources, real property, and business law. A significant aspect of Jeffery's practice is regulatory law: advising clients on regulatory obligations in the aquaculture, agriculture, forestry, and energy sectors and representing clients before the New Brunswick Energy and Utilities Board. Jeffery has a special focus on Aboriginal law, particularly with respect to Aboriginal consultation and engagement and advising stakeholders regarding economic development on reserve lands. His practice uniquely integrates his knowledge and experience in commercial, regulatory, and Aboriginal law to provide well-rounded advice. Jeffery is a founding and current co-chair of the Aboriginal Law section of CBA–New Brunswick. He shares his knowledge of the field with aspiring lawyers by serving as coach to the Kawaskimhon National Aboriginal Law Moot team at UNB.

Anthony (Tony) Charles is Director of the School of the Environment and a professor in the School of Business at Saint Mary's University in Halifax, as well as Director of the Community Conservation Research Network.

Daniel (Dan) Christmas served for five years as Band Manager for the Community of Membertou. Mr. Christmas worked for the Union of Nova Scotia Indians for fifteen years, the last ten as its director. He was actively involved in the recognition and implementation of Mi'kmaw Aboriginal and Treaty Rights in Nova Scotia. From 1997 to 2016, Mr. Christmas held the position of Senior Advisor with Membertou and assisted the Chief and Council and its management team with the day-to-day operations of the Community. He was also an elected councillor for Membertou for eighteen years. In 2005, Mr. Christmas was awarded an honorary Doctor of Laws degree from Dalhousie University. In December 2016, he was sworn in as an Independent Senator for Nova Scotia. Senator Christmas is the first Mi'kmaq to be appointed to the Senate of Canada.

Jeff Denis is an associate professor of sociology at McMaster University and a settler Canadian of mixed European ancestry. His research focuses on the social psychology of racism and colonialism, and the strategies, alliances, policies, and practices that can bring about more just and sustainable societies. He is the author of *Canada at a Crossroads: Boundaries, Bridges, and Laissez-Faire Racism in Indigenous–Settler Relations* (University of Toronto Press, 2020).

Shelley Denny is Mi'kmaw from Eskasoni First Nation and Director of Aquatic Research and Stewardship at the Unama'ki Institute of Natural Resource (UINR). She attended Acadia University, where she obtained her BSc in biology, St. Francis Xavier University, where she obtained an MSc in biology in fisheries ecology, and Dalhousie University for a PhD in the Interdisciplinary Program. Her research will build on her work at UINR in Indigenous and Western knowledge systems. Her research is focused on developing an alternative governance model for fisheries by exploring how inherent and treaty fisheries can be implemented in Nova Scotia.

Lucia Fanning is currently professor emerita, Marine Affairs Program, Dalhousie University. Her research focuses on understanding the value of all branches and sources of knowledge to better inform decisions affecting the sustainability of our coastal and marine ecosystems. For the past seven years, in collaboration with Indigenous partners from across Canada, she has worked on understanding how different knowledge systems (e.g. "Western" and Indigenous) influence fisheries decision making on Canada's Pacific, Atlantic, and Arctic coasts as well as inland fisheries in Ontario (see fishwiks.ca). An extension of this work focuses on the use of Inuit knowledge in Nunavut to identify and implement coastal restoration across the territory.

Susanna Fuller is Vice-President, Operations and Projects at Oceans North, which is dedicated to finding solutions for healthy oceans and coastal communities, with a focus on Indigenous-led solutions. Susanna's work focuses on achieving tangible conservation outcomes in sustainable fisheries and spatial protections in Atlantic Canada and the Arctic, as well as initiatives to protect high seas biodiversity. She completed her PhD at Dalhousie University, including research on North Atlantic marine sponge populations, and has worked for the past decade and a half on the science–policy interface for national and international fisheries and ocean conservation. Before joining Oceans North in

2018, she led the marine team at Ecology Action Centre in Halifax where she lives.

Amber Giles is Wolastoqiyik from Wolastoq territory and Mi'kma'ki and is currently living in the Arctic. She received a BSc in marine biology from the University of New Brunswick and a master's in marine management from Dalhousie University. Amber's graduate work was completed as part of the Fisheries Western and Indigenous Knowledge Systems (Fish-WIKS) research project and focused on the incorporation of Indigenous Knowledge Systems into policy-level decision making for commercial fisheries in Canada. Since graduating, Amber has worked in the area of Indigenous fisheries and Indigenous Knowledge Systems for various organizations, including the Atlantic Policy Congress of First Nations Chiefs, Assembly of First Nations, Nunavut Wildlife Management Board, and the Government of Nunavut.

Jim Jones was born in Grand Bank, NL, and is a graduate of Memorial University and the University of Alberta. He has worked in Atlantic fisheries for more than forty years, over thirty of those with DFO. From 1998 to 2009 he served as Regional Director General for DFO Gulf Region, a period that saw the development of Indigenous fisheries programs after the *Sparrow* and *Marshall* decisions, and the emergence of shellfish as the dominant industry sector. From 2017 to 2020 Jim served as DFO's lead negotiator for Rights Reconciliation Agreements across the Maritimes and the Gaspé.

Nadine Lefort is Communications and Outreach Manager with Unama'ki Institute of Natural Resources. She has managed environmental education and outreach programs across Canada, with a focus on making Indigenous Knowledge accessible and applicable in different scenarios through a Two-Eyed Seeing perspective. For over twenty years, Nadine has worked extensively with Albert and (the late) Murdena Marshall on Two-Eyed Seeing. She manages UINR's Nikani Awtiken, a summer program for Mi'kmaw youth. In addition to her work with UINR, Nadine teaches environmental science courses at Cape Breton University.

Constance MacIntosh is a full professor at the Schulich School of Law at Dalhousie University and is currently the acting Scholarly Director for the MacEachen Institute for Public Policy and Governance. Constance's research is far-ranging and includes deep dives into the intersection of federal law, policy, and practice with the governance rights and well-being of Indigenous communities, with a particular focus on public health and water quality. She served as an expert for the Council of Canadian Academies report on food security in Northern Indigenous communities and also on the independent report for Nova Scotia on whether to lift the hydraulic fracking moratorium.

 Albert Marshall is a highly respected and much loved Elder of the Mi'kmaq Nation. He is from the Moose Clan and lives in the community of Eskasoni in Unama'ki—Cape Breton, NS. Albert is a fluent speaker of the Mi'kmaw language. A passionate advocate of cross-cultural understandings and healing, and our human responsibilities to care for all creatures and Mother Earth, he is the "designated voice" for Mi'kmaw Elders of Unama'ki with respect to environmental issues. Albert is a survivor of the Indian Residential School in Shubenacadie, NS. Albert coined the phrase "Two-Eyed Seeing" (*Etuaptmumk*) to explain the guiding principle and an action-oriented invitation to recognize the strengths that exist within different ways of knowing.

 L. Jane McMillan, professor in the Department of Anthropology at St. Francis Xavier University, is the former Canada Research Chair for Indigenous Peoples and Sustainable Communities (2006–2016). Jane received her PhD from the University of British Columbia in 2003 and is a socio-cultural and legal anthropologist conducting primarily community-initiated research, focused on the intersections of Indigenous law with community strategies for implementing Treaty and Aboriginal Rights. She is the author of the award-winning *Truth and Conviction: Donald Marshall Jr. and the Mi'kmaw Quest for Justice* (UBC Press, 2018). She sits on the board of directors for Innocence Canada, is a member of the Mi'kmaw/Nova Scotia/Canada Tripartite Forum Justice Working Committee, and serves on the Atlantic Policy Congress AAEDIRP steering committee and the Research Advisory Board for the Mass Casualty Commission.

Naiomi Metallic is from the Listuguj Mi'gmaq First Nation in Quebec. She is a full-time faculty member at the Schulich School of Law at Dalhousie University and holds the Chancellor's Chair in Aboriginal Law and Policy. Prior to joining the law school, she practised law for nearly a decade with Burchells LLP in Halifax, and she remains an active member of the firm's Aboriginal law practice group.

John Paul is from Membertou First Nation and is Executive Director of the Atlantic Policy Congress of First Nations Chiefs Secretariat in Dartmouth, NS. Taking direction from the chiefs through frequent All Chiefs Forums and Executive Chiefs Board of Directors and Co-Chairs, Mr. Paul provides policy analysis and strategic advice on a wide range of policy issues facing First Nations in Atlantic Canada and Eastern Quebec. The APC Secretariat's mandate is to research, analyze, and develop alternatives to federal policies affecting its member First Nations communities. Mr. Paul received a BA in community studies from Cape Breton University in 1980 and his Master of Public Administration in Financial Management from Halifax's Dalhousie University in 1982. A strong and dedicated advocate for First Nations, Mr. Paul has worked toward positive change for First Nations communities in diverse policy areas for more than thirty-five years.

Tyson Paul is from Eskasoni and currently resides at Potlotek First Nation with his partner and children. He has a BSc in Community Studies as well as a Bachelor of Engineering Technology (Environmental Studies), both from Cape Breton University. He has been working at the Unama'ki Institute of Natural Resources for the past twelve years as Researcher for Integrative Knowledge Systems. In January 2022, he started a new position within UINR as Commercial Fishery Liaison Coordinator.

Kerry Prosper is from Paqtnkek Mi'kmaw Community, located in Eskikewa'kik, one of seven traditional territories in Atlantic Canada established by the Mi'kmaq. Kerry is an avid harvester, a highly regarded spiritual healer, and a leader. He is currently a band councillor and the Knowledge Keeper on Campus for St. Francis

Xavier University, Antigonish, NS. Kerry was Chief of Paqtnkek in 1993 when Donald Marshall, Jane McMillan, and Peter Martin were fishing eels in Welnek, or Pomquet Harbour, and the events leading to the *Marshall* decision occurred.

Paul (P. J.) Prosper is Regional Chief for the Assembly of First Nations and represents the Mi'kmaw Chiefs of Nova Scotia and Newfoundland. Prior to his appointment in 2020, he served as Chief of Paqtnkek Mi'kmaq Nation from 2013 to 2020. Paul is a proud graduate of the IB&M (Indigenous, Black, and Mi'kmaq) Initiative at the Schulich School of Law, Dalhousie University. He has extensive experience in Aboriginal legal issues from a research, litigation, and negotiation perspective. His work has been primarily devoted to advocating for the rights of Mi'kmaw people. Through the years, Paul has worked for several Mi'kmaw organizations in such areas as oral history, Mi'kmaw land use and occupation studies, claims research, citizenship, consultation, First Nations governance, justice, community development, and Nationhood.

Joseph Quesnel is a Métis research associate at the Frontier Centre for Public Policy. He specializes in Indigenous economic development and governance issues. He was lead researcher for the Frontier Centre's flagship Aboriginal Governance Index, and he completed an extensive study of the self-governing BC Nisga'a Nation. Quesnel's work has been featured in numerous Canadian radio and newspapers outlets. He has been called to provide expert testimony before the Standing Senate Committee on Aboriginal Peoples and the House's Standing Committee on Aboriginal Affairs and Northern Development. Joseph also served as a program manager at the Macdonald-Laurier Institute, overseeing their Indigenous resource economy project.

Ryan Stack is an assistant professor of accounting at the F. C. Manning School of Business at Acadia University, as well as a PhD candidate in social accounting at Queen's University. His awards include the Smith School of Business Fellowship and the

Norman Macintosh Memorial Fellowship in Accounting. His research interests include professionalism, accountability, non-profit organizations, and
accounting in Indigenous communities. He has co-authored several award-
winning and published teaching cases focusing on family business.

Allister Surette has been president and vice-chancellor of
Université Sainte-Anne since July 1, 2011. A native of West
Pubnico, NS, Mr. Surette served as MLA for the constituency
of Argyle from 1993 to 1998. He was special advisor on Acadian
and francophone governance within the public school system and Minister
of both Human Resources and Acadian Affairs. In October 2020, the government of Canada appointed him as a federal special representative to
act as a neutral third party to help rebuild trust between commercial and
Indigenous fishers after the unrest and violence in Southwest Nova Scotia.
He submitted his report, "Implementing the right to fish in pursuit of a
moderate livelihood: Rebuilding trust and establishing a constructive path
forward," to DFO Minister Bernadette Jordan on March 31, 2021.

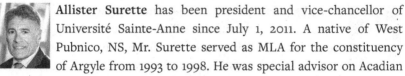

Kji-saqamaw/Grand Chief Norman Sylliboy grew up in Eskasoni,
part of a traditional Mi'kmaw family with a legacy of 103 years of
leadership in the Grand Council. This stems from his grandfather Grand Chief Gabriel Sylliboy, his father, Captain Athanasius
'Tana's' Sylliboy, and his uncles and brothers. Kji-saqamaw Norman
Sylliboy is honoured to continue the legacy of his grandfather. And just like
his grandfather did, he solemnly promises to serve his people, St. Anne, and
the church faithfully. Norman has been a social worker for nineteen years
and is one of the original social workers from when Mi'kmaw Family and
Childrens Services was created in 1985. He now works as a family support
program worker where he goes to Mi'kmaw communities throughout Cape
Breton and parts of mainland Nova Scotia to deliver programs for youth and
adults.

Gilles Thériault has worked in fisheries for over fifty years. In
the 1970s, he helped organize the Maritime Fishermen's Union
(MFU) and served as executive director for ten years. In 1987,
he launched his consulting career providing strategic services

for fisheries development across Canada and around the world. After the Supreme Court rulings on Marshall in 1999, Gilles represented the federal government in negotiating interim agreements with First Nations for access to fishing licences, boats, and other supports. He has since worked with many Indigenous communities in the Maritimes and Quebec supporting the development of their fisheries. After advising Elsipogtog First Nation on the purchase of the McGraw Seafood plant in Tracadie, NB, he served as general manager of the plant from to 2015 to 2019. He is currently senior business development advisor for McGraw Seafood and recently oversaw the construction of a new state-of-the-art processing plant.

Dan Vanclieaf was, at the time of writing, a lawyer with McInnes Cooper, focused on Aboriginal, environmental, and energy and natural resources law.

Lucia Westin was, at the time of writing, a litigation lawyer with McInnes Cooper, focused on Aboriginal, energy and natural resources, construction, and insurance law.

Fred Wien holds a professor emeritus appointment at Dalhousie University. A former director of the Maritime School of Social Work, he was seconded in the 1992–96 period to the Royal Commission on Aboriginal Peoples serving as Deputy Director of Research. He was appointed to the Order of Canada in 2015.

Richard (Rick) Williams is President of Praxis Research and Consulting Ltd., as well as the research director for the Canadian Council of Fish Harvesters. He was project director for a recent ACOA-funded research and consultation project on labour supply and intergenerational succession challenges in the Atlantic Canada fish-harvesting industry. From 2009 to 2013, he served as Deputy Minister to the Premier for Policy and Priorities, Province of Nova Scotia.

NOTES

I. OVERVIEW: THE COMMERCIAL FISHERY AND THE DEVELOPMENT OF FIRST NATIONS FISHERIES

I.I. AN OVERVIEW OF COMMERCIAL FISHERIES

1   This data is sourced from Fisheries and Oceans Canada's website for fisheries statistics (dfo-mpo.gc.ca/stats/commercial/sea-maritimes-eng.htm). The estimate for landings by inshore and midshore fleets is based on fisheries conducted predominantly by owner-operated vessels 65 feet or fewer in length.

2   There are more lobster licences than core enterprises in New Brunswick because, as DFO policies evolved, a limited number of part-time or occasional harvesters were allowed to continue fishing lobster with "B" licences. These non-core licences will leave the fishery when their owners retire. In contrast, a holder of a core licence can sell it to a new entrant who becomes the owner-operator.

3   DFO licensing and fisheries landed-value information is provided for the whole of Quebec including the North Shore and Îles de la Madeleine. Five of the Mi'kmaw and Wolastoqey First Nations impacted by the Marshall decision are located in Quebec, all in the Gaspé Region.

4   The variation in average snow crab landings per licence among the four provinces is explained by the fact that in New Brunswick, PEI, and to some extent Quebec, most snow crab is harvested by midshore vessels with much larger individual quotas than is the case for the many smaller inshore boats fishing crab, particularly in Nova Scotia.

5   This information comes from Statistics Canada tax filer data covering every person reporting taxable income from fish-harvesting employment.

I.2. DEVELOPMENT OF FIRST NATIONS FISHERIES SINCE THE MARSHALL DECISIONS

1   Supreme Court of Canada, Supreme Court Judgments, R. v. Van der Peet, August 21, 1996, scc-csc.lexum.com/scc-csc/scc-csc/en/item/1407/index.do.

2   "Food, social and ceremonial fisheries," Government of Canada, modified May 19, 2021, dfo-mpo.gc.ca/fisheries-peches/aboriginal-autochtones/fsc-asr-eng.html.

3   "Food, social and ceremonial fisheries."

4   "Netukulimk is a complex cultural concept that encompasses Mi'kmaq sovereign law ways and guides individual and collective beliefs and behaviours in resource protection, procurement, and management to ensure and honour sustainability and prosperity for the ancestor, present and future generations." Mi'kmaw leader Kerry Prosper quoted in "Netukulimk" (in-progress document, October 2020), Province of Nova Scotia, curriculum.novascotia.ca/sites/default/files/documents/resource-files/Netukulimk_ENG.pdf.

5   "Kespuwick Resources Inc.," Business, Acadia First Nation, 2022, acadiafirstnation.ca/kespuwick-resources-inc.html.

6   "Acadia First Nation: 2021/22 Netukulimk Fish Harvest Plan," Acadia First Nation, no date, acadiafirstnation.ca/notices/706-2021-2022-fsc-netukulimk-fish-harvest-plan/file.html.

7   "Acadia First Nation Neukulimk Harvest Plan."

8   The Canadian Press, "Ministers Announce Negotiators, Process for Long-Term Response to Marshall," February 9, 2001, cifas.us/ministers-announce-negotiators-process-for-long-term-response-to-marshall/.

9   Strictly speaking, access rights are not "leased." Under certain circumstances, DFO rules allow a licence holder to "designate" another person or business entity to fish the licence or the quota. As an example of the revenue that can be generated this way, a CBC News story from October 2021 described the potential income for Sipekne'katik First Nation from leasing one of its nine lobster licences to a non-Indigenous harvester in Southwest Nova Scotia as $450,000 per licence over the season. See Paul Withers, "Sipekne'katik backs out of commercial lobster season citing fears over safety," CBC News, October 30, 2020, cbc.ca/news/canada/nova-scotia/sipekne-katik-backs-out-of-commercial-lobster-fishery-1.5784133.

10   "'Landmark agreement' reached on lucrative surf clam fishery," CBC News, updated March 12, 2019, cbc.ca/news/canada/nova-scotia/arctic-surf-clam-landmark-agreement-reached-1.5052380. This agreement was made prior to the purchase of Clearwater by a consortium of First Nations and an outside corporate investor.

11   Government of Canada, "Our response to the *Marshall* decisions," modified April 19, 2021, dfo-mpo.gc.ca/publications/fisheries-peches/marshall-1999-eng.html.

12   While Indigenous communities in the region never stopped fishing for food and trade after European penetration, the introduction of limited entry licensing by the federal fisheries department in the 1970s effectively and systematically excluded First Nations from equitable access to commercial fishing. Donald Marshall was arrested in 1993 for fishing eels to sell without a DFO licence, resulting in the most significant legal challenges to this history of systemic racism.

13 Government of Canada, "Our response to the *Marshall* decisions."

14 Government of Canada, "Our response to the *Marshall* decisions."

15 Fisheries and Oceans Canada, "Reconciliation in action: Fisheries agreement reached between Government of Canada and the Elsipogtog and Esgenoôpetitj First Nations," news release, August 15, 2019, canada.ca/en/fisheries-oceans/ news/2019/08/reconciliation-in-action-fisheries-agreement-reached-between-government-of-canada-and-the-elsipogtog-and-esgenoopetitj-first-nations.html.

16 Fisheries and Oceans Canada, " Government of Canada and the Maliseet of Viger First Nation reach agreement on fisheries," news release, August 30, 2019, canada.ca/en/fisheries-oceans/news/2019/08/government-of-canada-and-the-maliseet-of-viger-first-nation-reach-agreement-on-fisheries.html.

17 The Canadian Press, "'A new chapter': Quebec First Nation signs five-year fisheries agreement with Ottawa," April 19, 2021, theglobeandmail.com/canada/ article-a-new-chapter-quebec-first-nation-signs-five-year-fisheries-agreement/.

18 "First Fishermen Seafood," Membertou Corporate Division, no date, membertoucorporate.com/seafood.

19 Report in AllNovaScotia.com, September 9, 2021.

20 "Fisheries," Sipekne'katik, 2016, sipeknekatik.ca/fisheries/.

21 "Fisheries," Ugpi'ganjig, 2019, ugpi-ganjig.ca/departments/fisheries/.

22 Ken Coates, *The Marshal Decision at 20: Two Decades of Commercial Re-Empowerment of the Mi'kmaq and Maliseet* (Ottawa: Macdonald-Laurier Institute, 2019), 4.

23 Government of Canada, "Our response to the *Marshall* decisions."

24 The Canada Census has used the term "Aboriginal" to describe individuals who self-identify as First Nations, Inuit, Métis, or as being from another Indigenous population.

25 See Rick Williams, *A Future for the Fishery: Crisis and Renewal in Canada's Neglected Fishing Industry* (Halifax: Nimbus Publishing, 2019), 34.

26 Government of Canada, "2021 moderate livelihood fishing," modified March 15, 2021, dfo-mpo.gc.ca/fisheries-peches/aboriginal-autochtones/moderate-livelihood-subsistance-convenable/2021-approach-approche-eng.html.

27 Tom Ayers, "Potlotek, DFO agree on first authorized moderate livelihood fishery," CBC News, June 4, 2021, cbc.ca/news/canada/nova-scotia/ potlotek-dfo-moderate-livelihood-fishery-1.6053723.

28 "4 Mi'kmaw bands launch moderate livelihood fisheries with federal approval," CBC News, October 13, 2021, cbc.ca/news/canada/nova-scotia/ mi-kmaw-bands-launch-moderate-livelihood-fisheries-1.6209852.

29 Fisheries and Oceans Canada, "Minister Jordan issues statement on cooperative path forward with Potlotek First Nation," June 4, 2021, canada.ca/en/fisheries-oceans/news/2021/06/minister-jordan-issues-statement-on-cooperative-path-forward-with-potlotek-first-nation.html.

30 "4 Mi'kmaw bands launch moderate livelihood fisheries."

31 Fisheries and Oceans Canada, "Interim understanding reached that will see Bear River and Annapolis Valley First Nations members fishing in pursuit of a moderate

livelihood," news release, October 13, 2021, canada.ca/en/fisheries-oceans/news/2021/10/interim-understanding-reached-that-will-see-bear-river-and-annapolis-valley-first-nations-members-fishing-in-pursuit-of-a-moderate-livelihood.html.

32 Vernon Ramesar, "Pictou Landing moderate livelihood lobster fishery to operate with DFO approval," CBC News, May 2, 2022, cbc.ca/news/canada/nova-scotia/pictou-landing-first-nation-moderate-livelihood-fishery-dfo-approval-1.6437212.

33 Haley Ryan, "We'koqma'q gets federal approval for moderate livelihood fishery," CBC News, May 22, 2022, cbc.ca/news/canada/nova-scotia/we-koqma-q-moderate-livelihood-fishery-gets-federal-approval-1.6462391.

34 Logan MacLean, "Moderate livelihood fishery opens in Lennox Island, PEI," Saltwire News, updated May 10, 2022, saltwire.com/atlantic-canada/news/moderate-livelihood-fishery-opens-in-lennox-island-pei-100730367/.

35 Paul Withers, "DFO redistributes quota in baby eel fishery to increase access for Mi'kmaw bands," CBC News, April 1, 2022, cbc.ca/news/canada/nova-scotia/dfo-hands-percent-of-commercial-baby-eel-quota-to-mi-kmaw-1.6404503.

36 Macdonald-Laurier Institute, "The Marshall Decision has a great legacy, 20 years on: John Paul and Joseph Quesnel in the Telegraph Journal," November 30, 2019, macdonaldlaurier.ca/marshall-decision-great-legacy-20-years-john-paul-joseph-quesnel-telegraph-journal/. (See chapter 1.4.)

1.3. A HISTORY OF EXCLUSION

1 This article draws substantially on Fred Wien, *Rebuilding the Economic Base of Indian Communities: The Micmac in Nova Scotia* (Montreal: Institute for Research on Public Policy, 1986).

2 One analyst of pre-contact times, Bernard Hoffman, concluded there were about forty-five Mi'kmaw summer villages in Nova Scotia, with about thirty-five of them located along waterways and the remainder in coastal areas. See Ashley Sutherland, "The Relationship between the Mi'kmaw People and the Fisheries: A Historical Perspective," no date, colchesterhistoreum.ca/archives/the-relationship-between-the-mikmaw-people-and-the-fisheries-a-historical-perspective.

3 William Wicken, Fact sheet on Peace and Friendship Treaties in the Maritimes and Gaspé, 2010, rcaanc-cirnac.gc.ca/eng/1100100028599/1539609517566, page 2.

4 Wicken, Fact sheet, 4.

5 Virginia Miller, "The Decline of the Nova Scotia Micmac Population, 1600–1850" (paper presented at the Eleventh Algonkian Conference, Ottawa, 1979), 26.

6 Wien, *Rebuilding the Economic Base of Indian Communities*, 13–14.

7 Abraham Gesner, 1847 Report on Indian Affairs, Nova Scotia Archives MG 15, vol. 4, no. 32.

8 Sutherland, "The Relationship between the Mi'kmaw People and the Fisheries."

9 Sutherland, "The Relationship between the Mi'kmaw People and the Fisheries."

10 In the early 1980s, I asked Mi'kmaw adults living on reserve whether they had ever spent more than a year harvesting in New England. Depending on the age group, responses in the affirmative ranged from 37 to 55 percent (Wien, *Rebuilding the Economic Base of Indian Communities*, 23).

11 W. S. Arneil, "Investigation Report on Indian Reserves and Indian Administration, Province of Nova Scotia," Indian Affairs Branch (Ottawa: Department of Mines and Resources, August, 1941), 4.

12 Union of Nova Scotia Indians, 2015–16 First Nation Regional Health Survey Version 2.0 (Sydney: Union of Nova Scotia Indians, Information and Governance Projects, no date), uploads-ssl.webflow.com/5b786757ee914c5f85ba8959/5c8bf87f7788864706 3e0a78_First%20Nations%20Regional%20Health%20Survey%20-%20Version%20 2.0.pdf.

13 Arneil, "Investigation Report," 3 and 9.

14 Sheila Steen, "The Psychological Consequences of Acculturation Among the Cape Breton Micmac" (master's thesis, University of Pennsylvania, 1951), 35. See also Wilson D. Wallis and Ruth Sawtell Wallis, "Culture Loss and Culture Change Among the Micmac of the Canadian Maritime Provinces, 1912–1950," *Kroeber Anthropological Society Papers* 8/9 1953, 100–29.

15 Wien, *Rebuilding the Economic Base of Indian Communities*, 72.

16 Mary Beth Doucette and Fred Wien, "How Does First Nation Social and Economic Development Contribute to the Surrounding Region? A Case Study of Membertou," submitted to Wanda Wuttunee and Fred Wien (eds.) *Engraved on Our Nation: Indigenous Economic Tenacity* (forthcoming, University of Manitoba Press, 2022).

17 Vanessa Minke-Martin, "The Long, Expensive Fight for First Nations' Fishing Rights," *Hakai Magazine*, October 23, 2020, hakaimagazine.com/news/ the-long-expensive-fight-for-first-nations-fishing-rights/.

18 Ken Coates, *The Marshall Decision at 20: Two Decades of Commercial Re-Empowerment of the Mi'kmaq and Maliseet* (Ottawa: Macdonald-Laurier Institute, 2019), 10 and 19.

1.4. THE *MARSHALL* LEGACY

1   See "The Marshall Decision has a great legacy, 20 years on: John Paul and Joseph Quesnel in the Telegraph Journal," Macdonald-Laurier Institute, November 30, 2019, macdonaldlaurier.ca/marshall-decision-great-legacy-20-years-john-paul-joseph-quesnel-telegraph-journal/. The original article has been modified slightly for this book.

2   Ken Coates, *The Marshall Decision at 20: Two Decades of Commercial Re-Empowerment of the Mi'kmaq and Maliseet* (Ottawa: Macdonald-Laurier Institute, October 2019), macdonaldlaurier.ca/mli-files/pdf/20191015_Marshall_ Decision_20th_Coates_PAPER_FWeb.pdf.

II. UNDERSTANDING THE LOBSTER FISHERY

2.1. UNIQUE CHALLENGES IN THE LOBSTER FISHERY

1   The Fisheries Act gives the DFO minister final authority to make "best use" decisions on fish resources. For more, see note 2.

2   Fish stocks are a public resource owned by the people of Canada, and the federal Fisheries Act gives the DFO minister sole authority to decide the "best use" of the resource. The minister can decide to close a fishery to protect an endangered stock, to allow more people into a healthy fishery by issuing new licences and quotas, or in rare cases to take an allocation away from one group and give it to another to achieve some "best use" purpose. Every fishing licence and quota is therefore a time-limited privilege not subject to permanent private ownership. Here is one key example of the DFO minister's power to reallocate a fishing privilege: in March of 2022 the minister announced that 14 percent of the TAC for the baby eel or "elver" fishery in the Maritimes would be transferred without compensation from non-Indigenous harvesters to First Nations to support moderate livelihood fishing. This occurred after efforts to negotiate a "willing seller" agreement broke down due to disagreement over the selling price for the quota. See Paul Withers, "DFO redistributes quota in baby eel fishery to increase access for Mi'kmaw bands," CBC News, April 1, 2022, cbc.ca/news/canada/nova-scotia/dfo-hands-percent-of-commercial-baby-eel-quota-to-mi-kmaw-1.6404503.

3   The one exception to this rule is the offshore lobster fishery in which Clearwater owned the only licence until it was sold to Membertou First Nation in 2020. This fishery did have a TAC set at 720 metric tonnes at the time of the sale. See Paul Withers, "Clearwater gives up piece of offshore lobster monopoly to N.S. First Nation for $25M," CBC News, September 8, 2020, cbc.ca/news/canada/nova-scotia/clearwater-membertou-lobster-licences-deal-1.5716085.

4   Each LFA has a limit on the maximum number of traps that can be fished at one time by a licence holder. The licence holder does not have to fish all the traps that come with their licence, but only they can fish them—they cannot sell or lease out any of their trap allocation that they don't use.

5   For a more detailed description of the Rights Reconciliation Agreements program, see chapter 1.2.

6   Background section, *Canada Gazette*, Part II, vol. 154, no. 25, Regulations Amending the Atlantic Fisheries Regulations, 1985 and the Maritime Provinces Fishery Regulations, November 2020, gazette.gc.ca/rp-pr/p2/2020/2020-12-09/html/sor-dors246-eng.html.

7   See chapter 4.5.

2.2. CONFLICT OVER THE MI'KMAW LOBSTER FISHERY: WHO MAKES THE RULES?

1   See, for example, Alex Cooke, "Fire destroys lobster facity in southwest Nova Scotia amid escalating fishery tensions," CBC News, October 17, 2020, cbc.ca/news/canada/ nova-scotia/lobster-facility-nova-scotia-fire-1.5765665.

2   dal.ca/faculty/science/marine-affairs-program.html.

3   dal.ca/sites/fishwiks.html.

4   Government of Canada, "Aboriginal Fisheries Strategy," September 24, 2012, dfo-mpo.gc.ca/fisheries-peches/aboriginal-autochtones/afs-srapa-eng.html.

5   The Constitution Act, 1982, Schedule B to the Canada Act 1982 (UK), 1982, c 11, canlii.org/en/ca/laws/stat/schedule-b-to-the-canada-act-1982-uk-1982-c-11/latest/ schedule-b-to-the-canada-act-1982-uk-1982-c-11.html.

6   First Nations Study Program, "Sparrow Case," Indigenous Foundations, Arts, UBC, 2009, indigenousfoundations.arts.ubc.ca/sparrow_case/; Supreme Court of Canada, Supreme Court Judgments, "R. v. Sparrow," May 31, 1990, scc-csc.lexum.com/scc-csc/scc-csc/en/item/609/index.do.

7   "R v Simon," Case Briefs, casebrief.fandom.com/wiki/R_v_Simon and Supreme Court of Canada, Supreme Court Judgments, "Simon v. The Queen," November 21, 1985, scc-csc.lexum.com/scc-csc/scc-csc/en/item/93/index.do.

8   Social Research for Sustainable Fisheries, "Highlights of the Marshall Decision," factsheet, June 2021, people.stfx.ca/rsg/srsf/researchreports1/FactSheets/Factsheet1. pdf; Supreme Court of Canada, Supreme Court Judgments, "R. v. Marshall," September 17, 1999, scc-csc.lexum.com/scc-csc/scc-csc/en/item/1739/index.do.

9   Megan Bailey, "Nova Scotia lobster dispute: Mi'kmaw fishery isn't a threat to conservation, says scientists," The Conversation, October 20, 2020, theconversation.com/nova-scotia-lobster-dispute-mikmaw-fishery-isnt-a-threat-to-conservation-say-scientists-148396.

10   See paragraph 44 (e), "R. v. Marshall."

11   See, for example, Shelley Denny, "Making room for Mi'kmaw livelihood fishery easier than you think," Saltwire, updated October 17, 2020, saltwire.com/nova-scotia/opinion/shelley-denny-making-room-for-mikmaw-livelihood-fishery-easier-than-you-think-509373/.

2.3. MOVING FORWARD IN THE LOBSTER FISHERY

1   Supreme Court of Canada, Supreme Court Judgments, "R. v. Marshall," September 17, 1999, scc-csc.lexum.com/scc-csc/scc-csc/en/item/1739/index.do.

2   "Netukulimk," Unama'ki Institute of Natural Resources, 2020, uinr.ca/programs/ netukulimk/.

3   Megan Bailey, "Nova Scotia lobster dispute: Mi'kmaw fishery isn't a threat to conservation, say scientists," The Conversation, October 20, 2020, theconversation.com/nova-scotia-lobster-dispute-mikmaw-fishery-isnt-a-threat-to-conservation-say-scientists-148396.

2.4. ATLANTIC LOBSTER AND MODERATE LIVELIHOOD

1   A. Gordon DeWolf, "The Lobster Fishery of the Maritime Provinces: Economic
    Effects of Regulations," Bulletin of the Fisheries Research Board of Canada 187
    (Ottawa, ON: Environment Canada, 1974).

2   L. S. Parsons, "Management of Marine Fisheries in Canada," Canadian Bulletin
    of Fisheries and Aquatic Sciences 225 (Ottawa, ON: National Research Council of
    Canada, 1993).

3   Landed value is the total revenue received by fish harvesters when they sell
    their catch on the wharf or at the plant gate. Current and historical information
    on landed value and landed volume (metric tonnes) by species and province is
    available on the DFO's website: dfo-mpo.gc.ca/stats/stats-eng.htm.

4   J. F. Caddy, "The State of Knowledge of the Lobster Resource in Miramichi Bay
    and Adjacent Waters," T. H. Huxley School of Environment, Earth Sciences, and
    Engineering, University of London, England, report dated August 9, 2001, waves-
    vagues.dfo-mpo.gc.ca/Library/257715.pdf.

5   Fisheries and Oceans Canada, "Fisheries and Oceans Canada and Listuguj Mi'gmaq
    Government Reach Agreement on a Fall Commercial Lobster Season," news release,
    August 14, 2021, canada.ca/en/fisheries-oceans/news/2021/08/fisheries-and-oceans-
    canada-and-listuguj-migmaq-government-reach-agreement-on-a-fall-commercial-
    lobster-season.html.

III. THE *MARSHALL* DECISIONS

3.1. FISHING WITH DONALD MARSHALL JR.

1   I am grateful for the teachings shared with me by members of the Mi'kmaq Nation.

2   See Tuma Young, "L'nuwita'simk: A Foundational Worldview for a L'nuwey Justice
    System," Indigenous Law Journal 13(1), 2018, 75–102. Kisa'muemkewey refers to the
    treaty diplomacy processes of the Mi'kmaq.

3   See Marie Battiste (ed.), Living Treaties: Narrating Mi'kmaw Treaty Relations
    (Sydney: Cape Breton University Press, 2016). Mawiomi is a formal gathering for
    establishing and renewing relationships.

4   Nova Scotia, Royal Commission on the Donald Marshall, Jr., Prosecution: Digest of
    Findings and Recommendations (Halifax: Lieutenant-Governor in Council, 1989), 1.
    See also L. Jane McMillan, Truth and Conviction: Donald Marshall Jr. and the
    Mi'kmaw Quest for Justice (Vancouver: UBC Press, 2018) and Michael Harris, Justice
    Denied: The Law versus Donald Marshall (Toronto: Totem Books, 1986).

5   See L. Jane McMillan, "Living Legal Traditions: Mi'kmaw Justice in Nova Scotia,"
    University of New Brunswick Law Journal 67 (2016): 187.

6   L. Jane McMillan, "Mu kisi maqumawkik pasik kataw—We Can't Only Eat Eels:
    Mi'kmaq Contested Histories and Uncontested Silences," Canadian Journal of
    Native Studies 32:2 (Fall 2012): 119.

7   See McMillan, *Truth and Conviction*, 113.

8   See Aaron Mills, "Rooted Constitutionalism: Growing Political Community" in Michael Asch, John Borrows, and James Tully (eds.), *Resurgence and Reconciliation: Indigenous-Settler Relations and Earth Teachings* (Toronto: University of Toronto Press, 2018), 133–73.

9   R. v. Marshall (1999) 3 S.C.R. 456, 177 DLR (4th) 513.

10 See McMillan, *Truth and Conviction*, 118, note 5.

11 R. v. Marshall (1999) 3 S.C.R. 456. See also Naiomi Metallic and Constance MacIntosh, "Canada's actions around the Mi'Kmaq fisheries rest on shaky legal ground," *Policy Options* November 9, 2020, policyoptions.irpp.org/magazines/november-2020/canadas-actions-around-the-mikmaq-fisheries-rest-on-shaky-legal-ground/.

12 Anthony Davis, "Demonizing commercial lobster fishers does no good," *Chronicle Herald*, October 21, 2020, thechronicleherald.ca/opinion/local-perspectives/anthony-davis-demonizing-commercial-lobster-fishers-does-no-good-511959/.

13 See Zoe Heaps Tennant, "The New Lobster Wars: Inside the decades-long East Coast battle between fishers and the federal government over Mi'kmaw treaty rights," *The Walrus* (Nov. 26, 2021), thewalrus.ca/the-new-lobster-wars/?utm_source=ActiveCampaign&utm_medium=email&utm_content=Canada+s+New+Lobster+Wars&utm_campaign=Nov+15+-+Weekly+newsletter.

3.2. THE INDIGENOUS RIGHT TO A MODERATE LIVELIHOOD

1   McInnes Cooper has prepared this article for information only; it is not intended to be legal advice. You should consult McInnes Cooper about your unique circumstances before acting on this information. McInnes Cooper excludes all liability for anything contained in this article and any use you make of it. © 2021 McInnes Cooper and Jeffery Callaghan. All rights reserved.

2   The Constitution Act, 1982, Schedule B to the Canada Act 1982 (UK), 1982, c 11 at s. 35.

3   R. v. Marshall (1999) CanLII 665 S.C.C. [*Marshall I*].

4   *Marshall I*, para. 59.

5   *Marshall I*.

6   Fisheries and Oceans Canada, "Reconciliation in action: Fisheries agreement reached between Government of Canada and the Elsipogtog and Esgenoôpetitj First Nations," news release, August 15, 2019, canada.ca/en/fisheries-oceans/news/2019/08/reconciliation-in-action-fisheries-agreement-reached-between-government-of-canada-and-the-elsipogtog-and-esgenoopetitj-first-nations.html.

3.3. CANADA'S ACTIONS ON MI'KMAW FISHERIES

1   R. v. Marshall (1999) 3 S.C.R. 456

2   R. v. Marshall (1999) 3 S.C.R. 533

3   R. v. Sparrow (1990) 1 S.C.R. 1075

4   R. v. Powley (2003) S.C.C. 43

5   R. v. Badger (1996) 1 S.C.R. 771

6   R. v. Gladstone (1996) 2 S.C.R. 723

7   R. v. Adams (1996) 3 S.C.R. 101

8   Emma Smith, "Scale of Sipekne'katik fishery won't harm lobster stocks, says prof," CBC News, September 22, 2020, cbc.ca/news/canada/nova-scotia/mi-kmaw-fishery-moderate-livelihood-megan-bailey-conservation-dalhousie-university-1.5734030.

IV. MI'KMAW VOICES

4.3. CHIEFS' POSITIONS ON MODERATE LIVELIHOOD

1   Gerald Toney, Chief of the Annapolis Valley First Nation, assumed the role of Fisheries Lead for the Assembly in November 2020.

4.4. A MI'KMAW APPROACH TO MANAGING FISHERIES

1   With permission from Springer Nature Customer Service Centre GmbH: Springer (Amber Giles, Lucia Fanning, Shelley Denny, and Tyson Paul, "Improving the American Eel Fishery Through the Incorporation of Indigenous Knowledge into Policy Level Decision Making in Canada," *Human Ecology* 44 [2016]: 167–83), link. springer.com/article/10.1007/s10745-016-9814-0.

2   N. J. Reo and K. P. Whyte, "Hunting and Morality as Elements of Traditional Ecological Knowledge," *Human Ecology* 40, 1 (2012): 15–27.

3   R. Barnhardt, "Indigenous Knowledge Systems and Alaska Native Ways of Knowing," *Anthropology & Education Quarterly* 36, 1 (2005): 8–23.

4.5. EXPLORING THE RIGHTS AND WRONGS OF THE MODERATE LIVELIHOOD AND EAST COAST INDIGENOUS FISHERY

1   "Netukulimk," Unama'ki Institute of Natural Resources, 2020, uinr.ca/programs/netukulimk/.

2   Allister Surette, "Implementing the right to fish in pursuit of a moderate livelihood: Rebuilding trust and establishing a constructive path forward," Final report by the Federal Special Representative, March 31, 2021, dfo-mpo.gc.ca/fisheries-peches/aboriginal-autochtones/moderate-livelihood-subsistance-convenable/surette-report-rapport-mar-2021-eng.html.

3   Elizabeth McMillan, "As tensions rose during N.S. fisheries dispute, province balked at paying for extra RCMP," CBC News, May 25, 2021, cbc.ca/news/canada/nova-scotia/fisheries-dispute-st-marys-bay-rcmp-staffing-costs-1.6032605.

4 "Implementation of the Mi'kmaw and Maliseet Treaty Right to Fish in Pursuit of a Moderate Livelihood," Report of the Standing Committee on Fisheries and Oceans, May 2021, ourcommons.ca/DocumentViewer/en/43-2/FOPO/report-4/.

5 Quoted in Report of the Standing Committee on Fisheries and Oceans, May 2021.

6 Report of the Royal Commission on Aboriginal Peoples, October 1996, bac-lac. gc.ca/eng/discover/aboriginal-heritage/royal-commission-aboriginal-peoples/Pages/final-report.aspx.

V. COMMERCIAL HARVESTER AND COMMUNITY VOICES

5.I. PERSPECTIVES FROM COMMERCIAL HARVESTER ORGANIZATIONS

1 "Who We Are," UFCA, 2021, ufca.ca/who-we-are.

2 "Home," Coalition of Atlantic and Québec Fishing Organizations, no date, 1fishery. ca/.

3 "Home," Canadian Independent Fish Harvester's Federation, no date, fed-fede.ca/.

4 Department of Fisheries and Oceans, "Regulatory Impact Analysis Statement," *Canada Gazette*, I, 153, 27: Regulations Amending Certain Regulations Made Under the Fisheries Act, July 6, 2019, gazette.gc.ca/rp-pr/p1/2019/2019-07-06/html/reg2-eng.html.

5 See DFO Statistics website: https://www.dfo-mpo.gc.ca/stats/commercial/licences-permis/licences-permis-atl-eng.htm.

6 With some variation across DFO regions, a new entrant to the fishery can qualify to become an owner-operator by working as a crew member for a minimum of two years and completing safety training courses required by Transport Canada. Quebec and Newfoundland and Labrador have apprenticeship systems with more extensive training requirements.

7 Courtney Langille, "The History of Owner-Operator and Fleet Separation Policies: Cornerstones to Protecting the Independence of Fish Harvesters," *Union Forum Magazine*, Winter 2021–2022, ffaw.ca/the-latest/news/history-owner-operator-fleet-separation-policies-cornerstones-protecting-independence-fish-harvesters/.

8 Department of Fisheries and Oceans, "Regulatory Impact Analysis Statement."

9 Coalition of Atlantic and Quebec Fishing Organizations, "Fishery Coalition leadership denounces violent actions," news release, October 16, 2020, newswire. ca/news-releases/fishery-coalition-leadership-denounces-violent-actions-801753971. html.

10 "What We Do," UFCA, 2021, ufca.ca/what-we-do.

11 I am grateful to Marianne Scholte for her blog post "Threads and Borders," which provides a concise summary of oral presentations to the House of Commons Fishery Committee hearings on the moderate livelihood issue. The following quotes by harvester leaders are taken from her report, which can be accessed at https://threadsandborderscowbay.blogspot.com/.

12 "2021 Polling Results," UFCA, ufca.ca/polls.

13　UFCA, "UFCA responds to government's announced deal with First Nations in southwest Nova Scotia," news release, October 13, 2021, static1.squarespace.com/static/5fe0f323dbe7005a219c1531/t/6168187db72976242d212fdd/1634211966402/UFCA_News+Release_August+13,+2021.pdf.

14　"Home," Coalition of Atlantic and Québec Fishing Organizations, 1fishery.ca/.

15　From Marianne Scholte's blog post, threadsandborderscowbay.blogspot.com/.

16　Scholte blog post.

17　Coalition of Atlantic and Québec Fishing Organizations, "Government Reports puts spotlight on the need for formal direct dialogue between Indigenous leaders, commercial fishing organizations and the federal government," news release, May 19, 2021, newswire.ca/news-releases/government-reports-puts-spotlight-on-the-need-for-formal-direct-dialogue-between-indigenous-leaders-commercial-fishing-organizations-and-the-federal-government-855363291.html.

18　"Support reconciliation, sustainable fisheries and listen to the voice of Canadian fishers," petition on change.org, change.org/p/prime-minister-of-canada-support-peace-reconciliation-conservation-for-canada-s-fisheries-and-the-voice-of-canada?utm_source=share_petition&utm_medium=custom_url&recruited_by_id=ab1ff940-1238-11eb-a265-516e34b079f8.

19　Canadian Independent Fish Harvester's Federation, "Canadian Independent Fish harvester's Federation participate in reconciliation workshops," no date, fed-fede.ca/wp-content-fed/uploads/2015/09/CIFHF-statement-on-reconciliation-workshops-ENG.pdf.

20　Quoted in Scholte blog post.

21　Greg Mercer, "Landmark deal involving Mi'kmaq and Clearwater Seafoods risks inflaming fishery tensions," *Globe and Mail*, updated November 12, 2020, www.theglobeandmail.com/canada/article-landmark-deal-involving-mikmaq-and-clearwater-seafoods-risks/.

22　Scholte blog post.

23　Scholte blog post.

24　Important to note that while the lobster fishery is managed by effort controls (e.g., limits on numbers of traps or fishing days) and not by a limit on the total catch, the same logic pertains: if one fleet increases their traps or fishing days, others will have to be reduced to compensate if overall conservation targets are to be maintained.

5.2. AN INTERVIEW WITH ALLISTER SURETTE

1　Mr. Surette's report can be found here: dfo-mpo.gc.ca/fisheries-peches/aboriginal-autochtones/moderate-livelihood-subsistance-convenable/surette-report-rapport-mar-2021-eng.html.

5.3. AN EXPERIMENT IN DIALOGUE

1　Allister Surette, "Implementing the right to fish in pursuit of a moderate livelihood: Rebuilding trust and establishing a constructive path forward," final report,

Government of Canada, March 31, 2021, dfo-mpo.gc.ca/fisheries-peches/aboriginal-autochtones/moderate-livelihood-subsistance-convenable/surette-report-rapport-mar-2021-eng.html.

2   This quotation and those that follow are from a press release authored by Arthur Bull, facilitator for the sessions, titled "New Dialogue Between First Nations and Fishermen's Groups" and dated September 13, 2018.

VI. CURRENT ISSUES

6.I. THE STATE OF THE RESOURCE

1   "A fishery decision-making framework incorporating the precautionary approach," Fisheries and Oceans Canada, modified March 23, 2009, dfo-mpo.gc.ca/reports-rapports/regs/sff-cpd/precaution-eng.htm.

2   "Sustainability survey for fisheries," Fisheries and Oceans Canada, modified March 3, 2022, dfo-mpo.gc.ca/reports-rapports/regs/sff-cpd/survey-sondage/index-en.html#wb-auto-4.

3   J. M. McDevitt-Irwin et al., "Missing the safety net: evidence for inconsistent and insufficient management of at-risk marine fishes in Canada," *Canadian Journal of Fisheries and Aquatic Sciences*, 72, 10 (2015): 1596–608.

4   "Regulations Amending the Fishery (General) Regulations: SOR/2022-73," *Canada Gazette* II, 156, 8 (April 4, 2022), gazette.gc.ca/rp-pr/p2/2022/2022-04-13/html/sor-dors73-eng.html.

5   Fisheries and Oceans Canada, "Stock Assessment of Northern Cod (NAFO Divisions 2JK3L) in 2019," Canadian Science Advisory Secretariat (2019), waves-vagues.dfo-mpo.gc.ca/Library/40872142.pdf.

6   R. Boenish et al., "The global rise of crustacean fisheries," *Frontiers in Ecology and the Environment*, 20, 2 (2022): 102–10.

7   M. K. Trzcinski & W. D. Bowen, "The recovery of Atlantic halibut: A large, long-lived, and exploited marine predator," *ICES Journal of Marine Science*, 73, 4 (2016): 1104–14.

8   Kathy Johnson, "Unit 1 Redfish Access and Allocation Decisions Expected in 2022," *Atlantic Fishermen*, December 1, 2021, atlanticfisherman.com/unit-1-redfish-access-and-allocation-decisions-expected-in-2022/.

9   "Sustainable Fisheries Framework," Fisheries and Oceans Canada, modified April 5, 2021, dfo-mpo.gc.ca/reports-rapports/regs/sff-cpd/overview-cadre-eng.htm.

10   "Netukulimk," Unima'ki Institute of Natural Resources, 2020, uinr.ca/programs/netukulimk/page/2/.

11   Office of the Prime Minister Office, "Minister of Fisheries and Oceans and the Canadian Coast Guard Mandate Letter," December 16, 2021, pm.gc.ca/en/mandate-letters/2021/12/16/minister-fisheries-oceans-and-canadian-coast-guard-mandate-letter.

12 A requirement that in a situation of scientific uncertainty, decision makers should err on the side of conservation or the least environmental impact.

13 "A fishery decision making framework incorporating the precautionary approach."

14 M. Wiber et al., "Participatory research supporting community-based fishery management," *Marine Policy* 28, 6 (2004): 459–68.

15 Paul Withers, "'Everything about the Gulf of St. Lawrence was warmer in 2021': federal scientist," CBC News, January 19, 2022, cbc.ca/news/canada/nova-scotia/another-year-of-record-warm-water-in-gulf-of-st-lawrence-1.6319664.

16 R. A. Wahle et al., "American lobster nurseries of southern New England receding in the face of climate change," ICES *Journal of Marine Science*, 72 (suppl. 1) (2015): i69–i78; and H. Y. Chang, R. A. Richards, & Y. Chen, "Effects of environmental factors on reproductive potential of the Gulf of Maine northern shrimp (Pandalus borealis)," *Global Ecology and Conservation*, 30, e01774 (2021).

17 Paul Withers, "Wharf price for Nova Scotia lobster has plunged in April," CBC News, April 26, 2022, cbc.ca/news/canada/nova-scotia/wharf-price-n-s-lobster-plunged-april-1.6430502.

18 "Cod Prices 2021," Food Fish and Allied Workers Union, 2022, ffaw.ca/our-fish-prices/cod-prices-2021/.

19 Paul Withers, "DFO redistributes quota in baby eel fisheries to increase access for Mi'kmaw bands," CBC News, April 1, 2022, cbc.ca/news/canada/nova-scotia/dfo-hands-percent-of-commercial-baby-eel-quota-to-mi-kmaw-1.6404503.

20 L. Harnish & J. H. M. Willison, "Efficiency of bait usage in the Nova Scotia Lobster Fishery: A first look," *Journal of Cleaner Production* 17, 3 (2009): 345–7, sciencedirect.com/science/article/abs/pii/S0959652608001911.

21 Paul Palméter, "DFO shutting down herring, mackerel fisheries on East Coast," CBC News, March 30, 2022, cbc.ca/news/canada/nova-scotia/dfo-shutting-down-herring-mackerel-fishery-1.6402779.

22 Matt Byrne, "Maine's elver season shut down 2 weeks early as off-book sales disrupt quota," *Portland Press Herald*, 2018, updated May 24, 2018, pressherald.com/2018/05/23/suspected-illegal-elver-sales-forces-early-closure-of-fishery/.

23 D. A. Algera et al., "Assessing a proponent-driven process for endangered species threat mitigation: Ontario's Endangered Species Act, American Eel, and hydropower," FACETS 7, 1 (2022): 153–73, facetsjournal.com/doi/full/10.1139/facets-2021-0058.

6.2. STRATEGIES FOR OVERCOMING RACISM

1　In keeping with the Royal Commission on Aboriginal Peoples, we find that it is more accurate and helpful to consider the various First Nations as peoples who may or may not share some physical characteristics and other biological markers, much attenuated by intermarriage, adoptions, and the like. What they do share, within each Nation, is a collective identity, history, culture, and legal status.

2 Union of Nova Scotia Indians, 2015–16 *First Nations Regional Health Survey Version 2.0* (Sydney: Union of Nova Scotia Indians, 2019), Figure 3.68, p.70.

3 We consider institutional racism to be the practices of collectivities such as governments, businesses, and other organizations whose functioning, whether intentional or not, has unequal and negative consequences for a particular group of people.

4 "Peace on the Water: Advancing the Full Implementation of Mi'kmaq, Wolastoqiyik and Peskotomuhkati Rights-Based Fisheries," Report of the Standing Senate Committee on Fisheries and Oceans, Ottawa, July 2022, pp. 32–34.

5 It was not all one-sided. There were a few isolated incidents of Mi'kmaw fishers responding in kind, one of which involved trashing the Acadian flag.

6 See the chapter 5.4 for an interview with Gilles Thériault, who was in the thick of the conflict in the earlier period.

7 In 2016, for example, Environics found that the majority of Canadians support the principle of reconciliation. However, reconciliation means a wide range of things to different people, as earlier research also shows (Denis & Bailey, 2016), and negative attitudes remained deeply entrenched (e.g., victim-blaming for economic and social problems facing Indigenous Peoples). Support for Indigenous control of land and resources was significantly lower than support for things like adding Indigenous history and culture to school curricula.

8 First Nations representatives would never accept non-Indigenous fishing organizations being direct participants in formal consultations with the Crown about their Treaty Right, but they do need to be involved and informed at separate tables so that their concerns are communicated.

9 F. Wien, S. Fuller, and R. Williams, "Finding a way forward on the Mi'kmaq and Maliseet treaty right to fish for a moderate livelihood," *Policy Options*, May 19, 2021.

6.3. THE CLEARWATER PURCHASE

1 Paul Withers, "First Nations partner with BC company in $1B purchase of Clearwater Seafoods," CBC News, updated November 10, 2020, cbc.ca/news/canada/nova-scotia/mi-kmaq-purchase-clearwater-seafoods-1.5796028.

2 Angel Moore, "The deal is sealed, Mi'kmaq coalition partner with B.C company to buy seafood giant Clearwater," APTN National News, January 26, 2021, aptnnews.ca/national-news/the-deal-is-sealed-mikmaq-coalition-partner-with-b-c-company-to-buy-seafood-giant-clearwater/.

3 "About Us," Premium Brands Holdings Corporation, accessed 2020, premiumbrandsholdings.com/aboutus.htm.

4 R. Yerema & K. Leung, "Clearwater Seafoods LP Recognized as one of Atlantic Canada's Top Employers (2021) and Nova Scotia's Top Employers (2021)," Mediacorp Canada, 2021, reviews.canadastop100.com/top-employer-clearwater (page since replaced).

5 Clearwater Seafoods Incorporated, "Clearwater Seafoods Incorporated to be Acquired by Premium Brands Holdings Corporation and a Mi'kmaq First

Nations Coalition," November 9, 2020, clearwater.ca/news/clearwater-seafoods-incorporated-to-be-acquired-by-premium-brands-holdings-corporation-and-a-mikmaq-first-nations-coalition/.

6   First Nations Finance Authority, "First Nations Finance Authority (FNFA) Congratulates Mi'kmaq First Nations Coalition for Historic Clearwater Purchase," news release, November 10, 2020, fnfa.ca/wp-content/uploads/2020/11/2020-11-10-_FNFA_PressRelease_Clearwater-Final_ENG.pdf.

7   See National Centre for First Nations Governance, "Governance Toolkit Best Practices: Accountability and Reporting, Membertou First Nation," 2020, fngovernance.org/wp-content/uploads/2020/10/AR_Membertou.pdf; and Public Policy Forum, "Rebuilding the Local Economy: Inside the Mi'kmaq-Clearwater Deal & Frank McKenna Awards for Leadership in Public Policy," 2021, ppforum.ca/event/atlantic-panel-on-indigenous-ownership-frank-mckenna-award-for-leadership-in-public-policy/?utm_source=MC&utm_medium=quarterly&utm_campaign=dec2020.

8   Premium Brands Holding Corporation and Mikmaq Coalition, "Premium Brand Holdings Corporation and Mi'kmaq First Nations Coalition Announce the Acquisition of Clearwater Seafoods Incorporated," news release, November 9, 2020, premiumbrandsholdings.com/pdf/press-releases/2020-11-09-Clearwater-press-release.pdf.

9   Public Policy Forum, "Rebuilding the Local Economy."

10 Public Policy Forum, "Rebuilding the Local Economy."

11 Public Policy Forum, "Rebuilding the Local Economy."

12 See Clearwater Seafoods Incorporated, "Clearwater Seafoods Incorporated to be Acquired by Premium Brands Holdings Corporation and a Mi'kmaq First Nations Coalition"; Public Policy Forum, "Rebuilding the Local Economy"; Chief Terry Paul, Letter to Membertou, November 9, 2020, membertou.ca/wp-content/uploads/2020/11/Letter-to-Community-Transformational-Announcement-CLR-2020.pdf.

13 First Nations Finance Authority, "First Nations Finance Authority (FNFA) Congratulates Mi'kmaq First Nations Coalition."

14 Paul Withers, "First Nations partner with BC company."

15 IntraFish Media, "Clearwater, Canadian First Nations groups enter 'historic agreement' for surf clam fishery," IntraFish, March 12, 2019, intrafish.com/fisheries/clearwater-canadian-first-nations-groups-enter-historic-agreement-for-surf-clam-fishery/2-1-562688.

16 Alexander Quon, "Clearwater Seafoods selling 2 offshore lobster licences to Membertou First Nation for $25M," Global News, September 8, 2020, globalnews.ca/news/7321806/clearwater-seafoods-lobster-licences-membertou-first-nation/.

17 Angel Moore, "The deal is sealed."

18 Seafax, "Premium Brands, Coalition of Mi'kmaq First Nations to Acquire Clearwater Seafoods for $1 Billion," First News, November 10, 2020.

19   "Corporate Divisions," Membertou Corporate Division, accessed 2018, membertoucorporate.com/corporate-divisions.

20   Chief Terry Paul, Letter to Membertou.

21   Jason Smith, "With decades to wait for cash-flow, First Nations bet on Clearwater's growth," *Undercurrent News*, January 26, 2021, undercurrentnews.com/2021/01/26/with-30-year-wait-for-cash-flow-first-nations-bet-on-clearwaters-growth/.

22   Angel Moore, "The deal is sealed."

23   Public Policy Forum, "Rebuilding the Local Economy."

24   Public Policy Forum, "Rebuilding the Local Economy."

CONCLUSION: FLASHPOINTS AND POSSIBLE PATHWAYS

1   Supreme Court of Canada Judgment in R. v. Marshall, November 17, 1999, scc-csc. lexum.com/scc-csc/scc-csc/en/item/1740/index.do.

2   Government of Canada, "Government of Canada and the duty to consult," modified December 9, 2021, rcaanc-cirnac.gc.ca/eng/1331832510888/ 1609421255810.

3   Fisheries and Oceans Canada, "Minister Jordan issues statement on a new path for First Nations to fish in pursuit of a moderate livelihood," statement issued March 3, 2021, canada.ca/en/fisheries-oceans/news/2021/03/minister-jordan-issues-statement-on-a-new-path-for-first-nations-to-fish-in-pursuit-of-a-moderate-livelihood.html.

4   See Paul Withers, "Atlantic Canada seafood sectors surged in 2021," CBC News, February 3, 2022, cbc.ca/news/canada/nova-scotia/atlantic-canada-seafood-sectors-surged-2nd-year-pandemic-1.6337406.

5   The Maritime Fishermen's Union (MFU) is certified, and collects mandatory dues, under provincial legislation on the Gulf coast of New Brunswick, but harvesters on the Bay of Fundy coast are not certified. The PEI Fishermen's Association is certified as a unified industry voice with membership dues under provincial legislation.

6   Atlantic Policy Congress of First Nations Chiefs Secretariat, "Fisheries and Integrated Resources," Fisheries, 2022, apcfnc.ca/fisheries/.

7   "About Us," Kwilmu'kw Maw-klusuaqn, 2022, mikmaqrights.com/.

8   Lobster "B" licences are a holdover from the time before the current limited entry and "core" licence systems were introduced by DFO in the 1980s. "B" licence holders were part-time or occasional harvesters for whom fishing was not a primary occupation. They were allowed to continue fishing with fewer traps, but their licences will not be reissued when they retire.

9   "DFO says there's 'no plan' to cut commercial lobster catches to implement treaty fishery," CBC News, April 26, 2022, cbc.ca/news/canada/nova-scotia/dfo-no-plan-to-cut-commercial-lobster-catches-mi-kmaw-fishery-1.6431186.

10   From a press release authored by Arthur Bull, the facilitator for the dialogue sessions, titled "New Dialogue Between First Nations and Fishermen's Groups," September 13, 2018.

11   Allister Surette, "Implementing the right to fish in pursuit of a moderate livelihood: Rebuilding trust and establishing a constructive path forward," final report, Government of Canada, March 31, 2021, dfo-mpo.gc.ca/fisheries-peches/aboriginal-autochtones/moderate-livelihood-subsistance-convenable/surette-report-rapport-mar-2021-eng.html.

12   Surette, "Implementing the right to fish."

13   Surette, "Implementing the right to fish."

14   Similar circumstances prevailed after the *Marshall* decisions were handed down, when violent and racist incidents occurred in parts of Nova Scotia and New Brunswick.

15   Quoted in Canadian Independent Fish Harvester's Federation, "Canadian Independent Fish Harvester's Federation participate in reconciliation workshops," November, 2020, fed-fede.ca/wp-content-fed/uploads/2015/09/CIFHF-statement-on-reconciliation-workshops-ENG.pdf.